THE SEA IS ONLY KNEE DEEP

VOLUME 2

Paulina Zelitsky, Paul Weinzweig

Paulina Zelitsky, Paul Weinzweig

ISBN 978-0-9918538-4-7

The Sea is Only Knee Deep

VOLUME 2
CONTINUED FROM VOLUME 1

Paulina Zelitsky, Paul Weinzweig

Table of Contents

19. She wanna be a plain old Jane, She likes the taste of sugarcane[1].. 1

20. The Sky is Falling... 15

21. It was Hello and Goodbye at the Hotel Capri 31

22. Walking on Broken Glass...................................... 50

23. *Kaddish*[10] for Pelta 63

24. In the Shadow of SMERSH.................................... 74

25. Time Travel through a Wormhole........................... 91

26. Odessa Quandary.. 100

27. Freedom is not Free... 118

28. Don't Ask Questions about Fairy Tales................. 135

29. With the sad whisper of lowered flags.................. 154

30. Necessity Breaks Iron[57] 168

31. My Metamorphosis in the City of Franz Kafka...... 181

32. Parting the Red Sea... 197

33. You are to be Deported to your Country of Origin 207

34. Tensions in a Safe House 220

35. The Sun Shines Brighter after a Shower[67] 232

Epilogue: Reset for the Cold War Waltz 250

Appendix 2: Excerpt from the article of Boris Ioffe "Special Secret Mission" 266

About the Authors 272

Other Published Books by these Authors: 275

ENDNOTES 277

19. She wanna be a plain old Jane. She likes the taste of sugarcane[1]

Don Quixote of America (Havana)
by Cuban sculptor Sergio Martinez

Though Boris recovered physically, I was afraid that he would become vindictive following my threat in the heat of his attack to complain to his wife, my husband, and my father. He was obviously hurt emotionally and fearful that I would damage his reputation with everybody in authority, including his wife, with the same expediency as I put him out of action during his attempted rape. I had good reason to be worried. He was shocked by the force of my response and made preventive moves to protect his reputation. To short-circuit my complaints and accusations, he denounced me for security noncompliance on the very next day to our KGB officer at the

Soviet embassy. His charge against me of uncooperative behavior and carelessness would fall on fertile ground because it was not so far-fetched. Their records of my compliance were unflattering.

All of us were obliged to file a monthly report with security at the embassy about the people we were working with, their comments, attitudes, and their relations with Cubans and other foreign acquaintances at work or even socially. I struggled to produce my initial monthly report describing my delight over my good luck to work and learn from such capable and serious people as my senior colleagues. I stopped reporting because I had nothing to add in any future reports except to reiterate how responsibly and carefully they always carried themselves—repeating the same report with nothing new to add seemed ridiculous. Still, it was better than inventing intentionally stupid and false but frivolous accusations, just for the sake of keeping good accounts with our political officers. I was simply incapable of this and could not force myself to write the subsequent reports, a procedure I found utterly disgusting and degrading, not to mention nonsensical. I had no desire to damage other people with slanderous accusations.

Over the year, I continued to ignore this requirement, never confronting our security officers with actual refusal but simply failing to comply. When reminded, I repeated the same excuse of having nothing new to add to my first report about how lucky I was to work with such terrific people! I even attempted some light humor to trivialize the matter, a traditional Odessan escape mechanism. I maintained my devious excuses, and so far, thanks to my youth and good looks, I have gotten away without punishment. In much the same manner, I had avoided membership in Komsomol. Eventually, I relaxed since no one was harassing me. There were reminders, but no penalties for my lazy attitude towards reporting.

Until now, the KGB coordinator at the embassy and our

2

The Sea is Only Knee Deep

Pompa had never raised questions regarding my non-compliance. They were always pleasant to me. To be honest, I was amazed that I was able to get away with my reckless attitudes for so long, but I was young and took everything for granted. Undoubtedly, before our violent encounter, Boris was protecting me (he told me so repeatedly) by giving me positive references, but after the incident, my threats to tell about his attack to his wife and my father, in addition to my absence from work the next day, raised a red flag. Fearful that I would report on him to Pompa, he decided on pre-emptive action. The best way to stop my complaints from being taken seriously would be by destroying my credibility. Then, everyone would believe that I was attempting to retaliate against him because he had brought attention to my careless behavior.

Too many men consider it culturally acceptable to act out their primitive sex instincts like a beast driven by hormones. Despite the record of accomplishments in modern civilized living, men can still justify their primitive behavior when sex is concerned. They feel it is their right to allow their base instincts to take over without asking for the woman's consent. Why did I need to study for a professional career for many years and sacrifice my youth on a construction site if all I wanted was to be valued as a sexual object? How could these men fail to understand that I studied for a career to be valued not simply for my sex appeal but mainly for my intelligence and character? I wanted men to recognize me as a strong and competent person and not as weak and stupid prey. We humans are so proud to have evolved from the stage of primates. Why then should this evolution not change our expectations regarding male sexual behavior? Why should so-called civilized men still consider women as prey or a product to purchase? The proper place for such men is with their simian forebears - in the zoo or the jungle.

All I could do was to avoid such aggression through caution and vigilance. Physically, I was not strong enough to counter a sexual assault. Still, thanks to my Papa, I learned how to defend myself against an uninvited offender. Karate could be more effective protection than the burqa (Islamist tradition), or wearing a wig (Jewish Hassidic tradition), or wrapping our heads with scarves as we have done in Eastern European cultures throughout history.

There was no escape, however, from my office and from Boris, who now had in his possession my documents, including the Soviet passport that I brought with me to the Soviet Cojimar compound to prove my citizenship to enter. There was no way I could avoid Boris. I had to go back to work as soon as possible. When I returned to the office, I noticed that Boris was at his desk, but he did not raise his head to acknowledge my presence. Nor did I attempt to look directly at him or greet him. Instead, I went to greet our other colleagues and apologized for my absence, which I said was due to illness. However, I did not show a medical certificate, a traditionally valid excuse in the case of illness. The exercise of returning to my work routine helped lower my anxiety while I tried to figure out how to ask Boris about my purse with all my documents.

Boris left early before lunch without speaking to me. When I returned from lunch, I found, to my great relief, my purse with documents as well as a note from the embassy to come to a meeting after work. I was uncertain what Boris had said about me to Soviet officials. At the embassy, our Pompa received me with the KGB officer present. They informed me of complaints about my careless behavior and dodging my obligations to submit a monthly report, which all Soviet employees in Cuba were obliged to write. I immediately suspected Boris of snitching on me. 'Move by the knight, as we say in Odessa, for a preemptive strike. It could have been even worse if Pompa himself forced my reporting compliance by requesting Boris create a *'kompromat'* (compromising material) on me.

I knew that there was no use in attempting to counter-complain about the attempted rape. They would think that I

4

was trying to slander Boris in retaliation. Therefore, I kept my mouth shut about Boris and only said that I was not feeling well lately and was even thinking of resigning. My tactics were successful in the short run. The security officials eased off, but the encounter left a sour taste in my mouth. This meeting alerted me to the fact that from now on, Boris was dangerous. Being afraid that, sooner or later, I would disclose his attempted rape to his wife or my parents and husband, he was trying to discredit me. I became depressed with the realization that there appeared to be no exit from my predicament. If I could never have imagined that Boris would act towards me in such a despicable way, how could I expect anybody else to believe in this incident? Suddenly, everything was spoiled for me. I no longer felt safe in our office under the pretense that nothing happened. I was traumatized, humiliated, and frightened. In the office, I had nowhere to escape from Boris and couldn't share with anyone the stressful consequences of my conflict with him. The stigma of being merely a young, ideologically unstable female was discrediting. In contrast, my supervisor was a respectable, mature member of the Communist Party. In the opinion of others, I should have been only grateful for his guidance and oversight.

I returned to the office wearing the mask of indifference as if nothing happened and acquiesced robotically to my tasks, but the office atmosphere became toxic for me. I began to imagine that everyone on our Soviet team was taking the side of Boris. I felt like an insect under a microscope with my every move scrutinized for some damning report to Pompa. I was becoming paranoid and imagined that other members of the Soviet team acted unusually short and formal with me. Later, looking back, I thought it quite probable that the chill was due merely to the tightening of security surrounding the Soviet naval base project and not because Boris was slandering me.

The situation was driving me nuts. I was a prisoner and knew that I could not and should not continue working with Boris on the same team. We would clash again, and it would be unendurable. I began looking for alternative employment, but outside of our Soviet group in the Ministry, there were no positions created yet in my field. If I left employment altogether, where would we live? The Ministry of Transport was sponsoring our hotel and the right to purchase food in a special store for foreign assessors. If I quit my job, we would lose our residence and the purchasing rights in this store.

Finally, I found an immediate and temporary solution. It was the autumn of 1970. Every year, the Cuban employees of MITRANS, just like those from all other Cuban companies, schools, institutions, wives, and mothers, were sent to the countryside to cut sugarcane between December and June. Even Eduardo, during his short stays in Cuba over this period, occasionally traveled for a day of work in the sugarcane fields. Such mass mobilization to the sugarcane fields was due to the famous promise of Fidel Castro, made personally to the Soviet leadership, to deliver 10 million tons of sugar in 1970 to cover Cuba's trade debt with the USSR.

Instead of working and producing in their respective industries, according to their skills, masses of Cubans were sent daily by cargo trucks and buses to the sugarcane fields. Even the yellow taxis of Havana were sent to the countryside. The taxis were driven by Cuban ex-prostitutes as a result of a government measure to re-educate them. These taxis became extremely popular with the male clientele despite the double billing: one for the metered fare and another for the sex service.

I heard many people complaining about the futility of this sugarcane enterprise. Foreign assessors were not involved except for bearing the effects of complete chaos in local transportation and labor force misallocation. For me, however, it appeared to offer the opportunity to escape from the office. Besides, I wanted to see and experience it for myself. More important was the opportunity to distance myself from Boris and the Soviet embassy. Mind you, I was not obliged to go to the *Zafra* (sugar harvest) as were all Cubans who did not have any say in the matter. In my case, it would be simply a gesture of goodwill. The truth was that I used this excuse to liberate myself from the company of Boris by declaring my decision to join the Cuban sugarcane cutters. This was meant to look like an expression of my patriotic solidarity with the revolutionary enthusiasm of the Cuban people. All my colleagues were surprised. The KGB operatives at the embassy were probably having a good laugh at my attempts to escape their influence. I declared my decision to our Cuban coordinator in MITRANS to join a sugarcane MITRANS brigade.

Sugarcane harvesting brigade

Starting the very next day, I delivered my children to the daycare center of MITRANS very early in the morning and entered one of several sugarcane brigade buses for the long drive to the sugarcane fields.

The experience of harvesting sugar cane was abominable. The heat could reach over 40 degrees Celsius. On the open fields, strong winds whipping up the fiber of freshly cut cane would sting all of my exposed and sweat-covered skin. This work was incredibly hard; very quickly, it saps your energy and irritates your skin. Women were expected to do the easy work of collecting the cut cane and piling it up in a few collection points. Still, the brutal hardship of this work dampened my enthusiasm pretty fast.

Following an inedible pretense of a lunch consisting of some nameless paste between two pieces of stale white bread, we broke into separate groups with the men joining the women in conversation in an attempt to forestall their return to the cutting job. They were just too exhausted. It reminded me of our life in the Soviet Union, when, during harvest time, all workplaces, institutions, and schools had to send their employees and students to the harvest fields. I went many times after grade five. The effect was the same: a feeling of total uselessness. We were neither trained nor experienced in this kind of work. We did not know how to do it correctly, and we did not care; it was not our product, and we had no connection to it. We were only wasting time and wasting much of the agricultural produce through sloppy, unproductive work. It was a waste of fuel spent to deliver us there and back. The peasants did not care either - the fields were not theirs, the product was not theirs, and they had no personal interest in collective farming or in instructing us how to do this work properly.

All of us were only slaves who pretended to work. It amounted to hypocrisy, corruption, and waste practiced by everyone: by the government being indifferent about our progress in school or at work, and by farmers who would prefer us to waste their collective farm produce to allow them to blame us for poor productivity. Most importantly, it was a real-life school for learning hypocrisy and cynicism by a new generation of Soviet youth. What a shame. Why did Cubans not study the history of Soviet errors? Why did they feel compelled to repeat them? Privately and cautiously, people like Eduardo and I recounted our Soviet experience to Cubans, but they did not want to hear because any thinking different from that of Fidel's was dangerous.

I could not understand why Cuban leaders counted on the efficiency of inexperienced and, in most cases, forced labor for such a difficult and skilled task as the cutting of sugarcane. To that effect, they were wasting a lot of precious fuel to transport daily much of the urban population to faraway sugarcane fields. The nation sacrificed all other industrial production and services in this country because all plants and institutions went shorthanded or completely stopped working during the Zafra. The country came practically to a standstill for several months every year in a quixotic display of patriotism. Like Don Quixote tilting his lance at windmills that he imagines are giants, his Cuban counterparts swing their machetes in the sugar fields to demonstrate the power of the prophet Fidel to move the masses to miracles, no matter how absurd the undertaking.

I shared my impressions with Uncle Angelito, who was a hardworking and efficient self-made small furniture manufacturer. The Cuban Government confiscated his business and sent him and all his employees to a Zafra, a sugarcane harvest. He told me that as long as there were some resources left after the Revolution, the island would survive; but after the wealth produced by previous Cuban generations had been consumed, it would be the Soviet Union and the Soviet Bloc who would have to undertake the burden of maintaining the economy of the island. He told me that he had lost hope and would find a way to use all his savings to leave Cuba.

I understood that it was unrealistic to expect a decent quality of life at the expense of the Soviets. We were living in a country where the blind was guiding the blind. Counting on the Soviet Union would not be long-lived. According to the grumbling of Pompa, the USSR was already paying unrealistically high sums for the military protection and economic survival of many Third World nations in addition to other Soviet Bloc countries. Over the past ten years, since the political takeover by Fidel Castro, Cuba had already inflicted on the Soviet Union expenses of many billions of US dollars (5-6 billion USD per year). The only payoff for these expenses and the costs to come was the Soviet military advantage in the hemisphere, thanks to Cuba's geopolitical location.

Our secret submarine base in Cuba, built to service new Soviet ultra-quiet submarines with strategic and tactical nuclear weapons on board, was precisely that advantage, but it was also the most dangerous and provocative action in history. A leak, an accident, or an error could have horrific consequences, at least for Cubans.

Since I lost respect for Boris and my trust in him, his assurances of the "good and safe game" with the Americans also lost credibility for me. I began to realize that our *koshki-mishki* (cat and mouse) game with nuclear weapons in Cuba was entering an extremely dangerous stage. I was also in peril because Boris was a vengeful type.

When I returned to the office after a week of sugarcane experience, the relationship between Boris and me had calmed down, but only on the surface. I continued to feel trapped and nervous. As well, I began feeling that others on our Soviet team were not so friendly with me anymore. They no longer invited me to join them for social gatherings or their field trips to Cienfuegos. I was made to understand that the construction stage of the Cienfuegos navy base project was progressing well. They were preparing for the service operations of the Soviet ships and submarines, but they stopped involving me in the daily routine work of the Navy project. So, I returned to the structural design of berth facilities for bulk and general cargo. It seemed that I was now better off.

This lasted until I suspected that the complaints against me had reached the KGB in the Soviet Union, and my horizons were shut down once again. This information arrived in the traditional conspiratorial manner of a hand-delivered envelope, a form of covert communication developed by ordinary Soviet citizens over the past half-century of government-inspired random mass terror. When I received the envelope, handed to me personally by my father's friend who was on an official visit to Havana, I understood that this was my 'knock on the door' (a popular expression reflecting fears of arrest by the KGB).

It looked as if the personal danger was imminent. I could not attempt, in the risky manner of many Cubans, to use an old truck tire for swimming to the Florida coast with two small children. I felt the sky was falling. I was anticipating trouble and began to consider my options, but I had to act fast before "Chicken Little" got her pretty head cut off.[1]

Following an inedible pretense of a lunch consisting of some nameless paste between two pieces of stale white bread, we broke into separate groups with the men joining the women in conversation in an attempt to forestall their return to the cutting job. They were just too exhausted. It reminded me of our life in the Soviet Union, when, during harvest time, all workplaces, institutions, and schools had to send their employees and students to the harvest fields. I went many times after grade five. The effect was the same: a feeling of total uselessness. We were neither trained nor experienced in this kind of work. We did not know how to do it correctly, and we did not care; it was not our product, and we had no connection to it. We were only wasting time and wasting much of the agricultural produce through sloppy, unproductive work. It was a waste of fuel spent to deliver us there and back. The peasants did not care either - the fields were not theirs, the product was not theirs, and they had no personal interest in collective farming or in instructing us how to do this work properly.

All of us were only slaves who pretended to work. It amounted to hypocrisy, corruption, and waste practiced by everyone: by the government being indifferent about our progress in school or at work, and by farmers who would prefer us to waste their collective farm produce to allow them to blame us for poor productivity. Most importantly, it was a real-life school for learning hypocrisy and cynicism by a new generation of Soviet youth. What a shame. Why did Cubans not study the history of Soviet errors? Why did they feel compelled to repeat them? Privately and cautiously, people like Eduardo and I recounted our Soviet experience to Cubans, but they did not want to hear because any thinking different from that of Fidel's was dangerous.

I could not understand why Cuban leaders counted on the efficiency of inexperienced and, in most cases, forced labor for such a difficult and skilled task as the cutting of sugarcane. To that effect, they were wasting a lot of precious fuel to transport daily much of the urban population to faraway sugarcane fields. The nation sacrificed all other industrial production and services in this country because all plants and institutions went shorthanded or completely stopped working during the *Zafra*. The country came practically to a standstill for several months every year in a quixotic display of patriotism. Like Don Quixote tilting his lance at windmills that he imagines are giants, his Cuban counterparts swing their machetes in the sugar fields to demonstrate the power of the prophet Fidel to move the masses to miracles, no matter how absurd the undertaking.

I shared my impressions with Uncle Angelito, who was a hardworking and efficient self-made small furniture manufacturer. The Cuban Government confiscated his business and sent him and all his employees to a *Zafra*, a sugarcane harvest. He told me that as long as there were some resources left after the Revolution, the island would survive; but after the wealth produced by previous Cuban generations had been consumed, it would be the Soviet Union and the Soviet Bloc who would have to undertake the burden of maintaining the economy of the island. He told me that he had lost hope and would find a way to use all his savings to leave Cuba.

I understood that it was unrealistic to expect a decent quality of life at the expense of the Soviets. We were living in a country where the blind was guiding the blind. Counting on the Soviet Union would not be long-lived. According to the grumbling of Pompa, the USSR was already paying unrealistically high sums for the military protection and economic survival of many Third World nations in addition to other Soviet Bloc countries. Over the past ten years, since the political takeover by Fidel Castro, Cuba had already inflicted on the Soviet Union expenses of many billions of US dollars

(5-6 billion USD per year). The only payoff for these expenses and the costs to come was the Soviet military advantage in the hemisphere, thanks to Cuba's geopolitical location.

Our secret submarine base in Cuba, built to service new Soviet ultra-quiet submarines with strategic and tactical nuclear weapons on board, was precisely that advantage, but it was also the most dangerous and provocative action in history. A leak, an accident, or an error could have horrific consequences, at least for Cubans.

Since I lost respect for Boris and my trust in him, his assurances of the "good and safe game" with the Americans also lost credibility for me. I began to realize that our *koshki-mishki* (cat and mouse) game with nuclear weapons in Cuba was entering an extremely dangerous stage. I was also in peril because Boris was a vengeful type.

When I returned to the office after a week of sugarcane experience, the relationship between Boris and me had calmed down, but only on the surface. I continued to feel trapped and nervous. As well, I began feeling that others on our Soviet team were not so friendly with me anymore. They no longer invited me to join them for social gatherings or their field trips to Cienfuegos. I was made to understand that the construction stage of the Cienfuegos navy base project was progressing well. They were preparing for the service operations of the Soviet ships and submarines, but they stopped involving me in the daily routine work of the Navy project. So, I returned to the structural design of berth facilities for bulk and general cargo. It seemed that I was now better off.

This lasted until I suspected that the complaints against me had reached the KGB in the Soviet Union, and my horizons were shut down once again. This information arrived in the traditional conspiratorial manner of a hand-delivered envelope, a form of covert communication developed by ordinary Soviet citizens over the past half-century of government-inspired random mass terror. When I received the envelope, handed to me personally by my father's friend who was on an official visit to Havana, I understood that this was my 'knock on the door' (a popular expression reflecting fears of arrest by the KGB).

It looked as if the personal danger was imminent. I could not attempt, in the risky manner of many Cubans, to use an old truck tire for swimming to the Florida coast with two small children. I felt the sky was falling. I was anticipating trouble and began to consider my options, but I had to act fast before "Chicken Little" got her pretty head cut off.[2]

20. The Sky is Falling

Throughout the brief but tumultuous history of the Soviet Union, anyone who could be accused of any kind of real or even imaginary contact with a foreign citizen or had a relative residing abroad was automatically suspected of treason and usually arrested; unless, of course, these people were commissioned by the MID (Ministry of Foreign Affairs). This was the reason why, in the 1960s and 70s, everyone was still afraid to even glance at a foreign person. For example, the family of my father had to discontinue all correspondence with Papa's older sister Rachel, who was fortunate to immigrate to the United States before the Russian Revolution when she was only 14. The family pretended that Rachel did not exist and never mentioned her in numerous questionnaires, which everybody was obliged to fill out. When my parents informed their relatives of my plan to marry a foreigner, my relatives were shocked and begged me not to commit such an error. When Eduardo and I were finally married, most of my relatives refused to meet with Eduardo in my home and never invited him into theirs. It was as if my new husband was an "untouchable" from some ancient caste system.

In our insulated Soviet world, any contact with a foreigner, however accidental or innocent, could result in losing one's job and even the arrest of the so-called 'contaminated' Soviet citizen. What my relatives chose to ignore was that Cuba had become a close strategic ally of the USSR. Eduardo, as a Cuban citizen, was accepted as a trustworthy fellow traveler. When I argued this point, my relatives usually replied that in recent Soviet history, foreigners who were trusted at one moment could be labeled as enemies the next. I could not blame my relatives for their fears because I knew from my father that millions of ordinary Soviet citizens had been arrested and killed or had been sent to Soviet labor camps where they suffered horribly for such purely imaginary crimes.

My parents survived by carefully following two guidelines. First, to avoid membership in the Communist Party, although not enforced, the absence of such membership limited their careers and opportunities. Secondly, by never aspiring to or accepting administrative, 'visible' positions in Soviet society. My father said that these two conditions – the Party membership and management position - were laced with 'high-risk danger'. He explained to me that it was better to sacrifice job promotion, privileges, and ambition than to be unable to sleep at night because of fear or a guilty conscience.

Only those with Communist Party credentials could ever aspire to climb the ladder of administrative management. Both of my parents carried the titles of deputy heads in their respective technical departments. Only members of the Communist Party could become departmental heads. They explained that they acted for their directors by preparing all plans, proposals, and reports to be presented to the Minister of Transportation in Moscow. They were not allowed to sign any of their work, including technical patents; only the head of the department and the director-general could sign. Each new project had to be initially defended in Moscow in front of ministerial committees. To that end, good technical knowledge, experience, and innovative capacity were instrumental. This was the main reason why my parents were kept in their jobs all those years despite their political non-affiliation and their 'certain nationality' (meaning Jewish ethnicity).

I was my parents' only child, and my well-being was more important to them than fears of punishment by the authorities. Nevertheless, my father has always been cautious and calculating about any matter that might attract the attention of Soviet authorities. I was surprised by his two apparently conflicting communications. One was a letter that came by regular mail, mentioning that lately, he was suffering from high blood pressure and urging me to return to Odessa for a visit this summer. Around the same time, he also sent me a hand-delivered envelope containing several cryptic messages of a different kind. The hand-delivered messages arrived with his friend, who came to Havana for a week to consult the Port of Havana about improvements required in their water supply.

My father took advantage of his friend's visit to Havana to ask him personally to meet with me and to assure me that I should stop worrying about his heart condition because he had recovered and is currently doing well. Through his friend, Papa explained that we had not seen each other for over two years and that I might be worried about his previous mail, indicating that he was ill. Papa asked his friend to ease my worries by giving me the latest news about his full recovery and a few recent photographs as proof of his robust health.

Papa had explained to his friend that the regular mail sent abroad is read by the security services that are overburdened with the sheer volume of correspondence, which results in long delays for mail delivery. On the other hand, a personal meeting and a few photographs were taken outside in nature, and showing a cheerful and healthy father should alleviate my worries about his health. Papa's messenger was unaware of any ulterior motives. He felt that such an innocent request from my father was only natural. Papa did not have to warn his friend against reporting this personal request to authority because everybody knew that carrying letters privately was prohibited; however, this was not a letter but only a few photographs, so his friend had a good excuse to keep it confidential.

He came to my hotel in the early morning on the weekend without bothering to telephone me in advance (a very Russian way of dropping over). I took the children, and we went to the garden of the Hotel National, where the boys could play and where the sea breeze was refreshing. He handed me an envelope with a few photos and assured me that my father wanted me to know that his health was fine and that I should

17

not worry about him. We spoke about Cuba, and I advised him about the best spots for snorkeling in Cojimar. At the end of his visit, he said that he would return to Odessa the following week and tell my father that the children and I were doing well, and we're grateful to hear good news about his recuperation.

After he had left, I examined the photos. On the back of several photos, there were some cryptic expressions written in our Odessan jargon. One photograph of him looking very serious was taken beside the sign of Bebelya Street. On the back of the photograph, he wrote: "From your loving father recovering after *mandrazh* (big scare)."

Another photograph of him was taken against the background of a stormy Black Sea. Written on the back was a sentence with Odessan double meaning: "*Mansi pishut, Volni goniat no eschio ne storm*" (literal meaning: stories are written, waves are angry, but there is no storm). In Odessan dialect, the implied meaning: the stories are a pretense and not true.

A third photo showed him in our city garden. The atmosphere appears cold and windy, and Papa sits on a bench looking gloomy, all bundled up in his coat. On the back of this photograph was written: "The weather is cold; it is better in the tropics."

The last photograph was taken of both him and Shura smiling happily. On the back was written: "Many kisses from your loving parents, hoping to visit you in Havana."

What does all this mean? What was the big scare? Was Papa frightened by his heart condition? Why was one photo taken on such a despised street as Bebelya? It is an ugly street without trees and far from our neighborhood. At first glance, I was confused by this photo and by Papa's message. It took me a day and a night to unravel the mysteries of these messages.

The Sea is Only Knee Deep

**I kept the fourth photo of my parents
but destroyed the other three as a precaution**

By the next morning, the meanings took on some clarity. I reflected: everybody in Odessa knows that there are two blocks of KGB buildings occupying two city streets: Bebelya and Pereulok Griboedova. There was a popular joke in Odessa about Bebelya Street being the longest street in Odessa because from there, you could easily get to Kolima and Magadan (forced labor camps in the northern extremity of the Far East). Did he want me to understand that he had been through a big scare with the KGB?

The second "stormy seas" message seems to warn that what was written to me in Papa's mailed letter was a lie. The third photo's message about the cold weather and "better in the tropics" is probably a warning for me to stay in Cuba and not to come home. It seemed that the last photo of my happy parents was a confirmation to stay in Cuba. We all knew that my parents could not possibly obtain permission to travel abroad because foreign travel for the individual Soviet citizen was not allowed; besides, the KGB would refuse their permission to travel, justifying it by the risk to national security because of possible exposure of presumptive secrets in the Black Sea Institute. This was the traditional protocol to justify

19

the denial of foreign travel. It appeared that Papa intentionally sent me contradictory messages. Thanks to the constant fear of the KGB, all Soviets had conspiratorial frames of reference. My father appeared to be warning me to cancel my visit to Odessa this summer, despite the advice in his previous letter, possibly written under pressure from the KGB (from Bebelya Street). It meant that his encrypted message on the back of the photographs was to be taken very seriously.

My father survived the purges of the Great Terror, which did not entirely stop even after the 20th All-Union Party Congress in February of 1956, when Khrushchev delivered his 'secret' report for the Central Committee on *Errors of Stalin, Molotov, and Malenkov*. The attack by Mikoyan two days later on *The Personality Cult and its Consequences* went a bit further. Initially, he blamed the mass extermination of innocent members of the Communist Party only on the 'cult of personality' of Stalin. He still did not reveal the persecution and murder of millions of ordinary, innocent Soviet citizens. To retain absolute control over the country, the Soviet state simply changed its tactics after these revelations from mass terror to selective terror, this time using a larger variety of labor camps and prison institutions, especially mental hospitals.

As soon as the Politburo got rid of Khrushchev, the Communist Party and the KGB were able to rehabilitate Stalin and justify his genocidal policy against Soviet citizens. Now, the KGB was controlling everything in the country. Yuri Andropov, the Chairman of the KGB, became the second man to Brezhnev, and after the death of Brezhnev, he became the General Secretary and Chairman of the Presidium of the Supreme Soviet. This is why, even after Stalin's death, during the current 'vegetarian period', my dad would be frightened by the prospect of my having attracted special interest from the KGB. Such interest was never innocent.

It looked as if the KGB had interrogated my father about me. Neither my father nor I seemed to know what the KGB wanted from me. Only when I finally met with my father in person did he confirm that the KGB had interrogated him in Odessa. He said that a KGB agent called him at work and asked him to come to the public park. Two agents were waiting on a park bench, reading copies of Pravda to mark their identity as indicated in a telephone call to Papa. They told him that the discussion would relate to me, but they were not accusing me of any specific wrongs. They said that they needed additional information about my character and me, and requested all corresponding details regarding our family (three generations back) and friends. Papa felt intimidated by them and answered the best he could; he worried that they were secretly tape-recording his answers. Then, they asked him when he expected me to return home. He answered that we had not yet discussed it. They urged him to ask me to return home as soon as possible because they needed to meet with me. He said that it was possible, but he was not sure if I would come this summer (on my holidays) to Odessa. They insisted that he should call me repeatedly to apply pressure so that I return to Odessa this summer for my holidays.

He answered that his communal apartment in Odessa still had no phone installed despite his soliciting one for the past twenty years and that he was only corresponding with me by mail. The KGB agents agreed that Papa would write a letter asking me to come home for a visit as soon as possible. The agents told him they wanted to read all correspondence between us. They said that he should tell me that his health is delicate because that would expedite my decision to return. They also said that as soon as he learns from me the date of arrival in Odessa, he should notify them right away. In the end, they added that he had nothing to worry about because, otherwise, they could easily find me in Cuba. Their assurances did not calm my father; he was extremely worried and wanted me to know that it might be safer for me to stay in Cuba for the time being. Relating to the story, Papa expressed his surprise at the spy novel theatrics of his meeting.

In the USSR, all of us lived in constant paranoia, terrorized by the KGB. We always imagined the worst; it would never enter my head at that time that their inquiry might be harmless. I could not conceive any other reason, such as enlisting me as a spy, for example, nor could I afford any curiosity about that. I was afraid that my knowledge of classified work, as well as my feelings of anxiety over refusing to report on my colleagues, made me a suspect in their eyes, and now they will punish me. Whatever it was, I could not afford to risk testing their intentions. The shadows were gathering, and the foxes were expecting us. Any of their plans could inflict extreme pain and danger, not just for me but also for my children. In this, I was certain. I began to think seriously about the alternatives. The frightful idea that my children might be condemned to grow up in slavery to a totalitarian state, labeled as the so-called 'socially dangerous', was not bearable. These children, even when spared special state orphanages and allowed to stay with their relatives, could not aspire to university studies or a decent career; indeed, they would be discriminated against throughout their lives.

How lonely I felt! The only person in the whole world who would understand me was my papa, my *tateh* (father). He was the only soul who understood me. We were very similar individuals. I trusted my father unquestionably because I was convinced of his loyalty to me as well as his honesty and rationality. I did not have the same relationship with Shura, nor with Eduardo, nor with any other family member or friend. The rest of the people around me were affected, in various degrees, by fear or ambition. The majority would simply switch sides with the current, but not my papa.

I also began to discover differences with Eduardo. Despite the physical attraction and our shared love for the children, we had quite dissimilar personalities. He seemed to avoid problems instead of dealing with them. His natural temperament was to conform and to avoid any trouble. The rebel I believed that I had married was nothing of the sort. This tendency to accommodate and this reluctance to rock the boat

22

were reinforced when he landed in a job that any Cuban could only dream of. Initially, he was sent for postgraduate courses in London, England, and later to Poland. After that, he traveled extensively, selecting the ships for Cuba to purchase and the yards to build them in. He enjoyed his work and benefits. We could not correspond or speak on the telephone during his trips, but he always returned loaded with beautiful gifts for the children (made possible by economizing on his food) and me. On his return to Cuba, he would take the children and me for strolls around the city and on outings to the beach. He was a very affectionate father, often inventing personal songs for each child. He was caring and tender with them, and I felt grateful for this shared love, but isolated because I could not share with him my fears related to my Soviet colleagues. Entrusting such knowledge to Eduardo could become a serious liability for him.

It was also important to remember that we grew up in different circumstances and with quite distinct characters. He was still very idealistic and irrationally preferred to stay this way. Besides, his life experience under the communist totalitarian system was all too recent and comfortable. His family belonged to a middle-class Spanish background, and none of them were ever subjected to the same psychological grinder of fear and misery experienced by the majority of Soviet people during a half-century of Soviet history. His whole family, including his parents and siblings, were attractive, elegant, well-groomed, and active participants in the Cuban Revolution. His father occupied an important directorship in the Cuban Ministry of Transport and appeared to be a very distinguished and serious man, though not so serious as to abandon his wife and family for his 22-year-old secretary, in keeping with the revolutionary spirit of social change on all fronts.

When I met Maria, the mother of Eduardo, for the first time, I was impressed with her beauty and elegance: her healthy skin, her slim figure, and her hair always professionally styled. She even wore nylon stockings in the tropical heat. She was soft-mannered and maternal. Never before had I met a woman of her age in the Soviet Union who was so well preserved. Middle-aged Soviet women and men wore dreary and colorless clothes, looked worn down, and were often overweight. I admired Maria for her stoic and proud behavior during her marriage crisis, which occurred shortly after my arrival in Havana. She suffered from emotional shock and cried during the nights, but never attempted to retaliate against her husband, who took her submission for granted. Their behavior surprised me. I was not used to this philosophy of 'civilized machismo', nor did I favor it. Russian women would fight hard in an attempt to save their marriage. But this was a Latin culture, very different from Soviet society. Latin women were not expected to make waves. Men were to do as they pleased, and women were to accommodate them and to forgive.

Eduardo's whole family beamed with naïve revolutionary idealism, oblivious to their future misery under subsequent stages of Cuban communism. Since his high school days, Eduardo has participated in student movements, even in student leadership. He went through revolutionary military training. However, at that time, Fidel Castro and his political party, the M26J, declared everywhere, nationally and internationally, that the Cuban Revolution and Castro himself were never communist. Communists, he emphasized, were dictators, while the Cuban Revolution is a democracy where all political parties will participate.

Two years later, when he suddenly declared that he was a communist and would lead Cuba on the road to communism in a nationally televised newscast, the Cubans were so shocked that they could not believe he was serious. Neither did Eduardo. He thought the Cuban Revolution would transform itself into something very different from the Soviet Union; actually, into a democracy, according to Castro's promises. He did not know then that Castro's concept of democracy was opposed to the Western idea. Castro understood democracy as the right of all citizens to follow and

24

obey the 'supreme leader' explicitly and his apparatchiks without doubts, questions, or expectations of any personal benefits for their slavish work. Democracy in Cuba also means the right of Cuban citizens to die in the name of the 'supreme leader'. This is why the entire island nation was covered with billboards with the message: **"PATRIA O MUERTE"** (My country or death). Nothing new here: we practiced this kind of democracy under Stalin, as did the Germans under Hitler.

Despite the radical changes in Cuban politics over the ten years that had passed since the victory of the Revolution, Eduardo stubbornly continued to accommodate his personal hopes. It was a popular pastime among Cubans to justify their government's policies: Cuban socialism is only a temporary measure, and, over time, it will become different from the Soviet experiment because of Cuban geography and history. In the final analysis, they believed that the Cuban character would fall into its natural state of tropical *pachanga* (happy Cuban Reggaeton music and sexy Caribbean dance). Only, they forgot one thing: Fidel Castro was the biggest *Gallego*[3] in Cuba and was never captivated by music or by the Latin temperament. He did not dance.

Personally, I never found him magnetic or attractive; the way so many people expressed their enthusiastic impressions after meeting with him. His personality was that of a domineering *Caudillo,* which was reflected in his behavior and the countenance of those in his court. He was extremely arrogant and could hear only himself. He was utterly confident, as well as vindictive and merciless to any opposition. He was the archetypal creature in the Eurythmics' song *Missionary Man.*[4] His character reminded me of the zealous false prophet: self-righteous, stern, stubborn, and obsessed with his unique mission to become the savior of Latin American souls. Hernan Cortez, the infamous Spanish *conquistador*, claimed, and might even have believed, that the salvation of souls was his main objective as he ravaged and robbed Mexico.

Doris was an older Cuban woman who used to babysit my children occasionally. She was originally from Biran in the Province of Holguin, where Fidel's family lived. She told me in confidence some stories from Biran about Fidel Castro. I couldn't verify her testimonies, but she would not have an ulterior motive for lying. There were so many details whose plausibility could be affirmed only through a personal and intimate connection with Fidel's family in Biran. She said that her parents often worked in the Castro household.

Doris was a simple woman of Spanish origin and very friendly; she was a Catholic and also superstitious. She was too talkative and reminded me of our chattering communal apartment neighbors in Odessa. She attributed the bizarre qualities in Fidel's character to episodes in his childhood. According to her, Fidel Castro was born out of wedlock and baptized only at the age of eight as a son of the Haitian consul in Santiago with the name of Fidel Hípolito Ruz. When Fidel was 17 years old, Angel, his real natural father (a Gallego or Spanish immigrant), finally accepted him as a legitimate son and permitted him to change his name to Fidel Alexandro Castro Ruz (the surname of his natural father).

Doris made a big fuss about the influence of the Cuban-Haitian (originally Nigerian) religion of *Santeria* on Fidel Castro because he spent his childhood with his Haitian adoptive parents in Santiago and not with his natural parents in Biran. In her opinion, the Haitian population of Santiago had integrated the weird and superstitious *Santeria* pagan practices with Catholicism, and the mix became a cult of its own. She also said that Fidel's family members were obsessed with their Spanish roots and were strong supporters of General Francisco Franco. However, being a supporter of fascist Franco was not considered a very patriotic posture in Cuba during World War II.

But why bother with Cuban sentiments if Angel, the father of Fidel, initially came to Cuba as a Spanish soldier to fight against the Cuban independence movement led by Antonio

Maceo? All his neighbors in Biran knew that Angel was a passionate pro-fascist *Gallego*. Fidel, too, was an ardent supporter of Franco's ideas of *Hispanidad*.[5] According to Doris, as a teenager, Fidel brought back from his Jesuit College Nazi literature, which he kept in his room at his father's home. Doris also insisted that the only explanation she and many other Cubans had for the continued survival of Fidel and his brothers, while so many of their brothers-in-arms disappeared, was the power of magical tricks learned from the priests of *Santeria*. As a devoted Catholic, she was indignant about Haitian tricks or black magic.

She said that Fidel dominated and bullied everyone in the family and scared the hell out of the local kids. He often burst out angrily at his parents, probably because of the humiliation due to his illegitimacy and early Haitian upbringing. His vindictive attitude was also displayed in his extortion of money from his father without showing an ounce of appreciation. His father bought him an apartment in Vedado (an expensive neighborhood of Havana), bought him a car, and financed his education at a prestigious Jesuit school in Havana (*Collegio de Belen*) and later his law studies at the University of Havana. He spent vast amounts per month to finance Fidel's expensive bourgeois tastes in everything. Still, she said, his father never won his affection or gratitude; instead, Fidel despised his father and mocked him, and finally, confiscated all his land. Such could be the fate, I thought, for his other sponsors, especially the Soviet Union, whose leadership was slow to understand the psychological complexity of Fidel and his unconscious transference of a neurotic relationship with his father to other authority figures.

I felt Doris was somewhat melodramatic. I was not impressed with her fears about *Santeria* and did not take her concern seriously. I considered *Santeria* a superstitious cult of poor and illiterate Haitians. My Soviet origins contained sufficient antidotes against any kind of supernatural explanations not supported by science. Still, the dramatic story of unwanted children sounded to me more like the traumatic childhood upbringing of Stalin and Hitler, both of whom, coincidentally, shared with the Castro brothers a similar childhood of cruel abuse and neglect by their father. The low social status of an illegitimate child and the absence of family love and guidance during childhood produced profound suffering and a strong desire for vindication.

The prospect of another Caribbean dictator (after Batista) would alarm any thinking person in Cuba. Everyone, including Eduardo, hoped that this dark side of Fidel would disappear after Cuba got from the Soviet Union all it needed. Then, the island will become a civilized society with a rich economy, social justice, and a progressive educational system. This was the dream of many Cubans and non-Cubans with whom I spoke. They refused to accept that Fidel's charisma and intelligence would not, one future day, be employed to guide them to a better democratic society. Fidel indeed had many talents, but he also had serious pathological traits. His frigidity, absence of empathy, paranoia, and megalomania were far from the easy-going, emotional character molded in the traditional Latin culture from family love and Caribbean music, dance, and tropical food.

I did my best to convince Eduardo that he, too, should not rely on the duplicity of his government. Regardless, everyone believes in what they want to believe: fundamentally, in their hopes and dreams. Most people take a long time, if ever, to give up their dreams in the face of changed realities. Eduardo had a wonderful job, which he enjoyed. He traveled abroad and was relatively much better off than most recent Cuban graduates. This made him more protective of the Cuban State, and he felt annoyed with my negative interpretations of events. Still, I was unable to share with him my most serious problems: the attempted rape by Boris, his denunciation of my security carelessness, and my fears of the KGB, who, according to my papa, had a special interest in me and wanted to speak with me in Odessa.

It was not possible to share with Eduardo the cryptic

warnings from my father because that would endanger my father and implicate Eduardo personally. With Eduardo, I had to use less dramatic reasons in my attempts to convince him to change his political loyalties. Unfortunately, and understandably, while these arguments would be valid for ordinary young couples with children anywhere in the civilized world, for revolutionaries as we were supposed to be in Cuba, personal appeals were not sufficiently important, and my attempts failed. However, my nagging about the inconveniences for our family having to live permanently in hotel rooms, absent of any kitchen facilities, resulted in some change.

The Hotel National did not allow guests even to boil water in their rooms. None of the rooms were equipped with a kitchenette or a boiler, much less with a device to sterilize milk bottles or the means for sterilizing diapers, which had to be re-used daily for a whole year until the baby grew out of them. (Disposable diapers were not available. To accomplish this task, I had to wash diapers and our clothes in the room's bathtub daily. It was prohibited to use any electrical or other type of cooking appliance in the hotel rooms. I was not allowed even to warm milk for the children or to cook very simple meals for us when our salaries were not sufficient to eat in restaurants regularly.

Of course, I found ways to break hotel rules. I smuggled into our hotel suite a small hotplate with exposed electrical coils as well as two ordinary aluminum water pails, which my parents had to send me from Odessa as ship cargo. Such useful and prosaic items were not available in Cuba in those times. In the beginning, I used my hot plate in secret only for sterilizing the bottles and the milk for the children. Little by little, I became accustomed to breaking the rules and began to improvise simple meals for the family when our financial resources were drained, and we could not afford to eat in the hotel restaurant. The hot plate became something I now took for granted in attending to the needs of the children. Eventually, one day, I got caught. The only available electrical outlet in the entire suite was beside the bed, where I accommodated my hotplate on a night table, topped with an aluminum pail for boiling baby bottles. One day, the bed cover caught fire, setting off the hotel fire alarm. Sure, we put out the fire right away, but the hotel made a big scandal, and justly so, about my breaking their rules. As a result, we were transferred to the nearby Hotel Capri (only a few hundred meters away), which offered us a special two-level suite equipped with hot plates and a kitchenette. Initially, I thought: what a paradise! However, the same night we moved to Hotel Capri, we discovered its major disadvantage.

21. It was Hello and Goodbye at the Hotel Capri

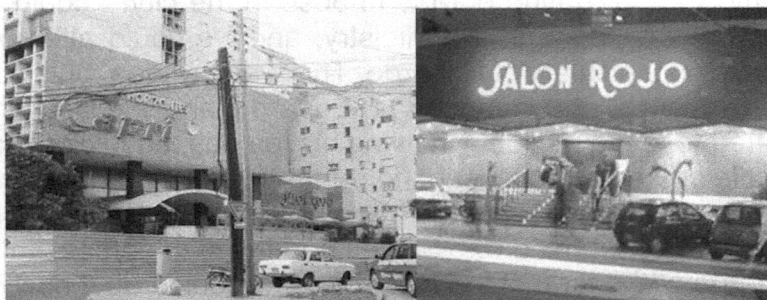

The night show at Salon Rojo in Hotel Capri from 11 p.m. to 4 a.m. Located on the ground floor beneath our windows

Havana's Hotel Capri, built as a casino-cabaret hotel in the late 1950s by American mobsters, was famous for its luxurious nightclub located on the first level and now called Salon Rojo. Our suite, with a kitchenette, like the rest of the suites equipped with a kitchenette, all rooms were located right above the cabaret on the second level. The lights and music from that nightclub penetrated everywhere and lasted until the early hours of the morning. We couldn't sleep. The loud life of an all-night cabaret was not fit for families. Yet, who could blame the hotel? After all, they were within their rights. Their famous Cabaret Salon Rojo was their main business. The hotel made us understand that we had no right to complain because their business was not a family service but a famous nightclub.

Eduardo was furious with me. Justifiably, he blamed me for the fire incident in the Hotel National and our transfer to Capri. We needed to get up very early in the morning to leave for work; however, he was unable to sleep because of the loud

31

Cabaret music playing all night long. Eduardo's mother continued to remind us that our first objective was to obtain housing and that nobody else besides us could force a solution. The hotel was only a temporary residence. We needed a permanent housing resolution, which I was hoping would allow me to change my employment or quit working altogether, freeing me from confronting Boris and the KGB at the Soviet embassy. The only alternative on the horizon seemed to be renting our own house in the city. I could quit my work with Boris in the Ministry, and we could attempt to survive on the salary of Eduardo. This was my idea, but I could not convey all the nuances to Eduardo and explain why I wanted to leave my job. Knowing his jealous, suspicious, and volatile character in sexual and romantic matters, I was afraid to tell him the story about the attempted rape by Boris and that Boris had denounced me. Since I had failed to confess this to Eduardo at the time of the incident, how could I do it now? If I did, it would probably cause an undesirable 'macho' reaction, which would create a dangerous rift between us.

So, without explaining the true reasons behind my decision, I still insisted on a change in our residence. Initially, Eduardo attempted to convince his mother to consent to our returning to her apartment. She objected by repeating that we were now sufficiently important functionaries for the Cuban economy to demand from the Ministry our own housing. She said that her apartment will always have an open door for us because we are her children. Still, we must insist that the Ministry allocate a residence suitable for our family of four.

All residential space in Havana was distributed among the state institutions. Only the state institutions could assign an available residential space to their employees. There was no other method, and it was illegal to rent privately in somebody else's house. Nobody would take such a risk because the Cuban Government would confiscate the property as soon as it was discovered. The only possibility to obtain a roof over our head was if the Ministry would assign us a housing unit. Nagging Eduardo to address our residence problems at the

Ministry did not get me very far. Eduardo wrote a formal letter to the administration soliciting residential space. In the beginning, they were reluctant, but afterward, they suggested a small two-bedroom house, which became available because the owners were *gusanos* (maggots - a derogatory Cuban term for those Cubans who were allowed to leave the country).

The administrator from the Ministry took us there in her car because public transportation was not available in that neighborhood from the moment that Fidel started the *Zafra* (sugarcane harvest) campaign. The administrator was extremely proud of the fact that all the belongings of this house from its previous owners were still there intact, and now they would belong to us. However, I did not get a good feeling from her proud statements. I did not want to own the belongings of the poor previous owners who, while immigrating to the United States, were forced to leave all of their possessions behind. Worst of all was the situation with the water. The whole neighborhood experienced regular electrical blackouts and lacked running water for the past two years. This meant that I would have to fetch the water with my pails early every morning before work from an industrial district of Havana. Of course, only if the water was available. Quite often, it was not.

I would have to carry it by myself since Eduardo was often traveling abroad and was rarely present in Havana. If I was expected to carry the water, when and how could I be expected to travel with the children to work when all the public buses were commandeered for the *Zafra*? Where and with whom could I leave my small children while I am fetching water? I cannot leave such young children alone in a house for a couple of hours, nor could I take them with me, carrying two pails of water from far away so early in the morning. Most of all, I disliked the idea of benefiting from the deplorable drama of those poor owners who left. No, I was not interested in stealing their possessions! The administrator from the Ministry, a middle-aged accountant who brought us there, could not even advise me on this matter. She was sympathetic to the fact that I had to look after two small boys; nevertheless, she also appeared to be insulted by my reluctance to take possession of other people's expropriated property.

"We are presenting you with a gift of a two-bedroom house with all its possessions: furniture, stove, refrigerator, expensive dishes, silver cutlery, bedding, and even some clothes of the previous owners, and you are not happy! Anyone else in Cuba would be extremely happy and grateful."

From my previous experience of living in Maria's apartment, I knew the hardship of carrying by hand two pails of water every day for an hour or so, even if I quit my job. Also, in the case of Maria's apartment, there were only sporadic water shortages, and there was running water at other times. By contrast, this neighborhood did not have any water at all because the local municipal water pipes were damaged beyond repair, and the distance to another district, where water could be fetched, would require a walk of 40-45 minutes in each direction, plus the interminable lineups at the water pump. I could not afford a problem like this with two very young children. The situation with public transportation was also a nightmare in this neighborhood. Eduardo would not even aspire to ask for the right to purchase a personal car because they were not for sale in Cuba. No surprise here: in the Soviet Union, the right to a personal car belonged only to the *'apparatchiks'* (senior officials and bureaucrats of the Soviet Union). My parents, who worked all of their lives as senior engineers for the state, could not even hope to dream of such an exclusive privilege.

I felt compelled to refuse this offer because, without running water, this housing was not practical, and the appropriation of other people's goods did not inspire me. I was hoping to hear of a better offer, but the Ministry of Transport never followed up with any further attempt to solve our need for adequate accommodation. We continued to live in our suite at the Hotel Capri. Eduardo's repeated reminders for

34

accommodation were dismissed with the rationale that, as far as the Ministry was concerned, our problems were solved because our children were awarded places at the nursery of the Ministry. They made clear that once I turned down their sole offer, they had no further obligations to our family life outside the workplace. Their excuse was that Cuba was not building new housing in Havana, and only those houses in Havana that became available belonged to *'gusanos'* who immigrated to the United States. Current Cuban emigration policies harassed those who decided to leave the island by forcing them to abandon all of their possessions and delaying their departure for as long as possible.

Also, the Ministry officials told us that their priority was first to accommodate the prominent revolutionaries. We could not help but notice that the revolutionary VIPs were taking over all the best real estate that became available. It meant no hope for ordinary professionals like us. We had nowhere to go. The apartments of our parents (Eduardo's and mine) had been too small and too cramped. If we moved back in with our parents, we would inflict suffering on them. My parents in Odessa lived their lives in one room in a communal apartment, sharing the bathroom and kitchen with five other families. If we returned to Odessa, the four of us would have to share with my parents the same room, which my father divided into two small rooms, but the division was made of pressboard and would not prevent the noise from my children driving my parents to distraction.

At this point, Eduardo gave up and suggested that, since I turned down his efforts, I should seek a solution by myself; after all, they should be more interested in helping me than him because I was a foreigner. I answered that I did not trust favors from either Soviet or Cuban authorities because they come at a price, which I am not willing to pay—in the case of Soviet citizens, denouncing their colleagues to the Soviet embassy and in the case of Cubans, denouncing neighbors to the local neighborhood 'vigilante committees'. I also told Eduardo that I heard from other foreigners from the West, who were living in our hotel, that in capitalist countries, when two people are working professionals, they can easily afford to rent or buy an apartment. They do not need to depend on anyone else for a permit to rent an apartment. I began to wonder why it was that if we were working, we did not have the right to rent our own place privately, because private rents were considered illegal and punishable by law. Meanwhile, Soviet and Cuban revolutionary *'nomenclatura'* (key administrative bureaucrats) could get anything they needed or wanted.

Since I began living in Cuba, I heard persistent rumors about Cubans who were leaving the country to immigrate to the USA or about their defections abroad or their escape by boats or by truck tires across the Florida Strait. If those people were brave enough to do this, maybe we too could figure out something. One thing I knew for sure, I did not want to continue working with Boris. I found him repugnant, and working with him was very difficult. I was afraid that, eventually, he would retaliate in an ugly fashion to prevent me from talking about his attempt to rape me. My father also hinted that, for the time being, I should not return to the Soviet Union because of the interest in me by the local KGB. For the first time, the idea of escaping to the West began to take root.

I tried to convince Eduardo to abandon his revolutionary zeal and told him that I wanted us to attempt to escape together to the West. I believed, simply and naively, that if he decided not to return from his next trip abroad, the children and I could join him after escaping from a Czechoslovakian airline while returning to the USSR. Eduardo's mother agreed with me. She said that we were young and still had time to start a new life, but Eduardo was somewhere between negative and reluctant. He was confused. He wanted assurances. We continued to argue like this, and, initially, I won. Eduardo promised to consult with his uncles in Spain during his next working trip there. I was optimistic that his family in Spain would also support our decision morally, if not financially.

The Sea is Only Knee Deep

I told him that he should not return to Cuba from Spain. When Eduardo had decided not to return to Cuba, I said that his aunt in Spain could call her sister Maria, Eduardo's mother, who had her own telephone. Receiving his aunt's message, I would depart from Cuba with the children, pretending to return home to Odessa. I would attempt to escape with the children during a refueling stop en route to the Soviet Union. From there, I would join Eduardo in Spain. I was very happy with this proposed arrangement. However, the normally placid Eduardo began to show signs of anxiety. He became nervous and angry, obviously burdened with this new responsibility. A couple of weeks later, he departed on his next business trip to Spain.

Maria and I kept our fingers crossed that he would decide to stay there with his family and that his aunt would call her sister, Maria, only to say that he would not return. Of course, we both lost sleep in nervous anticipation. Maria confessed to me that her sister in Spain had offered to sponsor her and her daughter's immigration to Spain based on family reunification. However, Maria refused because of her illusory hope of returning to her ex-husband, whom she still loved. Nevertheless, she believed that there could be an opportunity for Eduardo to escape the consequences of her indecision after she refused to accept her sister's offer to leave Cuba.

In the case of Eduardo's escape, his mother and I would simply pretend that we knew absolutely nothing about his intentions. However, instead of a call from his aunt, which we were awaiting so impatiently, he returned to Havana just a few weeks later, saying that his uncle and aunt turned him down, disapproving of his decision to leave Cuba. They told Eduardo that he should not leave his mother because, after her husband abandoned her, the eldest son was obligated to look after her and his teenage sister.

Eduardo took her advice as a command, and now he refused categorically to escape with the children and me. He said that the escape itself was very dangerous and that he was afraid for himself and us. He tried to discourage me by saying that after his escape, the children and the KGB would watch me closely. He added that only those English or French immigrants by nationality had a chance for a decent life in the civilized world; all other immigrants were discriminated against. Eduardo believed in the racist policies of Europe and America, as these were described in communist propaganda. To justify and solidify his emotional conviction, he converted into a fervent revolutionary and patriot, claiming that we would never have a chance in a Western country.

I did not believe him. Eduardo was telling me that I was wrong, that there was nothing else to do but to adjust to Cuban conditions; therefore, we should stay in Cuba because he was certain that things would change for the better. He said that we could return to live with his mother in the worst case, very conveniently ignoring her clear preference that we should not move in with her. He concluded that his decision was final: he would never abandon the Revolution. Cuba will be free and democratic as soon as it becomes strong enough to stand on its own. He trusted in the Revolution. He would not abandon it.

Today, I realize that Eduardo's reasoning reflected a clear case of 'cognitive dissonance syndrome', which psychology describes as the pressure to resolve the discomfort caused by holding conflicting ideas. According to this popular theory, people are motivated to reduce the discomfort of such conflict by altering their perception of reality. This is exactly what Eduardo did. Being fearful of committing a mistake and feeling powerless, he talked himself into voluntary submission. Escape was too dangerous, and the Revolution would bear fruit. In this way, he felt better about himself and resolved his confusion and anxiety, at least for the time being. Again, I could not confide in him my troubles with Boris and the KGB. Would those facts have changed his mind? At any rate, I had neither the time nor the peace of mind to continue waiting for the revolutionary fruit to fall from the trees by itself. The KGB was not waiting either.

I was afraid the report of Boris had reached the security service in Odessa, and this is why Papa was sending me hints about the KGB. For Boris, it was a pre-emptive action; for me, it could be a KGB investigation. Boris rushed to report on me to prevent any damage to him should I spill the beans to his wife and my family. To assure that nobody would believe my complaints about him, he slandered me. Now, the security service would think that I am a "conflicted person" (that is how they brand people with independent thinking, people they deem antagonistic to the government's ideals for the common good), and God knows what else. They will find me uncooperative because I refused to write monthly reports on my colleagues; consequently, they will screw up my life and the lives of my children.

Alternatively, they will keep me on the hook if I become overwhelmed with fear and agree to cooperate under pressure. They will use me as an informant to spy on colleagues, probably on senior Cuban personnel, and probably as a 'swallow' (a virtual prostitute pimped by the state). This is how they used my treacherous friend Carmen (her story is described later) or Tatiana, Che Guevara's girlfriend, who, according to Carmen, was a KGB secret agent mandated to keep an eye on Che and sideline him when he became a nuisance.

Could this be the reason they want to meet me formally in Odessa and not in Havana, where the Cuban DGI has percolated everywhere and was not trusted by the KGB? I will be damned if I do and damned if I do not. It is better to escape before they catch up with me. The rumors were that should an agent, once conscripted by the KGB security service, attempt to escape, he would be kidnapped or killed by KGB assassins at any cost. It is a matter of internal corporate regulation that they must implement anywhere on this planet, even when the agent they have to eliminate is not important to them and does not merit such a complex effort. They still must eliminate him or her as a lesson for all others. I heard such rumors several times from different sources.

If I dared refuse cooperation with the KGB, they would harass me until I agreed to it; additionally, they would never again allow me, or anyone in my family, to travel abroad. Why should I become their puppet? And for what - mediocre Soviet privileges of an apartment and a few other relatively small perks? I was young and only starting my life's journey. I had no interest in becoming their slave or their victim.

Whichever way I construed my dilemma, I refused to participate in security services games. I will fight for our freedom. I had to be firm with Eduardo, even though it was very hurtful and came at the price of our distancing from each other. I now felt that there was no alternative for me except to escape alone with the children and without Eduardo. I explained my decision to Eduardo. Both he and his mother, being decent and caring people, agreed that I had the right to do as I wished. Eduardo was terribly hurt; so was I. We carried on living, but the air around us was filled with needles - every move pierced our hearts. I began working to arrange my travel, but first, we would go to the office of the registrar to register our divorce to protect him and his family following my escape.

Eduardo even hesitated to ask me about any details of my escape plan because, in the case of interrogations by the security services, such knowledge would become a serious liability. I pretended that the details of our escape were all worked out and that my friends from the foreign diplomatic corps would help us in Canada. He did not ask about the identity of these friends or how I might have had such wonderful friends. I just knew that I had to tell him that everything was prearranged and I would have the necessary help after my escape; otherwise, he would consider my plans unrealistic and suicidal. In that case, he would try to hold me back.

The truth was, I did not have any friends in the Western world - nobody in the whole world outside the USSR and Cuba. How I could accomplish an escape and survive afterward with two small children and no money was a complete mystery to me. Over the past couple of months, I slept fitfully, fretting about our imminent leap into the abyss.

My only acquaintances in the foreign diplomatic corps were Perez and his wife, a couple from Israel. He was the Israeli consul in Cuba, whom I asked once if it was possible to seek refuge in their consulate as a means of immigrating to Israel. I did not explain the nature of my work or my fears of the intelligence services. He and his wife were friendly and sincere people. They listened to me with kindness when I came to their residence one night for a meeting arranged by Dr. Nader, my Czechoslovakian friend. I asked for their advice and their assistance in obtaining refuge on the grounds of my desire, as a Jew, to immigrate to Israel, our historic homeland.

Perez told me that he could not turn me down, but it would be highly damaging for the consulate and dangerous for the children and me. He and his wife urged me not to jump from Cuba from their consulate in Havana because the Israeli consulate could not afford to provoke a scandal with the Soviet Union. They would be accused of inciting my escape if it took place from their consulate, or they would be accused of smuggling a Soviet citizen out of Cuba. It was certain that Fidel would come down on the Soviet side. Under angry Soviet pressure, Cuba would expel Israel's diplomats from Havana altogether, arrest me, and extradite me to the Soviet Union. They said it took 20 years for Israel to obtain a diplomatic agreement for the consulate of Israel in Cuba, and it still had only marginal legitimacy. The objective of this consulate in Havana was to help Cuban Jews and not foreign citizens. They were right, and I felt embarrassed for making a request that might jeopardize their mission.

My timing was not propitious. It was not long after the Israeli victory in the Six-Day War of 1967 that the political and economic interests of the USSR in the Middle East emerged. It was also close to the Dymshits/Kuznetsov aircraft hijacking affair (a failed attempt by Soviet Jews to escape from

Leningrad in May 1970) when relations between Israel and the USSR, including all Soviet Bloc allies such as Cuba, were more hostile. I sympathized with the consul and respected their delicate situation in Cuba, which was a Soviet satellite. I told them that I understood their constraints and that I would manage my situation on my own. Still, I never admitted to Eduardo that the Israeli consul could not help me; instead, I kept him under the illusion that when it became necessary, they would assist us.

Suddenly, Eduardo came up with his latest scenario: he would not travel with me and would allow my departure from Cuba with our two children. He will permit me to travel with only one of our children; the second boy will stay with him in Cuba. He begged me to understand that he arrived at this decision only to help me logistically during the escape. Because our boys were so young (aged two and four), this would make my escape with them too risky, if not impossible. In the case of success, our survival afterward with two very young children would be much more difficult.

Of course, he was right about this. Sure, it was more difficult with two children than with one. Yes, it was crazy! This was particularly true of Ernestico, our youngest child, still a toddler, whom I would have to carry in my arms. However, this truth was unacceptable to me. I intended to leave with both children because both of them deserve to be delivered into freedom. I argued with him passionately, almost violently. All the time, I was intentionally misleading him and his mother by pretending that our Israeli friends would help us once we escaped.

Despite my knowledge that I was lying about my friends in the West, I was convinced that I had to do everything possible to save the children. If I had not told him this lie, he would not have let us go. Still, he delayed making his final decision. I became depressed and lost sleep. I had constant nightmares with crazy dreams of fights with Eduardo. These unconscious fights tended to end with dramatically gruesome and colorful results. One night, I even had a nightmare that I had killed him and that he was bleeding. This was terrible insanity, and I could not share my agony with anybody. I was going crazy because I couldn't imagine abandoning one of my children under any circumstances, especially now that I felt it was the only chance to secure their freedom. At the same time, I wanted to win over Eduardo, hoping that his love for our children would give him the strength to leave his mother and defect with us.

Then, without warning, I was deluged by a wave of treachery that transfigured our agitated emotional state into a serious Spanish melodrama involving two young families. One of the Spanish families was from the second generation of "niños" who were assigned to work in Cuba as assessors.[6] Luis was a tall, slim, undistinguished 27-year-old European who was an expert in something or other. He did not bother to explain the field of his expertise even to Carmen, his young and strikingly beautiful wife. Carmen was 22 years old, very sexy, with long black hair and long legs. She did not work and possessed no other discernible skills than her lovely body. Luis and Carmen had a two-year-old son named Lusito.

At the time, I had no idea that Luis's area of expertise was related to the organization and training at DGI (Cuban intelligence). Nor did I have any notion of how corrupt and frustrated the arranged relationship in this family was. I met Carmen in the park of the Hotel National, where I took our children to play after work. The park was a green and safe place with sea breezes from the ocean, a blessing in a tropical climate. While Lusito played with our boys, Carmen and I chatted to kill time. She surprised me on some occasions with her wild confessions about her daily sex requirements for new lovers. Such a promiscuous scenario was so remote from my experience and imagination that I thought she was inventing these fantasies because she had such a bore for a husband. After a while, we began inviting each other with our husbands and children on Sunday evenings for social get-togethers. Everything appeared harmonious between both families; the adults talked and drank while the children played together. Then, one day, both Carmen and Eduardo disappeared.

I learned about it from Luis. Eduardo failed to return home after work for the second day, and, naturally, I assumed that he went to visit his mother and spent the night in her apartment. I never suspected Eduardo would run off with another woman because I had never seen him even looking at other women. It would simply never enter my mind because I completely trusted in his devotion and reliability. It was Luis, who was visibly angry when he suddenly appeared at the door of our Hotel Capri suite, holding his son by the hand.

"*Hola*. Where is your husband?" asked Luis.

"I don't know. I just returned from work and never saw him there. I was thinking at this very moment that I should call his mother and ask her. He probably spent last night at her apartment, which he often does whenever we disagree about something or the hotel music is too loud. He didn't come here last night."

"Well, go ahead and call your mother-in-law because I have some news for you. Your husband and Carmen have run away together!" said Luis with anger.

I was stunned by his announcement. I lost the ability to reply. I could not understand how it was possible to make such an absurd accusation about our spouses.

"She left her child with me and did not return last night either," he continued, seeing my shock and disbelief. "I was looking for her everywhere. Then, I received reports that she was seen with your husband in another province at a beach cabin. I went there immediately, but when I arrived, they were already gone. I have no idea where they are now. All I know is that they took both of us for stupid fools."

I called Maria straight away. She did not know the whereabouts of Eduardo. Luis could be right. I could not understand it; Carmen was my friend. How was such treason possible? How was it possible for Eduardo? He was always very quiet, respectful, and almost shy with other women. How was it possible for Eduardo to behave with such disrespect towards both Luis and me? What an incredible blow! I was traumatized.

"If they have done this to us, you and I shall do the same. You and I shall also have sex!" sternly demanded Luis in an angry tone, still holding the hand of his son.

"No, Luis, her son is also your son. You must shut up out of respect for him, for me, and my children. You are completely insane! Get out of here immediately, and don't ever again come near me."

From somewhere, I found the strength to push him out the door, despite his resistance and his shameless outbursts in front of the children. My anger against Eduardo and Carmen turned against Luis at that moment.

As a family counselor, Luis was in a league of his own. Instead of help and empathy, he brought me terror. As an operative in the Cuban intelligence agency, he displayed a complete lack of self-control in the egotistical pursuit of his retribution. Clearly, he would have failed basic KGB training that demanded detachment and cool composure in any crisis.

Such treachery from those I trusted left me mentally and emotionally unhinged, even two weeks later when Eduardo finally returned home. I felt numb and depleted after two weeks of the night crying. Yet, I responded with the traditional female guilt syndrome. I blamed myself because I imagined that I had inflicted this pain by driving him into another woman's arms on account of all my troubles stemming from the implacable desire to escape from Cuba. Possibly, my pressure on him to escape with us might have been the spark that triggered his rebellion against me and the deep wound to our relationship.

My choice was to continue to suffer the guilt and inflict pain on myself or to block the entire, emotionally draining episode from my conscious mind and concentrate, like a train in a tunnel, on escaping toward the light of freedom, as difficult and painful as it already was. Strange, but I could not imagine that the problem did not arise from me, but rather from Carmen. I preferred to assume that if Eduardo and I do not talk about it, the problem will disappear because it is not real. I completely dismissed the idea, which I learned from Carmen many years later, that Eduardo was utterly captured by her extraordinary sexuality and really lost his mind to her, caught like an innocent beetle in a *Venus Flytrap,* and was chemically devoured over the next two weeks.

When, 25 years later, I met Carmen accidentally in Florida, where she lived in a lesbian relationship with another woman, she confessed that she had lied to Eduardo, saying that I had been disloyal to him. This falsehood relieved him of any guilt for his romantic frenzy.

When they returned two weeks later to Havana, Eduardo brought Carmen to Maria's apartment, where he asked his mother for permission to stay with Carmen in his bedroom. Maria was furious at her son and threw Carmen out. Maria answered that only Eduardo's wife and her grandchildren could stay in her apartment. After his mother's rejection, Eduardo returned to our hotel to talk with me. Carmen also returned to Luis, but shortly after, she abandoned her husband again.

During our chance meeting in Florida, Carmen recalled that Eduardo became obsessed with her after their two-week sojourn and continued to pursue her aggressively. Luis reacted violently. To avoid a crisis with her husband, she acquired protection from Ramon Mercader, a famous Soviet-Spanish NKVD (KGB) colonel residing in Cuba, when she went to live with him in his beautiful house in the upscale Havana district of Miramar. She told me how, on orders of Stalin, Ramon personally killed his friend Leon Trotsky in

Mexico in 1940 with an ice pick to the back of the head. For this murder, he received a 20-year Mexican prison term.

His prison, she said, had special comforts: a shortwave radio shop to conduct transmissions, receiving international daily publications as well as regular conjugal visits from Raquelia Mendoza, who was a Mexican nightclub dancer but not his wife. The Soviet KGB arranged all this for him. Prison conditions were better than in our post-Revolutionary Cuban hotels, so he was in fine form when his sentence expired. When he was released in 1960, he moved to Havana, where Fidel granted him a beautiful private house in the secluded, privileged district of Miramar. In 1961, he moved to the Soviet Union, where he was presented with the prize of "The Hero of the Soviet Union" (the country's highest decoration) and a large *nomenklatura* apartment in Moscow.[7] He divided his time between Cuba and the Soviet Union for the rest of his life. He died in Havana in 1978, having shared his privileges with Carmen, who had kept him under surveillance at the behest of the KGB.

Of course, in 1971, I was not aware of any of these details; Eduardo made it look as if he regretted his escapade with Carmen, and neither of us ever discussed it again. At that moment in my life, my emotional resources were already strained. For my escape plan to succeed and to muster the necessary courage, I needed to perceive reality strictly through tunnel vision. All my neurons were tensed for our escape to freedom. Unless I could sublimate all of my senses and feelings towards this task, I would stumble and fail.

In the meantime, I was well aware that should Eduardo refuse me his permission for the children's departure, I would not be able to leave Cuba. I would have to face my defeat and submit because I would not be able to abandon either of our children. For Eduardo, this decision to separate was just too traumatic, beyond his human limits. If anything bad happened to the children and me, he would feel guilty that he did not restrain us; he may never again see his beloved children.

Surprisingly, our dilemma was resolved by Eduardo's mother. It was she who supported my plea. She insisted that he must let both of his children leave with me. It was how, thanks to Maria, we finally agreed that if Eduardo does not escape with us, he will do everything possible to support my departure with both children.

I continued to agonize over the changes in his character. Where was the revolutionary rebel that I married? If he is honest with himself, he will pay attention to the great disparity between Cuban revolutionary promises and the reality on the ground. Why did he become so docile and obedient? Why did he refuse to take the risk with us? I was afraid to even analyze his reactions because it could destabilize me in favor of staying with him at any price, just as he had asked. No, I had to be single-minded in my decisiveness to consummate this extreme task: to jump into the void, the precarious unknown. To be able to do that, I had to shut down all emotions, all reactions, all doubts. It was incredibly difficult, but there was no alternative.

A few weeks before our flight, we went to the marriage office and registered for a divorce, giving me legal custody of both children. This needed to be done to protect Eduardo and his own family after our escape. Eduardo would be able to answer interrogators that he was already divorced from me and had no knowledge of my intentions. I imagined that if everything developed satisfactorily for the children and me during and after our escape, he would join us, and we would be together again. Later, we could return easily to our marriage since our divorce was only a false cover-up.

There was one serious test left: he still had an obligation to issue his legal permission for both children to depart Cuba, and this permission had to be granted right at the airport just before the flight. I knew how much Eduardo was suffering because he adored his children and how agonizing this decision was for him. I felt, however, that I had no choice. I must escape from the intelligence services before they recruit me or even before they initiate a formal meeting. I knew that if I did not escape now, later would become impossible.

This was the reason for my state of permanent anxiety about this last moment at the Havana airport. Both of us, Eduardo and I had by now accepted the need to sacrifice our feelings for each other, but we could not bring ourselves to think the same way about our children. I knew that Eduardo was a kind, generous, and loving father, but the despair of not seeing his dearest children ever again could persuade him to withhold permission at the airport and force our continued stay in Cuba.

22. Walking on Broken Glass

I failed to fall asleep the previous night, tormented by everything that might go wrong in the hours ahead. This was to be expected since today is the day of our second chance to escape. This could be the last opportunity for my flight, and it will determine the rest of our lives. We were up early but proceeding slowly because we still had a few hours before Eduardo would pick us up for the drive to the airport. A sudden call from the hotel reception interrupted me while dressing the sleepy children. It was Eduardo.

"Hi, Poli. I am early to avoid a late arrival at the airport. I don't want to miss your flight again," said Eduardo, speaking in a soft voice without irritation, which until now was regularly present in our relations over the past month.

It was a matter of sheer good luck to find a taxi anywhere in the city, even at hotels, and, in particular, near a hotel for Cubans. The available state taxis were rare, and private car owners were drastically rationed for fuel. Cuban fuel reserves were allocated for the "war" on the sugarcane fields. Moonlighting with a car was also punishable by law. Despite state appropriation of private cars, the few lucky private car owners who managed to survive were not allowed to purchase fuel above their monthly ration, which was often sufficient for only a few days of driving per month. During the 1960s, and even the early 70s - the years which followed the Revolution - there was no formal tourism and no system for ordering a taxi beforehand by phone because it was considered a decadent privilege of the rich from whom Cuba was now free. It was even less practical to rely on stopping a rare taxi on the streets.

This situation was due to the government policy to

transport the city's residents to cut sugarcane, the so-called *Zafra*. All fuel was expected to be used for the daily transportation of thousands of city residents to the sugarcane fields. The residents of Havana felt senselessly tortured for six months each year because the brutal cane cutting work (extremely hard physical labor) required the skill of experienced cutters, which city people did not possess. At the same time, the economy of the island was paralyzed because so much of the population was forced to abandon their real work in the national industries, in administrative services, in schools, or at home for wasteful and inefficient jobs in the sugarcane fields.

"Hola, Eduardo. Thanks for coming sooner than later, but the children are not yet dressed. They are acting up, and I have problems dressing them and packing our luggage at the same time. Could you please ask the hotel reception for a favor to allow you to come up to our room to help me with the children?"

I did not have to tell him the truth; he knew it. My nerves were falling apart, and I was begging for help.

"You know this is what I would like to do as well, but I am afraid the hotel manager will not allow me to come up to your room. You cannot be late today for your flight. Try to arrange everything on your own in case they don't allow me into your room. Remember, I brought the taxi with me, but the driver might refuse to wait. He may take off if we make him wait."

"Please try your best to come up to our room and help me with the children. They are still half-awake and are naughty this morning. I am afraid I will forget to pack some of our documents and necessities for the children. My head has been splitting from pain since last night, and I badly need your help."

Breaking a family apart is not simple when you share so many feelings for each other and two little children. Now, at this last moment, I found myself drained of energy, feeling weak, lacking confidence. I needed the reassurance of Eduardo's physical presence.

"My head is splitting too," he answered and hung up the phone. I had to finish dressing the children by myself because he did not come. Obviously, the hotel manager refused him permission. I prepared and packed their milk bottles and their jackets in my handbag together with our documents and started to carry our only piece of luggage, a large suitcase with all of our belongings. Both children followed me from behind. There has been no bellhop since most of the hotel service staff were working in the sugarcane field. The elevator on the eighth floor was not working again. It never does!

Once in the airless stairwell, I began sweating profusely. Worrying about the children, I begged them to hold onto the stairway railing. Fear gripped me again. All I needed now was one of my kids to fall or for me to fall and break my neck or leg! I told the kids to stop, lifted the youngest in my arms, and went downstairs, leaving our suitcase on the eighth-level landing. I had to rush downstairs after Edik, our five-year-old, who seems never to have learned to walk, only to run or to jump. Finally, we reached the lobby level safely, and the children went running to hug Eduardo.

Eduardo, looking pale and somber, was still arguing with the manager. He was not allowed by the rules of the hotel to come up into my room because we were by now formally divorced, and Cuban hotels, just like all Soviet hotels, allow visitors to the room only with a valid marriage license; ours was taken away by the registrar after our divorce was registered. Eduardo continued to exchange angry arguments in Spanish, which always sounds like a fight in Italian movies. Probably, he was venting his built-up frustration at the manager. Russian is a much calmer language, at least to my ear. Between ourselves, we spoke in Russian when we wanted to prevent others from understanding our conversation.

The hotel manager, dressed in the military uniform of a

Cuban officer, was annoyed because he was uncertain what to do. He looked relieved to see that we were able to come down without his having to break the rules, and he graciously permitted Eduardo to pick up our luggage from the eighth-floor landing as if he was doing me a favor. Then, he checked us out under the spiteful gaze of the receptionist. We paid, and Eduardo picked up our suitcase and proceeded outside. I followed behind, holding on to the children, one in each hand. I did not see any taxi beside the hotel and asked where it was. Eduardo did not answer. He was walking very quickly ahead of us down the block, carrying our suitcase. The luggage was heavy because I had attempted to cram most of our possessions in one suitcase, which might allow us to start a new life wherever we wind up. All our worldly possessions were contained in one suitcase. Only after we were at a safe distance from the hotel, he admitted that he could not find a taxi but had succeeded in hiring a private car. Eduardo struck an illicit deal with a driver who worked for a Cuban *apparatchik* (big boss) who had his own state car. I imagined that the driver requested a large payment to compensate him for the risk of getting nabbed. His car was waiting for us at the corner of the next block. If the driver got caught moonlighting for private passengers using state fuel, he would lose his job; maybe, even be imprisoned.

I was grateful to Eduardo for these arrangements. Still, my heart was in terrible pain, torn between compassion for him and my fears of unexpected complications if Eduardo should change his mind about letting both children go at the very last moment in the airport. We took our seats in the car and drove in silence, oppressed by the forthcoming trauma. Each of us was petrified by our grief over the imminent separation, possibly forever.

Sometimes during previous days, Eduardo had said that he honestly believed it would be easier for me if one of the children stayed back with him. I won this argument and not without a fierce battle. He knew I could not leave without both children. Still, *'Ne ver bez prover'* (don't believe until you have tasted it) is an old Russian proverb. The stakes were too high; a desperate person in the last critical moment might act unpredictably. Who was to judge him? To be honest, even I could not blame him if he changed his mind. Should this happen, I, too, would remain in Cuba for the sake of my children. Something similar already took place in Havana. I heard the story from a Spanish woman from the Soviet Union who had come to Moscow with her husband after the Spanish Civil War. Now residing in Cuba, she told me about the drama with her daughter, who was also living in Cuba with her husband. Both were *niños*, second-generation Spanish nationals from the Soviet Union. The daughter had quarreled with her husband because she intended to return to the USSR, but her husband prohibited their only son from leaving Cuba. She had no choice and did not leave for this reason. I heard about similar cases with other couples and was afraid that it could happen to me as well. Fear of Eduardo's change of mind during the last moments put my brain in a pressure cooker. While my rational mind debated the awful scenarios, my sanity stayed intact because, in my heart, I trusted Eduardo and his capacity to sacrifice his feelings for the good of his children.

When we arrived at the airport, and our flight was announced for documents check at immigration, we had to separate. The children and I needed to line up to cross through a glass door to the tarmac. Eduardo was not allowed, only the passengers. "I want my Papi. Why did Papi not come with us?" cried five-year-old Edik, upset about his father being left on the other side of the glass door at immigration.

"Edik, *mi Corazon* (my dear), your Papi is going to join us soon when our turn comes up. You will see. Stop crying; it will be soon." I was trying to calm him down; he was very upset, as if his instinct was warning him about the separation. He cried, apparently for water, but I knew that he was caught up in our drama. In my bag, I had only the baby bottles with milk. The crying of Edik granted me an opportunity to ask the immigration officers to allow Eduardo to join us to calm down our child, but they refused. Later, one of the officers kindly brought some water for the children. The boys became subdued.

The line of passengers started forming on the tarmac beside the tables of security and immigration officers standing under the blistering midday Cuban sun. All of us were sweating uncomfortably. Finally, when our turn came, the immigration officers called Eduardo to join us for questioning because of the requirement for his official permission to allow our children to leave Cuba. I kept a stronghold on both boys because I was afraid to let either of them go, just in case Eduardo would change his mind and refuse his permission for one of our boys. In such a circumstance, Ernestico, born in Cuba and being our youngest, would be the most likely candidate to stay behind with Eduardo.

A week ago, I missed the last flight of CSA Czech Airlines to Moscow. Consequently, we would now have to board the Soviet airline Aeroflot instead. It was unfortunate for us because my attempt to escape from Aeroflot would be much more difficult, if not impossible. I wanted badly to take the CSA-Cubana flight (Czech airline) rather than Aeroflot because of my perception that the state security agents of Czechoslovakian Airlines (CSA) were mere 'puppies' in comparison with their KGB counterparts. The Czech agents probably would not shoot at Soviet citizens (especially children) even if suspected of escaping. I reasoned that they would be afraid to err; ultimately, it was not their business to persecute Soviets but rather the job of the KGB.

It was a stroke of incredible luck to have obtained special permission from the Soviet consulate in Havana to purchase a flight from Havana to Moscow with CSA Airlines. Soviets were not allowed to take any of the foreign airlines when Aeroflot was available. Now, however, my good fortune was wasted because I missed the last scheduled flight of CSA Airlines from Havana to Moscow a week ago. These direct CSA flights to Moscow were now discontinued.

It was a big deal to gain such permission to fly CSA Airlines, Havana-Prague-Moscow, while the direct route of Aeroflot Havana-Moscow was also available. The previous Soviet consul in Havana was hopeless, and I would not even attempt to ask him because he was not the type to break the rules for me. However, in January of 1971, I met the newly arrived Soviet consul, a young, already balding, and optimistically disposed fellow from Moscow. My fortunes looked brighter. Right away, I characterized him as a spoiled brat from the *'nomenklatura'* (only the privileged sons of very senior party bosses were granted these juicy jobs abroad). I ventured to apply my considerable charms on him. I inquired innocently if it was possible to visit Prague and to do a little shopping there on my way to Moscow, because we have a real shortage of goods in Cuba, and the products in the USSR were of very poor quality. He was surprised but not angry at my naiveté. He told me that I probably spent too much time abroad, if it was news for me that Soviet citizens are not allowed to travel unofficially as tourists to Prague following the Soviet takeover of that country. Unless I was commissioned by the Soviet State for an official visit to Czechoslovakia, there was no chance of my getting a KGB blessing for my travel there. His answer was formal, but he did not sound irritated as the previous consul always did when I asked him a stupid question. I thought there was a chance to bend this new consul, who seemed to regard his rather short and ordinary self as a Don Juan, and to get such permission from him by applying a little more pressure.

I confessed to being blissfully ignorant about travel regulations, and we changed the topic of the conversation to the Cuban resort of Varadero, where the most beautiful and huge seashells were consistently discovered by our Soviet colleagues at the office. The new consul was now upbeat and very interested to learn from me where precisely the best shells could be found. He said that he was planning to take a week's holiday in Varadero to hunt for seashells, which he heard were much better there than in Cojimar. This was my good luck, an opportunity to convince him to permit me to purchase my flight with Czechoslovakian Airlines. It did not look suspicious; all the wives of Soviet diplomats would aim for the same. To shop in Czechoslovakia was the dream of all wives of the Soviet diplomatic elite working in Warsaw Pact communist countries. Even after the recent Soviet invasion and repression in 1968, Prague (as well as Berlin) was still long known for a much better quality of goods and shopping opportunities than anywhere else in the Communist Bloc.

The truth was that I was not planning to shop anywhere but to defect, and not in Prague, but in Gander, Newfoundland, Canada, during the 30 to 45 minutes refueling stop of the aircraft on its way from Havana to Prague.[8] Aeroflot also used the same refueling stop in Gander on its direct flight to Moscow, but I was afraid of the tight security of KGB guards over Aeroflot passengers. I preferred to escape from the Czech airliner because, as a Soviet citizen, I would be considered a safe passenger, a positive role model for Czechoslovakian security officials.

I got the idea of using Czech Airlines for our escape from Dr. Nader, the Czechoslovakian doctor in Havana who operated on the tonsils of our Edik in the Havana clinic for foreign assessors. During his coffee break, which we took together in the clinic's garden while my son was sleeping after the operation, he confessed to me in secret about the efforts of Czech assessors working in Cuba to look for escape routes after the Soviet aggression against Czechoslovakia. He told me in great confidence that his Czech friends and colleagues were considering the possibility of escaping in Gander, Newfoundland, during the refueling of Czechoslovakian aircraft. Being Czechoslovakian nationals, they all were approved automatically to fly with this airline, but they had serious concerns about the practical execution of their plan. This was because, after the Soviet takeover of Czechoslovakia, the KGB operatives had retrained the Czech security agents who were now present on board during all flights and were given orders to shoot all suspects attempting to escape. No Soviet citizen, yet, as far as I could discover, had ever attempted this escape route. I thought to myself that this might be the only viable possibility for us. I was hoping that, thanks to the Soviet stereotypes, the Czech security agents would be less suspicious of Soviet citizens. Thanks, Dr. Nader, for the tip!

My coquettish ways with the Soviet consul had to be carefully instrumented not to allow any suspicions about my scheme to jump ship. I planned to arrive at his door just before his departure for Varadero to beg him for a permit to purchase the flight to Moscow with CSA Airlines. It worked. When I arrived at the consulate, his secretary told me that he might not have time to receive me because he was departing for Varadero that very evening. Immediately, I inferred that he would be anxious to leave and would not have time to call Moscow for their approval of my request. My shopping expectations in Prague, combined with the good looks of a young female, worked a miracle on him. He received me, despite his rush. I spoke with him in his own language, that of a spoiled Soviet abroad. I told him that I would never forgive him if he did not issue my permission to shop in Prague. My silly rationale was that it would be a "stupid mistake" to classify my flight to Prague as a separate trip. It was only a transit stop on the route to Moscow.

I explained that I had only two weeks of holiday, which were starting early next week. I did not have time to wait for his return from Varadero. He agreed to make an exception for me and overlook the general prohibition for Soviet citizens to fly by foreign airlines. He put his signature and stamp on the requested permission. Of course, he also mentioned that I was now in debt to him for taking such a big risk with his diplomatic career, and we will have to continue our discussion about "shells" on our return to Havana. I anticipated that he would try to extort compensation for breaking the rules.

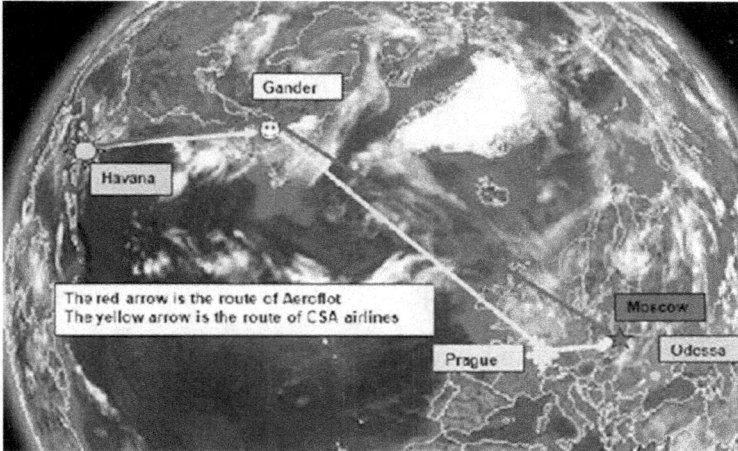

CSA and Aeroflot Havana-Moscow routes

However, I checkmated him by arranging it on such short notice before his departure to Varadero. A karmic settlement would have to be left for some vague future. He could not scare me with the promise to meet on our return to Havana from holiday because I was not planning to return. I even experienced some guilt about tricking him and jeopardizing his diplomatic career. I rationalized that this young diplomat obviously inherited his privileged position in '*nomenklatura*'; therefore, he belonged to the corrupt species I despised and probably deserved the trouble.[9] Anyway, I did not have a choice. I knew that he felt sufficiently secure about my trip through Czechoslovakia because Soviet tanks had only recently crushed this country into submission, and the KGB created very stringent security controls all over the nation.

So far, there was no precedent of any Soviet citizen attempting to escape from Czechoslovakia or Cuba using Czechoslovakia as a transit point. Aeroflot also had a refueling stop in Gander, and the advantage of flying with CSA Airlines for the purpose of escaping did not seem obvious. Anxious to depart for Varadero, the new council just ruined his life's career by issuing me a special permit for the purchase of our flight on Czech Airlines. Now, however, this victory was hollow since we were flying to Moscow by Aeroflot. My father had forewarned me in his photos with coded messages, which he sent personally with his friend, that the KGB may be waiting for a meeting with me on my return home, and that I should not return for the time being. This meant that now we must escape in Gander from the Aeroflot plane before it continues its flight to Moscow. This will be much more difficult since Aeroflot carries KGB agents to oversee the passengers on all its foreign flights precisely to prevent their escape. My Gander operation could be tough going.

By midday, it was becoming unbearably hot, especially on the tarmac under the sun. The children were very restless. When our turn finally arrived, the Cuban immigration agents and KGB security were also hot and uncomfortable. The agents hurriedly checked our documents and filled out the approval forms for the children's departure, which Eduardo was asked to authorize by signing. This moment was the most worrisome for me. I was in a stupor, not because of the blazing sun, but because of my frazzled nerves, or maybe because of both. I was frozen with dread and almost lost the ability to see or to hear. Everything will be decided now. It is as if I am in a dream. Should Eduardo refuse to give our children this authorization, I will stay. All will end here.

Despite his ghostly pale face and solemn expression, Eduardo acted decisively and signed his release on the children's forms. I was watching him as if I was not present, as if I would have been dead and was only flying over him, in an out-of-body experience, observing it all from above. It was a very strange feeling when I began to recognize that the moment of real separation had come and that our children and I might never see him again. Yes, we discussed many times before that if all turns out successfully, he will make an effort to escape and join us. I believed that when such a moment comes, he will do his utmost, but for now, there were no real expectations for anything at all. We had no idea what would happen to any of us.

He kissed the children, gave them a brief hug, and did not

even look at me. We did not need to use our eyes to communicate and to be aware of our emotional state; we were acutely aware of it without looking at each other. The flight attendant came to us and reproached me for delaying their flight, not walking quickly towards the craft's ladder. Still in a stupor, I obeyed her order and walked mechanically behind the stewardess and toward the plane, carrying Ernestico on one arm and holding the hand of Edik with the other.

When we reached the ladder, I turned to search for Eduardo, but he had turned his back and was walking away across the tarmac without looking at us. I felt my heart was being crushed. He is leaving without even waiting for the departure of our aircraft. Only then did I manage to force myself to walk up the passenger stairs. The flight attendant took us to our seats, from where I could look out at the tarmac through the small passenger window. Eduardo was there, again standing on the airport tarmac under the hot tropical sun, looking anxiously at the craft. The next moment, his eyes met mine, but immediately he turned his head away. His face had a dead, gray expression, as if he was not present, not alive, as if everything around us was not real. Probably, he, too, was trying to suppress his emotions; it would be monstrously hard on him. He stopped looking at my window while our aircraft went onto the runway. I tried to retain his image on the tarmac recorded in my memory, but my tears were clouding my view, and I could not control them any longer. The children were frightened at the sight of tears washing my face without any sound. They felt that something had gone very wrong. They, too, were afraid and sad but were unable to ask about what happened. The knowledge that we might never again see Eduardo overwhelmed me now with debilitating guilt, but I needed to gain control over myself. I did not know yet if we would succeed or we would fail. From now on, it was purely my responsibility. Still, the moment of physically abandoning Eduardo was emotionally more difficult than anything else that ever happened to me later in my life.

Paulina Zelitsky, Paul Weinzweig

Eduardo prior to our departure from Havana

When our plane finally began to pick up altitude, both my little boys became more tranquil, feeling drowsy from the movement of the aircraft. Soon they fell asleep, as did the majority of passengers in the cabin. After a day of walking on broken glass, I was still feeling too upset and exhausted to start organizing my thoughts. My mind, despite drowsiness, could not relax. I should not move in my seat so as not to disturb the sleeping children. Feeling deeply guilty about leaving Eduardo behind in Havana, cutting off myself and the children from my parents, from everybody and everything we ever knew, throwing away my professional career for which I had worked so hard - this was not an easy move.

"Is it smart?" Our neighbors in my parents' communal apartment in Odessa would ask. *Why was I prepared to risk our lives? What went wrong with me?*

23. *Kaddish*[10] for Pelta

While the children slept, I continued thinking about why I was simply unable to obey the rules and do what I was told; after all, in the opinion of many, compliance will result in a more comfortable life. Perhaps that rebellious streak in my character came from my grandma Pelta.

My father told me about her for the first time when I was about ten years old. We were studying Pushkin's romantic poetry at school, and I had fallen in love with it. I was not asking my father about grandma in particular. Quite the opposite: I never met her, and it never came to my mind to ask questions about somebody who in my little world did not even exist. In reality, my question was about my name, which I happened to dislike.

"Papa, I don't like my name, Paulina. No one else in our neighborhood or my class is named Paulina. I would prefer to be called Natasha, like the hero of Pushkin's poetic novel *Eugene Onegin,* or Ludmila, like the hero from his poem *Ruslan and Ludmila*. Pushkin gave his heroes beautiful names, but my name I can't find anywhere in poetry, and it doesn't fit with the other girls' names in our school."

"*Dochenka, Paulinochka*, what do you mean you don't like your name?" He answered softly, but was annoyed. "Why would you prefer to be called Natasha? You know that we Jewish people have a tradition to call a new child after a deceased member of the family, whose best traits they hope will be repeated in the newborn child. This is why I named you Paulina, and for a very good reason. You are named in honor of your Grandmother, my Mother Pelta. You see, I believed that the Russian version of Pelta is Paulina. This is why your name is Paulina, you little *'meshugge'* (the crazy one). If you would only know what kind of woman your grandmother was, you would feel proud to be named after her."

"Tell me, Papa, what was she like and why did she die? You never talk about her."

"*Dochenka*, the memory of her is forever in my heart, but your big mouth is a serious problem. Don't jump over your head; grow up first. If I tell you about her, you must remember not to mention it to anybody because it might become dangerous for us. Do you remember what your stupid bragging about so-called Uncle Lionia from Moscow brought to us a few years back? Remember how this almost got all of us arrested? They would arrest me and send you to a horrible state orphanage for socially dangerous children."[10]

"I was only seven years old then, Papa. I have grown up now. I already promised you with my life that I will never say to anyone what you tell me. I will simply keep my mouth shut. I never met Pelta. Would you tell me why she had such a strange name? It is even stranger than mine."

"It is from the Middle Ages. It was a Jewish-French name Bellette (a pet form of Belle), *Dochenka*. It was modified with a Yiddish accent after centuries of use in Poland, Russia, and Germany from Belle to Bellette to Pelet and finally, to Pelta. I wanted to name you after her, so you would grow up to be as beautiful, intelligent, and energetic as she was. Since we would not dare to give you a non-Russian name, we named you Paulina - the Russified version of Pelta. Now, listen about Pelta.

Her family emigrated from somewhere in Western Europe after the Jews, expelled by the Romans from their homeland, were forced to wander around the world. Remember when you were little and came to ask me who the Jews were, and I told you how they were expelled from their country? Periodically, they were collectively expelled from many nations that previously had allowed them to settle there, including England, France, Spain, Germany, and most other

Western European countries over the centuries. In your school books, life begins only with the Revolution. No? But for the family of Pelta, it started much earlier. I do not know exactly when her grandparents came to Odessa, but her father was born to an Odessan merchant. All that I was told, remember to keep this secret, was that her family belonged to a guild of registered traders. Pelta's father bought his merchandise in Brody (now in western Ukraine) and shipped it from the Port of Odessa to buyers in Italy and Greece. In Brody, he was introduced to the European Enlightenment, which was first brought to Eastern European Jews as the *Haskala*[11] European reform movement with an emphasis on the values of humanity, science, and the arts.

Pelta attended the Odessa Jewish school for girls. When I was a little boy, she told me that she loved it. There she learned Russian, French, and Italian, mathematics, geography, and bookkeeping. She told me that she particularly enjoyed learning these modern subjects of the Enlightenment, which were not available for Jewish female students anywhere else in Russia, only in Odessa. Her father supported her studies in science and the arts because he was hoping that she could help him in business when she grew up.

My mother told me how much she loved the choral works of Nissan Blumenthal performed on the Sabbath in her synagogue at Pushkinskaya and Zhukovsky streets, which you must know well. This is the Brodskaya Synagogue, now Odessa's public archive, since the Soviet Government shut it down as a place of worship. On her piano, she often played for us children her favorite piece, the *Kol Nidrei* prayer by Max Bruch. This music was traditionally performed in her synagogue during the evening service on Yom Kippur (Day of Atonement). It is very beautiful. It is about asking God's forgiveness for unfulfilled vows. Maybe, one day, you will be able to hear it.

Then, suddenly, everything was turned upside down for Pelta. When she was 14 years old, her life was changed forever. In 1905, once again, Odessa experienced mass pogroms (violent anti-Semitic attacks on Jewish residents). Okhrana (Tsarist secret police) organized these attacks in Ukraine. The mob of Ukrainian nationalists and Russian peasants were led by *Okhrana* agents to attack Jewish businesses in Odessa."

"Why Jewish, Papa? Why not Greeks or Poles or Russians?"

"Because the organizers used the Christian orthodox religious hatred to instigate the pogroms. The Greeks, Russians, and Poles all belong to the Christian (Orthodox) church as well. This is why it was easier to blame only Jews and to justify attacks in the name of the officially approved religion. The drunken mob attacked the business of Pelta's father. Her father and his employees were dragged outside their offices in the city. They were stripped naked and beaten mercilessly. Her father died, and his business was burned to the ground. No police intervened with these mob killings; quite the opposite, the Tsarist authorities and police encouraged it to relieve the upheavals and stresses among dispossessed Ukrainian and Russian peasants who were arriving in Odessa in large numbers to seek jobs in the port, especially in times of economic turmoil.[12]

After the death of her husband, Pelta's mother became very sick. She was frightened and depressed from grief. In this state, she was obliged to return to her family, who, in fright, blamed *Haskalah* for the misfortunes of pogrom victims. They advised my *bubeleh* (grandmother) to marry Pelta as soon as possible to a serious and righteous type of Jew, a Hassidic Jew,[13] to redeem the faults of the reformed *Haskalah*, which they believed was the reason that God was punishing Odessan Jews with pogroms.

The relatives of *bubeleh* brought their candidate for this marriage. He was a 43-year-old religious Hassidic Jew. Pelta was only 14 and adamantly refused to enter into this marriage. She pleaded with them to spare her, but her relatives refused to hear her objections. The *Hassidic Shadchen* (the matchmaker) tied her down on the bed and tickled her for hours. This was a traditional method in those years, practiced by the local Hassidic Jews, to overcome the objections of their daughters. Finally, Pelta agreed to marry Israel Zelitsky Shimilev-Manevich, who became my father.

He was a serious and righteous man and spent most of the day in the synagogue, leaving his young wife alone at home. Pelta did not complain about the situation. She was happiest when he stayed out of her hair. She continued to educate herself despite her husband's expectations that giving birth to their children and taking care of the household would claim all her free time. While her husband prayed, Pelta gave birth to a total of 14 children. Only four of us survived to adulthood. High child mortality was quite common for the time because of the pogroms and frequent plagues brought by ships from the Ottoman Empire or Europe, which periodically ravaged our city. Your Auntie Rachael was the oldest, then it was me, after me your Uncle Isaak, and the youngest was your Auntie Fania, whom you know well."

"Papa, I know only my Auntie Fania. Where are my Uncle Isaak and my Auntie Rachel?"

"Don't put the wagon before the horse. *Paulinochka,* that is another story. Let me finish this one. When I was about five years old, Pelta convinced her bankrupt husband (according to Pelta, he spent all his time praying instead of working) to allow her to join the workforce to earn money and provide for her family. He allowed Pelta to learn the trade of couturier or elegant dressmaking while working for a famous designer. She was very talented and was promoted rapidly at work. As a result, she was favored by the most prestigious clientele, making house calls for famous actresses and aristocratic ladies. They were so pleased with her work that she earned sufficient money to open her own fashion salon, where she employed seamstresses. Soon, she became famous on her own, and her clientele called on her for their special occasions. She became prosperous.

Pelta bought a house for her fashion atelier in the center of Odessa with her own money and personally hired talented Jewish, Russian, and Ukrainian girls to assist her in the laborious work of dressmaking. The girls who worked there were also taking care of our children. We were not permitted to play outside after school. I managed to play outside with other children only when I escaped from my prison guards, the seamstresses. All of us children (including the children of the seamstresses) were taught in the afternoon and at night in our home by official tutors from the expensive private Odessa Gymnasium because Jewish children were no longer accepted there. Such schooling was a very special privilege arranged and paid for by our mother for all of us, including the children of the seamstresses. The seamstresses supervised our homework, but I was always dreaming of escaping to play outside with other boys instead of learning with what I thought then were those boring, silly women. I would rebel and shout: I am a *'punia'* ("a man" in Odessan jargon) and not a woman, let me out! I badly wanted to be with other males, but my father was rarely at home, and my brother was only a baby.

I also remember how, in the morning when we woke up, we would run to the window to see which flag was flying from the city's Duma (City Council). Many different navies would arrive in the port of Odessa to unload their armies to occupy the new revolutionary Russia from the only access in the South. It was a real mess: today the French, a few days later the Italians, after that Germans, next week English, Greeks, Moroccans, then the Austro-German occupation, the Polish army, then Petliura[14] and Machno[15] (Ukrainian nationalists), the Whites of Denikin[16] (Czarist army), then roving Ukrainian gangs of bandits from the steppes, and after them the Reds.

When I succeeded in escaping from the seamstresses, I would run to the port and watch which navy would arrive next to claim Odessa. Once, I remember how I brought home a small, unexploded bomb, which I found on the street near the port. When some soldiers began knocking at our gates, I got scared and hid it in our fireplace. They never found it, but after they left, the bomb naturally exploded from the heat in the fireplace, and that wing of our house was damaged. I received a horrible spanking and was locked in my bedroom as punishment for a few days or maybe even a week; I can't remember for how long.

Ships came and went. Armies came and went. Each time Whites or Reds would take the city, they would raid the Jews. Especially dangerous were the Ukrainians, the people of Petliura. Pogroms became constant occurrences because all the invaders came for booty. Females were the most vulnerable victims because they were objects of rape. My mother decided to send my older 14-year-old sister, Rachael, to America by herself. The fashion business was not in fashion any longer. Anyone who had any money to escape dropped everything left behind his worldly goods and fled. It was difficult to arrange the departure permit for Rachael, and the long sea voyage was very expensive. Yet, my mother managed to arrange it all. Thanks to this opportunity, Rachael survived, became educated, married, and lived well in America. Unfortunately, we were unable to correspond with her because it would be a death sentence for any of us in the Soviet Union under Stalin. We had to ask her, specifically, never again to contact us. We lost all communication with her. I don't know if she is alive today."

"Then, what happened to you, Papa?"

"Life in Odessa was chaos. Residents of the city were constantly assaulted, and anti-Semitic attacks became routine. The Jewish population of Odessa created self-defense groups, which resisted many of the assaults from bandit groups: Whites, Reds, or Independent Ukrainians, all roaming across the steppes of the Pale[17] and attacking the civil Jewish population. The ferocity of anti-Semitic mobs only increased in response to efforts at Jewish defense. In January of 1920, we were attacked by the Ukrainian bandit Ataman

69

Struk,[18] a madman and an anti-Semite with 3000 drunken troops. They took Odessa in a battle and furiously attacked Moldovanka (the Jewish neighborhood of Odessa), where they killed and looted a defenseless population. Jewish self-defense consisted mainly of Odessa high school students and local youth. They bravely fought the overpowering troops of Ataman Struk, who were drunk from the vodka, but also crazed from the bloodbath of innocent civilian Jews, mostly the elderly and women with children, because all young males were fighting on the side of the Jewish resistance. Somebody denounced the salon of my mother as a Jewish self-defense cover. The drunken mobs of Struk attacked her salon, which was in the same house where we lived. They dragged her and my father out into the street. After beating and humiliating them, they killed them. The house was looted and set on fire. We never saw how any of this happened because our Russian and Ukrainian Christian seamstresses, who worked for my mother, escaped from the mob with three of us - Fania, Isaak, and me - pretending that we were their children. They removed us from Odessa altogether and hid us in the homes of other peasants in the region. The Christian workers and neighbors were allowed to leave by the marauding mob; if not, we would all be dead. My mother's seamstresses were very courageous and kindly spared us the agony of seeing what happened to our parents."

"Where did you go with the peasants?"

"They took us to a regional village and placed us to live with one Ukrainian peasant family. We worked for this family, helping them with the animals. When I became 14 years of age, our owner sent me to the Army of Budyonny (Reds), who finally won over most of the region.[19] It was not my choice. The peasants were forced to contribute by providing their sons as fresh warriors for the Red Cossack Army, or their houses would be burned. They contributed me instead of their son, and I became a Cossack in Budyonny's (Red) Army. I lived on my horse in the army for some years.

"Papa, do you have at least a photograph of Pelta?"

"I have only one photograph of Pelta with Fania when Fania was only a baby. One of my mother's seamstresses gave me this photograph (a gift from my mother to her) after I returned from the army."

"How old were you when the mob killed your parents?"

"I was eleven years old, Isaak was seven, and Fania five."

"Why are you keeping this story secret? You haven`t done anything wrong. You were only the victim of a pogrom and not the perpetrator."

"*Dochenka*, after I returned from the army, I dreamed of studying at the Naval Academy. To be accepted for this program, the recommendation from the Army was not sufficient. I also needed a proletarian background; otherwise, I would not stand a chance. You see, my mother, as I told you, had her own business: the fashion atelier where she employed others. This business would define her, in revolutionary terms, as a member of the bourgeoisie. Understand, this would be a very negative spot in my biography after the Revolution. I lied about my mother's occupation and was able to hide my bourgeois heritage (a serious disadvantage if you want to study for a professional career). I could do this only because I came to the Army of Budyonny as a farm laborer, meaning that my background was proletarian. This is how I filled out all the forms and documents. You, too, should keep the story of your grandmother secret; otherwise, it would damage my career and your future. '*Net Chuda bez dobra*' (There is no bad without good)," he concluded.

That was it! I returned to our Aeroflot reality. My question was answered: Paulina was the name given to me in honor of my grandma Pelta, the wellspring of my rebellious temperament. She took the long road. She educated herself, developed her talent, became wealthy by working hard, marketed and managed her own fashion business. She was a woman entrepreneur at the beginning of the 20th Century during the revolution in Ukraine, a God-forsaken country.

Grandma Pelta with my auntie Fania

Despite all the prejudices and persecutions, she made a good life for herself and her family. The anti-Semitic mob that killed her, just as they killed her father a dozen years before, had overlooked her son. My father is alive, and so am I, and I shall be very proud to continue her efforts. I hope that destiny will spare us the terrible experience of my predecessors.

With so much of our nation's history mired in conquest and cruelty, it is obvious why I want to leave to raise my children in a civilized country where hatred and discrimination are taboo and are neither promoted nor practiced by the state or by society. I want to be free, and I want my children to be free. When I arrive in the new country, I will educate myself on survival skills. I am determined to bring up my children in a society unshackled from hatred and ignorance, and allow my kids to break this vicious cycle of human history. These thoughts calmed me down, and I became capable of carrying on routine tasks with the children during the flight: feeding and washing them and making small talk after they awoke in their narrow Aeroflot seats.

Kaddish[20] *for Pelta!* I owe this adventure to her.

24. In the Shadow of SMERSH[22]

An announcement on the intercom woke up the children. We were arriving in Canada at the Gander, Newfoundland International Airport. How quickly time passed during the flight; I could hardly believe it. Now, the real test begins. With all the trials that went before, the most dangerous part was coming.

"This flight of Aeroflot IL-62M is now approaching Gander Airport for a scheduled refueling stop before continuing the flight to Moscow. We are asking all our passengers to follow the airline personnel to spend 40 minutes in the airport terminal lounge, where they will be served coffee or other refreshments. Please leave all your belongings with the airline except your travel documents. All passengers must leave; it is a safety requirement for the refueling procedure. Delays will not be tolerated since the refueling time is only 40 minutes."

Oh, no! What shall I do now? I am facing the moment of reckoning without any prepared plan. Only one condition is clear to me: I must hurry to store all our indispensable possessions in my brassiere. The limited size of my bra allowed only our most essential documents, such as our birth certificates, my engineering diploma, and our family photographs, to fit into a small envelope. My passport, in which both children were listed as Soviet citizens under my responsibility, and our airline tickets, I was required to hold in my hand when exiting the aircraft. No one on the flight should notice how and where I was hiding all my documents or become a suspect. I had everything stuffed in two envelopes, one for each side of my bra. It is not that much, but it is bulky, especially the family photographs. If I neglected to take these essential family photos, I might never again see those beloved images; it was unthinkable. I accommodated these personal possessions the only way I could, without anybody noticing: by bending close to the floor. This provoked an angry reaction from a flight attendant who had commanded the passengers to put their seats in the upright position and fasten their seatbelts.

After a nine-hour flight in a turboprop, Edik could not stay still for a moment. Passengers were climbing down the ladder to the airport tarmac. There was a cold rain falling. It was already May, but spring arrived late in Gander.

How can we escape? By running? To Where? The male Aeroflot attendants, with suspiciously military postures, could be the KGB agents who accompany passengers during refueling in foreign airports. Usually, the best agents are selected for Western airports. I counted six male and four uniformed female attendants who surrounded our group of approximately 170 passengers to escort us inside the airport terminal. How many agents are scattered among the passengers, dressed in civilian clothes? I will never know. When I slowed down intentionally, pretending that I needed to adjust my child's jacket, a male attendant immediately stopped beside me and asked us to keep pace with the rest of the passengers. He and several female attendants joined me on both sides to ensure that we did not delay the other passengers.

We walked along narrow corridors to the enclosed waiting room without being screened by Canadian immigration. My plan was crumbling quickly. I had been counting on stories from our Czech physician in Havana about Czech defectors who were given protection by immigration agents. But in our case, all other passengers were removed from the waiting room of the airport to allow the Aeroflot passengers full isolation and containment. The walls of this enclosure were glass. Canadian passersby would throw us curious looks from the other side. The Aeroflot attendants inside this glassed room and the Canadian officials lined up on the other side represented an impenetrable barrier.

I felt lost; my hopes evaporated for an immigration screening where I could request political asylum. We were locked in a glass ball until it was time to return to the plane. Despite Dr. Nader's assurances, immigration procedures appropriate for Czech passengers counted for nothing in the case of Aeroflot travelers who were confined to a protected transfer room during refueling. It was a terrible blow to my fragile plan.

I was hoping not to look desperate. The bar attendant offered free refreshments for the children and coffee for me. My thoughts were running in circles. My heart was pounding. We have only 30 minutes; what can we do? How does this little fish escape from the glass bowl? The only possibility that occurred to me was the same solution discovered by all kids on this planet when they wanted to escape from school authorities: the washroom!

However, I had to find out where the washroom was. I could not see one in the waiting room. I made a discreet inquiry of the bar attendant, who explained that the washroom was behind the bar, inside the service corridor. He added that Aeroflot passengers are not allowed to use it because it was reserved for service personnel. I insisted that I needed the washroom for my small children. He let me into the service corridor, where on one side, I could see the only door. I assumed it must be the washroom. Without looking behind to see if anyone was following us (so as not to look suspicious), I took the children into the washroom, hoping no one noticed. There were two narrow metal stalls, and I was not sure what to do. Then, I heard the announcement for the Aeroflot passengers to line up to be conducted back to the aircraft. Oh boy, the decisive moment has come. My naïve plan was to lock ourselves here in the washroom compartment, praying that the flight attendants and the KGB agents would forget about us or would simply consider us lost when counting the passengers returning to the Aeroflot craft. I entered with both children into the same narrow metal stall, locked the door, and begged the boys to stay quiet. Poor little children did not understand this game, but obediently stayed with me inside the stall. With great difficulty, the children accustomed themselves to the boredom of waiting in such a crowded place. After about 15 minutes, my thumping heart counting seconds like the beat of a metronome, I began to believe that the Aeroflot passengers might have left the bar and returned to their aircraft. I was hoping that this would present an opportunity for us to leave our hiding place for someplace more reassuring, like the company of one of those Canadian officials outside the glass waiting room. Since our return to the bar would be very risky, I hesitated. The children grew tired of staying still inside the small washroom stall and began protesting loudly.

Suddenly, somebody knocked very hard and rapidly on the door of our stall where we were hiding. **"Bang, bang, bang …"** I was terrified because I knew our game was over. I lifted Ernestico and opened the door. I found myself face-to-face with two Aeroflot female attendants.

"What are you doing here? Didn't you hear the announcement to return to the aircraft?" One of them shouted angrily.

"No, I have been busy with my younger child, who has diarrhea, probably because of the food served during the flight. I don't know what to do about this; maybe I could bring him to a doctor at this airport. I am sure the doctor will not refuse to see him; only a few minutes, please." I was trying without much hope to be clever.

"You are insane! We are in a foreign airport. Our flight departs right now, and we are already late because of you. Start walking with us to join the rest of the passengers immediately."

"Yes, I will. Please don't shout at me. These are only small children, and you scared them with your banging and shouting. Thank you for informing me. We will follow you right away."

A moment later, four additional uniformed, male Aeroflot agents surrounded us. They were waiting for us at the bar. Our escort through the narrow airport corridors to the aircraft was generous: two male agents in front and two behind us, with female attendants at our sides. When we arrived, the other passengers were already seated in the cabin. Everybody was now looking at us. My best defense for the security people in this situation will be pretending to be stupid. Let them think that I am a helpless young mother with two small children, overcome with stress and panic when her child had an upset stomach. Such a mother might become dangerous for the airline if she lays blame on the Aeroflot food. Of course, they might discover that my claims are false if they get a doctor to examine my sick child. Then, they will discover my claims were false, and my cover will be blown away. I thought that now our lives depend on how carefully I can manipulate the perceptions of these attendants or agents.

We returned to our seats, and the flight attendants were talking among themselves and looking at me. One flight attendant from their group took a seat behind us (she was probably a security agent) to ensure that we were supervised. I locked our seat belts and dimmed the overhead light. Now, a terrible dark fear began slowly to take hold of my mind. The children, tired after our stressful stopover, quickly fell asleep, but I was fighting my fears about what would happen upon our arrival in Moscow. If the flight security reports to their KGB department in Moscow about my washroom fiasco and a doctor examines my child, I could be arrested, and the children will be sent to my parents in the best case. Eduardo, the boys, and my parents could be spared, but I was in danger.

What charges could they make against me? What do I know about the precedents for similar charges? What were the results? News about defections never appeared officially in the Soviet press. It was as if such defections or attempted defections never happened at all. The subject was taboo. There was some public knowledge about SMERSH[21] tribunals regarding foreign spies in the Soviet media. SMERSH is the Russian acronym for *Smert Nemetskim Shpionam* or "Death to (German) Spies". It was the punishment department of GRU (Soviet Military Intelligence Agency) that arrested and sentenced all those military and sometimes civilian personnel who were imprisoned by the enemy in the enemy-occupied territories. I knew about one case: my Uncle Isaak Israel Zelitsky.

Isaak was my father's younger brother (five years younger). This is what I know, or rather what my father told me about him and his fate. After their parents had been murdered by a mob in 1920 during a pogrom, my father, his sister, and their younger brother began living with a Cossack family who saved the children. At the age of 14, my father was conscripted into the Budyonny Cavalry Army, where he met the famous Odessa writer Isaak Babel, who was at the time a war correspondent with Semyon Budyonny. After the civil war, my father went to Odessa Gubkom (the Regional Committee of the Communist Party) to arrange for the continuation of studies for himself and his brother Isaak. He was fortunate to meet Babel himself. Papa asked him to assist in arranging for further studies for his talented younger brother Isaak, who, before the pogrom, studied playing the violin from the age of four.

Thanks to the help of Babel, my Uncle Isaak was able to continue his studies and to live in the school residence. Papa, too, completed his secondary education and passed the examinations of the Odessa Naval Academy, where he wanted to study. The brothers settled in Odessa. Papa married my mother, Berta, but Isaak, who became recognized as a professional concert violinist, was still single because he traveled extensively across the country as a performing violinist and claimed to have no time to create his own family. Being a professional violinist, Isaak was not drafted into the army at eighteen like other Soviet boys; he was excused from military training. When the Second World War broke out, Isaak declared that he could not play the violin while his country needed defenders against German aggression. Inspired by patriotism, he volunteered during the very first days of the war. Since he had never received military training, he was conscripted as a junior communications technician and sent to the Soviet Ukrainian front. That was his very big mistake, according to Papa.

Germany and Romania attacked the Soviet Union unexpectedly, so there was no time to train recruits. Isaak was not only untrained; he was not even given ammunition.[22] Isaak was marched from the first days of the war to the Ukrainian front. The situation of the soldiers was tragically absurd since the majority of conscripts in his division were neither trained nor equipped for defense. Isaak had no rifle and did not know how to shoot. Isaak's Soviet Army battalion, cut off by the German army, lost all its provisions, ammunition, artillery support, and supplies. The Soviet Army leadership did not want to admit their delusions and errors due to Stalin's refusal to believe that German aggression was real because he relied on the Soviet non-aggression pact with Hitler. Receiving no orders from their military superiors, who panicked and became confused when Stalin went into hiding at the beginning of the war, Soviet divisions on the Polish and Ukrainian border were swept clean by German forces from the air and ground. The resulting chaos permitted the rapid advancement of the German Army through the heart of Ukraine.

From the first day of the war, my father lost all contact with his brother Isaak. The navy squadron where my papa was serving at the time was defending the largest Soviet submarine base in Liepaja, Latvia, on the Baltic Sea, which was attacked at the beginning of the war. Later, over the next two years, Papa was based in Murmansk with the Northern Fleet, whose mission was to organize a safe corridor for the fleet of allied forces. This is why he was unable to prevent

Isaak from committing this grave misjudgment of volunteering for the army. He heard nothing from his brother for the next two years.

My Uncle Isaak Israelevich Zelitsky

Suddenly, in 1943, agents of SMERSH called upon my father to present himself onshore in Murmansk for interrogation. SMERSH was in charge of finding and arresting all Soviet military personnel in German captivity, in addition to all repatriates and informal resistance fighters (partisans allied with the Soviet Army) operating in territories previously occupied by the Germans. They also backed all front lines to fire at retreating Soviet troops and, by this measure, assured the brave behavior of the Soviet Army.

My father came to this interrogation with more than a little foreboding. He thought it was the end because the infamy of SMERSH was even more terrifying than that of the Gestapo. No one invited for interrogation by SMERSH hoped to avoid the death sentence or, in the best case, years of forced labor in Gulag camps in the Far East and Northern Siberia. My father said that he was not frightened of battle with the Nazis but that he was terrified of SMERSH.

"Is Private Isaak Zelitsky your younger brother?" asked one interrogator.

"Yes, he is."

"Where is Isaak at present?"

"I don't know. The last news about him was that he volunteered to be sent to defend the Ukrainian front, but over the last two years, I haven't heard anything from him because, since the war started, I was involved in Baltic and Northern Sea operations."

"When did you last hear of him?"

"Before the war, when I was transferred from the Black Sea Navy to the Northern Navy. All I heard about Isaak was that he had volunteered with the Soviet Army on the Ukrainian front."

"You never heard from him since?"

"No, I never did."

"What do you know about Isaak's political fitness?"

"I believe the fact that Isaak, being a renowned violinist, volunteered to join the army as a private is sufficient evidence of his political fitness."

"What else do you know about him? Why is he not a communist?"

"I do not know what happened to him since we separated. All I know is that before that moment, he was not a member of the Communist Party."

"Why, if he is politically fit, he is not a Party member?"

"I think it is because he is a musician."

"You are not a musician, but we know that you are not a member of the Communist Party either."

"My brother and I are Jews by our ethnicity. Our priority is to defend our homeland with arms on the battlefield."

"What you said, the captain is very interesting, but we have news for you. Your brother was captured by the German Army. He claims that a bomb exploded beside him and left him unconscious. The Germans grabbed him in this unconscious state."

"Do you know if he is still alive?"

"His story does not end there. When, almost a year later, the Germans undressed him, they discovered that he was a circumcised Jew, and they sent him, together with other Jewish soldiers they found in the POW camp, to a Polish death camp to build additional cremation facilities to exterminate the Jewish civilian population in Poland. Your brother claims that Soviet soldiers were given two weeks for this construction. They rebelled before the end of the two weeks because they expected to be the first victims in the new crematorium. They killed some of their German guards and freed all other prisoners. Most of the prisoners escaped, but very few survived because of fire from German guards and the minefields they had to cross. Isaak claimed that he and eight others survived the ordeal and crossed the Soviet front line under fire to rejoin the Soviet Army and once again to fight Hitler. We arrested him because we could never believe that, being a Jew, he could escape the death camp. We suspect that he is a spy; otherwise, how did he survive? You must help us by confessing the truth."

"Thank you for the good news that he is alive. I am sure he is telling you the truth because it is a death sentence for a Jew to be captured by German troops. I know Isaak, and

I trust Isaak. He is a true patriot. For a Jew to survive a Nazi prisoner of war camp, there could be no other possibility but to fight and escape. I am sure if he said that he escaped from a German POW camp to join the Soviet Army, he is telling the truth."

"Well, we are not here to obtain your opinion, only the facts. As you know, according to Soviet law, all Soviet prisoners caught on territory occupied by the enemy are considered traitors, and traitors can never be trusted. All traitors are spies. If he came from the German-occupied territory, he is a traitor and a spy."

"Could you please tell me what will happen to him?"

"No, this is not your business. We have no further questions for the moment. You may return to your ship. When it is convenient, you will be notified if we need you again. Consider yourself very lucky that you are a Navy captain and we are in a war. You have not heard from him for two years, and because our country needs your services here, you will be saved from punishment as a direct family member of a traitor. Go away before we change our minds."

Papa left and went straight to the naval hospital in Murmansk, where my mother Berta, worked as a volunteer to be stationed close to my father. He told her what happened. She said that she would not rest until she found Isaak and tried to help him.

According to the penal practice in the Soviet Union, after someone was arrested, the authorities refused to reveal to his relatives and friends any information regarding the prisoner's whereabouts: to which prison or labor camp he was sent or what sentence was delivered. Papa was in the military service, and he could not request leave from the Navy to search across the country for his brother. If he applied for leave, he, too, would be considered a traitor. According to Soviet penal practice, all direct and often secondary relatives of the accused were also charged and sentenced to five years in a forced labor camp, followed by exile to the remote North or the Far East and confiscation of their property. This is how the Soviet leaders ensured that their soldiers would rather die than be taken alive by the enemy. The practice of arbitrary kidnapping and enslavement also guaranteed settlements in the northern regions and labor at little cost.

As soon as my mother, Berta, could take a leave from the Navy hospital where she was working as a volunteer, she collected some money from relatives and friends and traveled personally, in search of Isaak, to the forced labor camps of the Gulag containing the *catalog* inmates. These were specialized hard labor security camps built for ex-military Soviet prisoners. They were operated under especially draconian regulations. The guards of the prisons and labor camps where she went simply refused to answer if the prisoner Isaak was held there. To refuse to give out any information about a prisoner's whereabouts was standard government policy.

However, it was well known that when a visitor comes in person to the prison and asks the guards to send a prisoner a small food parcel, this parcel will either be accepted at the prison or refused. If the food parcel is refused, it means that the prisoner was not there; if the food parcel is accepted, it means he was there. The practice of not divulging information about the prisoner was intended to punish the family members. During the war, mothers or wives, with or without their children, were roaming the remote North and the Far East of the Soviet Union, home to the majority of Gulag camps, in a desperate hope to discover where their loved ones were held.

It took my mother more than three months to locate Isaak. She traveled under the most dangerous and desolate conditions across the country. A single woman in extremely remote cold areas, often traveling on foot, was risking rape and the possibility of being murdered for her possessions.

She visited some of those camps in the Far East containing the *katorga* inmates. These camps were known for starvation food rations and 14-16 hour forced labor workdays without rest in the northern uranium and gold mines.

A map indicating Berta's 3-month journey from Murmansk to Irkutsk across the USSR (over 4000 kilometers)

When Berta would finally arrive at the visitor's window of each forced labor camp, she would attempt to deposit a small food parcel for prisoner Isaak Zelitsky. She was in despair because not a single camp she reached accepted her parcel for Isaak. Finally, in the region of Irkutsk, in the Far East near Mongolia, in one *katorga* camp, the guard accepted my mother's bribe and recommended that she check with prison hospital Number Three. She had to make the perilous journey to the hospital location alone on foot, which took her an additional three days. When she arrived at that hospital and attempted to leave a food parcel for Isaak, she was told it was too late: he had died two weeks earlier. He perished from starvation. My mother returned to Murmansk, exhausted and disheartened. After her brief recovery, she went back to work at the Navy hospital, but in a poor state of health.

Six months later, a surprise: Papa's cousin Raya Murik from Novo-Ostankino in the Moscow Region received a letter from Isaak, which was almost unreadable because the writing was scribbled and the ink faded. The letter revealed his story and made the point that he was hospitalized not because of sickness but from starvation. This news brought fresh suffering to my mother because now she felt guilty. Her food parcel might have saved his life if she had arrived at the prison hospital just a few weeks earlier. Of course, it could happen only if the guards did not steal that parcel. My father tried to console her by saying that it was not realistic to believe that her small parcel would save Isaak because very little or none would be left of it after the guards and other prisoners expropriated its contents.

Six months later, a surprise: Papa's cousin Raya Murik from Novo-Ostankino in the Moscow Region received a letter from Isaak, which was almost unreadable because the writing was scribbled and the ink faded. The letter revealed his story and made the point that he was hospitalized not because of sickness but from starvation. This news brought fresh suffering to my mother because now she felt guilty. Her food parcel might have saved his life if she had arrived at the prison hospital just a few weeks earlier. Of course, it could happen only if the guards did not steal that parcel. My father tried to console her by saying that it was not realistic to believe that her small parcel would save Isaak because very little or none would be left of it after the guards and other prisoners expropriated its contents.

For ex-military prisoners, all correspondence was forbidden, but it seems that somebody took pity on Isaak when he arrived at the hospital and sneaked his letter into the postal system before he died. Well, it took another six months to arrive at the address of his cousin Raya. It is very sad to read from his letter about his almost fanatical loyalty to the Soviet Government, at any cost and by any means. Tortured to death now in the Soviet labor camp, he writes,

"If I had to repeat it all over again, I would act in the same way because absolutely everything that could be done to eliminate the German enemy should have been done at any price."

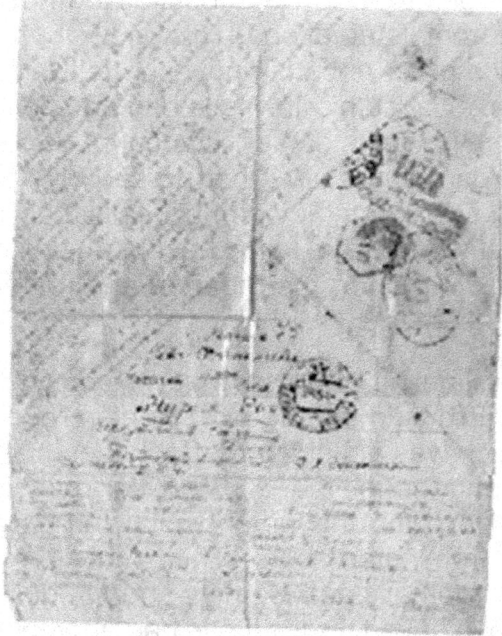

A letter from Isaak to his cousin Raya Murik arrived six months after his death from starvation

I wondered whether he ever questioned his decision to return across the front line only to be arrested and tortured in the Gulag as a wasted slave laborer. He tried to justify his actions as a patriotic duty to the Soviet Union when, under fire, he escaped with extraordinary effort back across the front line to join the Soviet army again.

It took another 43 years until Gorbachev publicly admitted that there was widespread and unjust persecution of innocent Soviet victims and agreed to exonerate the political victims, mostly postmortem. Between 1964 and 1987, only twenty-four people had been exonerated, according to Anne Applebaum.[23] Such was the fate of millions of returning prisoners of war who should have been recognized and honored as national heroes. Only in 1999 was the Certificate of Exoneration issued for Isaak, 56 years after his death and following anguished decades, during which my family continuously sent their formal requests for exoneration to the government. Until that certificate was finally issued, everyone in my family lived in fear, in the shadow of SMERSH, guilty by association of blood.

Certificate of Exoneration identifying Isaak as an innocent victim of repressions. It was issued 56 years after his death.

Finally, my family had the certificate, but Isaak was dead. This long-delayed formal recognition of his innocence could not bring back the life of this young man with so much promise. His life and his talent were wasted. In any other civilized country, he would be acclaimed as a national hero in the war against fascism. However, in my homeland, his name, and many thousands or even millions of others, are not even listed as victims of the Gulag, recorded by the Memorial Societies.

My papa said that if Isaak had discovered that he was not on those lists of victims, he would respond: "I don't care any longer because, finally, I am now free from all despots." My conclusion from this story was that Isaak managed to survive the German military camp and then the Nazi death camp. He managed to rebel and escape with his life. He succeeded in making it safely back across the active front line. Yet, he died, at the hands of those whom he selflessly served, from starvation in a Soviet Gulag forced labor camp.

I will probably perish even faster than Isaak because my health is not as robust as his. After all, he had good nutrition when he was a child until his mother was murdered by the mob when he was seven years old. My mother died when I was just two. Because of early childhood malnutrition, I developed anemia, which doctors insist I still have. This would not help me to survive the prison hunger and cold, especially after I became so spoiled by my tropical experiences in Cuba. I would not stand a chance of survival in the Gulag. My father was saved from arrest and similar torture, possibly death, only because he was needed for the war effort on the front line.

I do not have to be as naive as my Uncle Isaak or my husband, Eduardo. The outrageous cruelty and mask of the cynicism of our 'dear leaders' were sufficient for me to lose my trust in them. I do not want to become a traitor to the fatherland, but I refuse to become its victim and leave my children in its jaws. Homo Sovieticus is driven by herd instinct. The fate of the herd is the slaughterhouse. I will go my own way. It was dogmatic concepts of patriotism and decency that killed Isaak Zelitsky. He might have survived if he had remained in Europe, but I understood that his childhood experience of pogroms and the support of Soviet authorities for his privileged musical education inspired his patriotism. For the sake of my children, I had an obligation to be smarter.

25. Time Travel through a Wormhole

Our 18-hour trip from Havana to Moscow was exhausting. After our refueling stop, I worried about how to neutralize the flight attendants who may already have reported the Gander bathroom fiasco to KGB authorities in Moscow. I felt that the attendants were watching us during the flight. I had to use this as an opportunity. It would be convenient to make them think that I am a dumb provincial girl and that poor tiny Ernestico is truly not well with his tummy.

To prove this point, I took Ernestico to and from the washroom several times, despite his happy chirping. My older son thought this was a lot of fun and went running after us, making plenty of noise at the door. Yes, now we were noticed by the passengers who commented to the flight attendants on the difficulties of traveling with small children on long flights. Later, when I felt that the moment was right, I found the audacity to approach the same attendants, now seated at the back of the cabin, who had pulled us from the washroom in Gander. I tried to provide them with apologies and explanations.

"I am sorry for all this trouble, comrades. You can see for yourself that my child has an upset stomach, possibly from the airline food."

Normally, it would not be difficult for a young mother with small children to gain some sympathy. I was trying to impress our flight attendants and security personnel with the apparent distress of a young, helpless, and overwhelmed mother who was worried that the airline food made her child sick. If only I could convince them that this was the case, they would try to get rid of me when we arrive in Moscow by letting us go home as soon as possible, before I reported the sickness of my son to the medical authorities. The most important thing was to keep cool and not to overdo it.

"None of the other passengers complained. Why are you blaming the airline food? It is completely unjustified," answered a flight attendant.

"I am sorry. Possibly it was the effect of the refreshments at the airport. My children were not used to these kinds of drinks. I agree; it was not necessarily the food you served that caused my child's illness."

"Now, if your child had eaten a pastry at the airport, it could have been even worse. Be happy that all he had were drinks. Be careful with the food for your child until we arrive in Moscow."

"Yes," I chimed in, "we have a very good polyclinic and pediatric doctor in Moscow. I only hope that we arrive soon. Thank you anyway for your help. It is so difficult to travel alone with young children. I am desperate to arrive home." I was now addressing the female attendant who accompanied us out from the washroom in Gander.

"Where do you live?" she asked. The internal Soviet passports list on their first page the approved residential address and the ethnicity of each citizen. However, the external Soviet passports do not, possibly because it could be too embarrassing for the Soviet State that the Soviet passports used abroad indicate the ethnicity and approved address of residence of all Soviet citizens. My external passport, which they examined once again after we were returned under guard to the Aeroflot craft, had no such information. I instinctively lied about my residence address in an attempt to confuse our tracks and to pretend that our residence was near Sheremetyevo Airport. I was not prepared for the alternative of getting caught. My only plan had been to escape in Gander before the aircraft took off for Moscow. There were too many unknowns to be decided in one place and at one moment. Under these circumstances, it was impossible to plan for the failure to escape; that would be two jumps into the unknown. I was forced to improvise.

"I am from the town of Lesnoy in the Moscow Region," I answered. This was the address of the old wooden cottage of Auntie Raya, the cousin of my father, which was used as a summer *dacha*. We had stayed there overnight (because it is not far from the airport) when we visited my parents during the summer holidays two years ago. It was convenient to spend the night there between flights. Ernestico was just a baby at the time. This old, small peasant house in the middle of the forest, without a shower or toilet, but with beds, the stove for heating and cooking in the middle of the house, was located near the airport.

"Well, it is not far from the airport," observed another attendant.

"Thank you again for your help." I returned to my seat, congratulating myself on pacifying the annoyed attendants and security agents with my dumb provincial personality. It looked as if they had become more relaxed.

Let's just see what will happen next. I adjusted the children into a comfortable position, and soon we fell asleep, weary from the nervous energy expended in a failed attempt to defect. The call for breakfast awoke me. It was a tough task to wake up the boys. They sleep like bears in winter. There is a nine-hour time difference between Havana and Moscow. The children, unable to reset their body clocks, were overcome with drowsiness.

Our arrival was announced: "We are landing at Sheremetyevo Airport in Moscow. It is eight in the morning Moscow time. The weather is cloudy, and the temperature is six degrees Celsius. Please secure your seat belts and make sure your seat is in the upright position." The belts were too loose for the children; I had to spread my hands over them in an attempt to cushion them from the impact of a touchdown. The aircraft landed and came to a full stop on the tarmac, but the children didn't awake. The passengers were getting up, and I was still struggling with the sleepy children. I will have to force them awake and drag them behind the rest of the passengers. "*Grazhdane vichodite!*" (Citizens to the exit!) came the announcement.

Still worried about reports to the airport immigration about our Gander fiasco, I proceeded down the aircraft ladder. It felt good to stretch out our cramped muscles. Carrying Ernestico in my arms, he seemed much heavier than usual. Edik could not wait for me as I dragged my feet across the tarmac. He needed to expend all that energy stored up during the flight. He started running to the front of our group, which was moving slowly; everybody was tired after such a long journey.

My constantly running five-year-old son, always demanding my attention, forced me to overcome my fear and fatigue produced by physical, emotional, and mental strain. As we headed toward immigration and customs in the airport building, my concern resurfaced over possible reports of the Gander debacle. What happens if the KGB takes me away for interrogation? These thoughts were debilitating. By the time I lined up behind the others, Edik had slipped under the immigration screening tables and popped up on the other side. Now, I was compelled to ask passengers in front of me to allow me to proceed to the front of the line in order not to lose my son. Scared or worried, I still could not afford to lose Edik at the airport.

However, Edik turned out to be my lucky charm. My anxiety over losing him became the preoccupation of immigration officials as well. They had to grab him and hold on to him while asking me the required questions. I collected my strength and answered their questions, which were rushed thanks to my troublesome child. They asked me the location of our stay in the Soviet Union since my passport for traveling abroad did not reveal my address. I replied that it was the town of Lesnoy in the Moscow Region. This was a risky lie, which I felt compelled to repeat since I gave it to the flight attendant following my failed escape. Technically, I could claim this address because it was my relative's property, and I could hypothetically intend to stay there for the holidays. It would be my explanation if questioned by the KGB. Still, I would have problems explaining why I wanted to stay in Moscow if my parents lived in Odessa. Of course, I would not be able to reply to this question with the truth - my father warned me not to come to Odessa because the KGB was waiting for me there. In the end, the immigration agents did not question me; instead, they rushed to stamp my passport and let me grab Edik, my unruly child, who was waiting in their custody at the other end of the immigration tables.

I felt reborn. This was incredible luck. The KGB agents and Aeroflot flight attendants believed my story about the helpless mother with one sick child and his hyperactive brother. No one had reported us to the immigration officials. Everyone, it seems, was distracted by our domestic charade, our prolonged drama of a stupid young mother with nutty kids on a trans-Atlantic flight. I tried to compensate the long-suffering boys for their enforced immobility by playing games while waiting for our luggage. It felt as though we had been granted a renewed gift of life. Now, I felt strong enough even to carry our suitcase and catch a taxi while keeping hold of the boys.

Despite my sense of relief, I decided to go to the nearby cottage of Auntie Raya in the town of Lesnoy in the Moscow Region, just in case the KGB should follow us. If they put a tail on us, I could benefit from confirming the address I gave to Aeroflot attendants and later to the immigration officer at the airport. Besides, I could gain some time to decide what to do next, how to contact my father without calling attention, and arrive at Odessa unnoticed.

The taxi drove us to Lesnoy, located in a birch forest, still naked in the early spring. No other car appeared to follow us from the airport. The house was an old cabin. I knew where my Auntie Raya hid the key two years ago, and I opened the front door. Now, I was happy that I asked the taxi driver to wait for us because the cabin was uninhabitable: no running water or electricity, no sheets, blankets, or towels. No other car approached near the cabin, which meant nobody was following us. I began to feel safe. My fear of being followed was unfounded. However, with two small children, I could not stay in this cabin.

I decided that it might be useful to leave the cottage in disarray, pretending that we had stayed there and then to proceed furtively to Odessa. Papa warned me in his letter not to come to Odessa. I conveniently interpreted his warning to mean that if you come to Odessa, do so secretly. I turned both rooms of the cabin upside down and deposited the food leftovers from the flight onto the dining table. I locked the cabin and got back into the taxi with my kids. I asked the driver to stop at a long-distance telephone station where Soviet citizens usually make internal calls within the Soviet Union.

The taxi driver was quite happy with the kill he was making on our fare so far and took us to the closest intercity telephone station. Forced to leave our luggage with him while the children and I went into the station to make a phone call to Papa, I wrote down his license plate number. I purchased a 10-minute call to connect me with the office number for the department of my father's workplace in Odessa (we still did not have a phone at home). If anyone else besides my father answered, I would put the receiver down. I did not want anyone from my father's office to inform the KGB in Odessa about this call. In such a case, I would prefer to travel to Odessa unannounced and arrive at night when our neighbors are asleep. This was the best time to enter the apartment unnoticed. As if to confirm that the young and crazy are often lucky, my father was in his office while most of his colleagues were hunting for lunch.

"*Slushayu* (Hello)." Papa picked up the phone himself.

"*Papochka, Tateh* (affectionate names for father in Russian and Yiddish), we are here. I just arrived with the children in Moscow. I hope you are alone, and we can talk."

"*Dochenka, Paulinochka*, what a surprise! Yes, I am alone for the moment. We are well. How are you, my love, and how are the children? What happened?"

"We are fine, Papa, and I was not initially planning to visit you in Odessa, but now I have no alternative but to come home, and I am here in Moscow. I arrived with children in Moscow this morning."

"The time is not good here, *Dochenka*. I sent you a message. Didn't you understand what I meant? You wrote to me that most probably you were not coming this summer for the holidays. Why did you change your mind?"

"I have received your message, and I understood its meaning, but we are here, and we have nowhere else to go for now. I already checked the cabin of your cousin in Lesnoy, but it was not habitable. It has no electricity or water. We can't stay there."

"*Dochenka*, the cabin was closed for the winter, and it is too early in the season. There is no water because the pump will not function without electricity. It could be an electrical short circuit. No, you are right. You can't stay there with the children even if you are already in the country. Anyway, we did not ask for approval from my cousin, and she might not appreciate that. Come home, dear; we will think of something."

"Yes, I will. It is the best solution. We will drive to the Kievskaya Train Terminal and will purchase tickets to Odessa, if available."

"Come as soon as you can - the sooner, the better. I told you we would think of something. We are worried about you."

"We are completely well, Papa. Don't worry; we are just very tired. I will tell you later about everything. For now, I must arrange our travel to Odessa."

97

"Why are you taking the train to Odessa and not trying to catch a local flight by Aeroflot instead? Wouldn't that be easier for you with the children?"

"I don't want to register my name with the airline. The railways don't register passengers' names, which is why I want to buy train tickets. I do not want anybody to know that I am coming to Odessa. Please make sure that our neighbors and everybody else know nothing about my arrival. I will take a taxi from the train terminal. Please wait for me outside the building."

"I understood and will do all I can. If there is no train, please take a taxi to the Moscow apartment of my cousin Raya on Ferganskaya Street 14. Do you remember where? Do you have her phone number? If you need to go there, please call me, and I will arrange for your stay with them or somewhere else in Moscow."

"Yes, Papa, I will. I have her number, and I am very happy to be able to see you soon. Goodbye."

When we arrived at the Kievskaya station, we found an enormous, dirty, crowded, chaotic, and freezing railway station in the center of Moscow. We were lucky to purchase tickets for Odessa in a "soft" first-class carriage on an express train just before its departure.

Happy to be alone in our compartment, I made the beds for the children. The train steward brought us piroshki (stuffed dumplings) and hot tea as soon as we departed. The movement of the train in the dark of the night put the children fast asleep. I was very tired and soon dozed off, except that I would awake every time the train stopped at different intermediate stations. Then, I would fall right back to sleep. The stop-and-go jolting of the train coming in and out of stations managed to kill my good rest. So much for the express service. Usually, all these stops aimed to pick up contraband sellers with their vodka and other agricultural consumables. Anyway, tomorrow evening we will arrive in

The Sea is Only Knee Deep

Odessa, and I will have a good rest in my home and my bed. We were fortunate not to have been accused of attempted escape. I felt relieved and upbeat: our escape failed, but Aeroflot security spared us. Thanks to that, we could be reunited with my parents. For lonely me, it was such a gift!

I was elated. My parents were my sole security, and their room was my only true home, not the hotels in Cuba. The next day, the children were glued to the window of our compartment, fascinated by the frames of a film whizzing by the flat, light green, early spring landscapes of the Ukrainian steppes, the old ramshackle villages, the wretched intermediate train stations with their shabbily dressed peasants bent by hard labor and wrecked by alcohol, bad nutrition, and hopelessness. It looked as if we had traveled 100 years back in time. With difficulty, I kept the overzealous boys in our first-class compartment because the economy carriage was creepy.

We arrived in Odessa quite late in the evening and took a taxi through the dark and sleeping city to our apartment building. Quick hugs with my parents waiting for us outside 'na shucher' (on guard) on the street. They had the key to the building entrance, so I would not have to call them from the street, thereby awakening our communal neighbors. My parents took us silently to our room. They knew it was not a good idea to talk confidentially inside our communal apartment, and I was too exhausted for any meaningful conversation. My considerate parents just put us to sleep as soon as we arrived. There were two folding army cots for the children, one in my corner beside my bed for Ernestico and another beside my parents' bed for Edik. All three of us immediately vanished into a deep sleep, finally, in total peace. As I drifted into unconsciousness, an image came to my mind's eye of traveling back in time through a wormhole that linked two universes. I entered the vortex at the mouth of my current universe (Havana/Gander) and exited the time warp at an earlier universe of my childhood home.

26. Odessa Quandary

How sweet it is to awaken in your own home. This was my only home, or rather room, which I called home since the day I was born. You open your eyes and gaze out the same dear, old, childhood window at the tall, beautiful acacia tree with its white flowers decorating the aged Greek Catholic Church on the opposite side of our street. This church, closed since the Revolution, is light gray and very modest. Only the cross is made of gold, unusual for Russian churches, which are always covered in gold, especially on their domes. In 25 years of looking through my window at this church, I have never seen it open. Somebody keeps restoring the paint on its façade. Who is doing that and why?

The sun is warm, and the air outside my open window is redolent with the strong, sweet scent of acacias. Most of the streets in Odessa, including ours, are generously shaded by mature and aromatic flowering trees, especially acacias. Its foliage is typically bright green or bluish-green with small but abundant blooms of creamy white, rose, or pale yellow color with a strong and heavenly scent, very popular for its use in perfumes. My room corner feels like a paradise.

I get up and check on the boys who are still sleeping. My parents are up but have not yet gone to work. Shura is in the communal kitchen preparing our breakfast, giving Papa and me some privacy. I was hugging him as if I were still a little girl. Then we sat down and talked in whispers. "My heart is so very happy to see you, *Dochenka*. After your breakfast, we shall depart immediately."

Papa was looking around with demonstrative gestures indicating, in our Soviet lexicon of sign language, memorized from a half-century of persecutions, that he was afraid our apartment might be bugged.

"Later, I will explain more to you; for now, only the essentials. Please, we must go. The question and answer period will come later."

Papa cautioned me with a reminder to keep quiet. He pointed towards the luggage and some boxes packed with food supplies, all piled up in the corner of our apartment.

"*Poniatno* (it is clear)," I answered.

I understood that he did not want to speak inside the apartment, and he did not want our neighbors to see us. I understand that he prepared luggage and boxes with the food supplies, but I don't know yet where we will be going, and despite that, I am feeling safe for the first time during this past week. The practice of sign language, even in private at home, is something to which all Soviet citizens of my generation are accustomed from birth. People lived in communal apartments, and the sound insulation between their private rooms was poor. The police encouraged neighbors in communal apartments to eavesdrop on each other, and people learned to be careful even when there was no previous history of eavesdropping by their neighbors. It is my father who is in charge now; he knows what he is doing. It was really hard to awaken the boys. They were so tired. It took a while for them to shake off their sleep. I dressed them and fed them with milk and buttered bread.

An old pickup truck entered our *dvor* (the enclosed interior courtyard of our building). The driver called for my father, and together they loaded the back with the prepared luggage and the boxes with supplies. Fortunately, it is already late in the morning, and all our neighbors are at work or in school. Shura sat beside the driver in the front cabin. Papa took Edik, and I carried Ernestico from our apartment into the tarp-covered rear cargo bed, where we sat on makeshift benches. The driver started his truck and exited the courtyard to the main street.

The boys thought we were about to have a fun adventure and became excited. Soon, however, they discovered that my father and I were holding them tight and not releasing them because the benches were flimsy and the truck was without shock absorbers. We did not let them free, even to stand up to look through the opening of the tarp, because our ride was very rough. Now I could ask:

"Where are we going in such an early morning rush?"

"To Arcadia," he answered. Arcadia is the name of the nearby seaside resort where we have a dacha (summer cottage).

"Why do we move to Arcadia in early May? We have never moved to Arcadia before the second half of June! We will be cold, no?"

"It is better colder there than warmer in our situation. I am counting on the cold to avoid meeting with our neighbors from the dacha cooperative. When you called me yesterday, Shura and I solicited time off, but on such short notice, we were granted only one day off work, that is, today. We told them that I had a medical emergency. We will have to be back at work tomorrow. We will need time to talk and think about what we will be doing in the future. Until you decide what to do, it would be important to keep a low profile to prevent news about your return."

"Where did you get the truck and the driver? Do you know him?"

"He is the truck driver from a local fishermen's brigade. It is their truck. Many people, as you remember, often purchased fish from these brigades under the table. The Soviet law does not permit moonlighting fish for resale; so, they are used to confidential deals. When you called me yesterday at work, I went to see him, and we agreed that he would help us. Nobody knows of my connection with him."

The Sea is Only Knee Deep

Our truck arrived in Arcadia in 30 minutes. Everything is very close to Odessa. I jumped out of the back and lowered the children to the ground while the driver was helping my father to unload our luggage and boxes. Edik suddenly was fired up. He noticed the sea on the horizon and, thinking that he was back in the Caribbean, took off like a bolt of lightning.

"Playa, playa," (The beach, the beach), he shouted in Spanish, running madly downhill to the sea. I put Ernestico on the ground and sprinted after Edik.

"Stop, stop, stop, Edik, right now. You are a nutty kid! No, No, don't get into the water!"

Papa picked up Ernestico in his arms and watched us running down the steep slope towards the beach.

Nothing would stop our five-year-old runner; he was sprinting fast ahead, all the way to the sea, over the slippery clay slope. Seeing that Edik was not listening to my shouting, my father handed Ernestico to Shura and ran downhill after us. Edik was faster than both of us. He reached the beach first and ran directly into the cold seawater. The frigid water stopped him dead in his tracks. He looked surprised. Never before had he experienced seawater so cold. My father and I splashed into the water after him. Papa grabbed and lifted Edik on his shoulders, and we dragged ourselves back to the shore, totally soaked and frozen from the frigid sea. It was only the beginning of May. The air temperature was in the low 20 degrees Centigrade, but the seawater should have been about 10 degrees Centigrade.

I scolded Edik. "You will get sick. The water is too cold. It is only the beginning of May, and this is not Havana."

My father was now carrying Edik back uphill, and I followed behind them in soaked, wet shoes, complaining, "These are the only white summer shoes I have. Thank you, Edik."

"Edik, please, never do this again. The seawater in Odessa does not get warm until the middle or end of June. You will get very sick if you do it again, and the doctors will have to inject you with antibiotics, which hurts a lot. Remember?"

"Paulina, how did you manage to lose Edik in the water?" asked Shura.

"You would not believe it, but it was not difficult. Better not ask me. Edik is not a little boy but a Cossack like his grandfather. He runs so fast that neither Papa nor I could catch him."

Shura replied: "This boy has no fear of water, but he is suspiciously calm now. Is he inventing some new escape?"

"No," I admitted, "he is used to the Caribbean Sea and the Cuban beach. He can swim and is not afraid of water. The only thing that stopped him was the cold temperature of the water."

We moved into the garden house to dry off with towels and change before catching a cold. Odessa is not Havana. It was around 20° Centigrade, too cold for tropical Cubans. Once dry, we looked around. We were all alone in our dacha. Nobody had moved in yet, but everything was green, and all the trees were in flower. The air is filled with fresh scents of our fruit trees and the low rumbling noise of the sea. It is truly beautiful. What a wonderful idea to come here; we are on our own and can talk all we want. Shura started fighting with the kerosene burner, not an easy task since it had not used all winter. Papa, still carrying Ernestico, went around checking the condition of our beds. It is great; we have three beds in decent condition, except mine, which got too rusty and squeaked at any move. We unpacked the luggage and sat at the table to talk. My father started:

"When my friend told me that you received my coded messages on the back of our photographs, I thought that you understood what was going on here and that I was warning you not to return home on your holidays. I was hoping that you understood what it meant when I wrote that it was cold here and I dreamed of visiting you in Cuba. It's because the KGB agents ordered me to report on your arrival, which you planned for last week. When you failed to arrive, I called Eduardo, and he said that you missed the flight and that you became annoyed at him and took off somewhere else for your holidays with the children. I used his answer to report to the KGB agent that you did not arrive and that, according to Eduardo, you changed your plans and left for a little holiday with the children somewhere at a Cuban resort."

"Great, all went as I planned. I asked Eduardo to tell you these *'mansi'* (tales) for the KGB intentionally," I replied.

"I understood *Dochenka* everything when Eduardo told me that he did not know where you went; I also understood when he said that your message for me was: 'your sea is only knee-deep.' I recognized our old *chochma* (joke) when I rebuked you for doing the unthinkable. I figured out that you were up to something very *meshugenah* (crazy) again and that you could not talk about it."

"You bet, Papa, I couldn't; plus, I am afraid of these people from the KGB. I don't expect anything good from them."

"I don't recommend you, *Dochenka,* get involved either. Just as I said in my letter, it is a *tsuris* (trouble). However, this should be your own decision. I was hoping you would consider my advice and avoid returning to Odessa this year. I was very surprised to hear from you when you called me from Moscow, and I had to react very fast to make emergency arrangements for your undisturbed stay with us until you decide what to do. This is why I do not want those agents to learn of your arrival yet. To assure that, I had to prevent anyone, especially our neighbors, from spreading rumors that you are back. Until you decide what you want to do, it will be better if nobody knows that you are here. Do you know what they want from you? I asked them, but they ignored my questions."

"No, Papa, I don't, and I don't need it. There were other *tsuris* (troubles) that made my life more difficult. Anyway, don't you think they couldn't find me in Cuba if that is what they wanted to? After you told them that I was not returning to the Soviet Union, I am sure they would commission their Cuban KGB office to find out where I am. Do you know how many floors in the Soviet embassy belong to them? Aeroflot could inform them of my return. I am scared they will find me soon."

"In such a case, *Dochenka,* if they find that you are here, you will have to meet with the KGB in Odessa. I do not like it and would have preferred that you not come here. However, if you don't want to stay with your husband in Cuba, stay with your family here at your home. Our position is, and always will be, that you, your husband, and your children are welcome to live with us. I will arrange a recall for you and your husband to work with the Black Sea Institute in Odessa. I hope you know that all of this is possible only if the KGB approves of your transfer home. I do not know what they want from you, and I do not like to see you become involved with them. I avoided them all my life and took a very big risk to send you a message in Cuba to prevent you from coming here. Why did you come?"

"You are speaking as if it were easy, Papa, but it wasn't. I got on the very wrong side of Boris, and he denounced me to the embassy political security bosses. I could not continue working with him."

"*Dochenka,* you must know better. I will never help them, but I also would avoid provoking them. You are such a big *puritz* (important person) that you know everything better. The egg is teaching the chicken once again! In that case, make up your mind. Think carefully and take your time. You can rest here with the children. Nobody will notice you here in Arcadia, but be careful, please. Why have you fallen out with Boris? By the way, please don't call anyone, especially your girlfriends. *Dogovorilis* (agreed)? We don't want outsiders to know where you are."

"It is *gesheft* (a deal), Papa. You should not talk with anyone about my return, especially with your colleagues from the Black Sea Institute. I had a very ugly incident with Boris. I could not tell you before, and you would have had a very hard time believing me. Now, I will have to tell you the truth, Papa, even though I know it will hurt you. Boris wanted to rape me, and to prevent him, I used the kick, which you taught me when I was younger, for fighting off the men who would attempt to rape me."

The color of my father's face turned white: "He didn't hurt you, *Dochenka*? Are you all right?"

"I am fine, but I made an error when I threatened him by promising to tell you and his wife about his rape attempt. He got very scared that I would also report him to the Soviet embassy, so he took pre-emptive action by discrediting me at the embassy. He denounced me for being careless in security matters to the same KGB you are talking about. Can you understand now why I can't continue working for Boris?"

My father and Shura were speechless, completely stunned by my news. They had a hard time believing it and could never have anticipated anything of this kind. Then, anger appeared on my father's face, which now started to get red. He pushed his hand against his heart. It was frightening because we knew that he had high blood pressure. He was breathing with difficulty. He lifted his head back to breathe easier as if the pain was severe. We stood up. Shura was trying to help him.

"Volodya, be careful, or you will have a heart attack! Paulina, you can't talk like this to your father. You know that he has high blood pressure. You don't want him to have a heart attack. Let's stop talking before your father becomes sick."

She brought him pills for his heart condition. I was

embarrassed to upset my father like this. I hugged him tight and kissed him until his normal face color returned. Papa took his heart pills, rested, and said that he could never again, in his life, talk to Boris because if he saw him, he would kill him. I decided it was necessary to go for a walk with the children to escape the tension and get some fresh air.

Now the boys could run all around the whole territory of our "Cooperative of Scientific Workers" (our dacha) because we were the only members of the cooperative present so early in the season. Normally, this two-level, six-bedroom house with its surrounding garden grounds on the top of the hill overlooking the Arcadia beach was shared among six different privileged families. For now, and for the next two weeks, we had the whole cooperative, the whole house, and the entire large garden to ourselves.

Our family property consisted of one long room on the second floor of the house. It had an attached terrace. This room, Papa subdivided into two with a pressboard partition. However, there was no inside running water or a toilet. We also had our portion of the garden where, besides the fruit trees and flower beds, we installed a large garden shed where we kept the refrigerator and a dining table for family meals. Near the garden shed, Papa built a small kitchen with a water basin where we could wash our dishes as well as ourselves. The small outhouse terrified the boys; we had to find a substitute for their use. Still, the garden in our possession was six times bigger for the time being because none of our neighbors had moved in yet. The boys loved to play and run in the garden, and I was hoping that the sight and sound of them would heal the heart of my papa, hurt by my careless mention of the awful incident with Boris. It was sunny and a bit windy, which converted the sea into a loud and salty-smelling dragon, breathing invisible clouds of iodine.

The children and I were still asleep when my parents left for work early the next morning. They had to take the tram, which would deliver them to their office in only fifteen minutes.

When Edik awoke, he demanded to go straight to the beach, promising to stay out of the cold water. All he wanted, he insisted, was to play with his brother in the sand. I thought the children would be safe playing on the beach if we dressed them warmly. They will be entertained, and I will be sitting beside them, which would permit me to concentrate on the possibilities that my father mentioned yesterday. I decided to skip the fight with the kerosene burner for breakfast. All we needed were milk and bread with salami. Worries about cooking could come later when I have to make a proper meal for all of us after my parents return from work.

"We can't play now, boys. Both of you have to finish your milk and sandwich if you want to go to the beach."

"Poli (Edik always called me Poli), why does grandpa has so little hair on his head?"

"Because he is thinking a lot. Stop distracting me with your silly questions, and let me concentrate on what we shall take with us to the beach."

"Poli, but you have a lot of hair on your head! Is it because you don't think?"

Right, the innocent child sees that 'the emperor has no clothes', I thought, but answered, "We all have hair, the grandpa is the smartest among us; he knows more than I do. Is that what you wanted to hear? By the way, if you continue thinking and not chewing your *'kolbasa'* (salami), you will lose your hair too. Ernestico, you must chew by moving your mouth. Please do it for me."

Our garden is suffused with the aroma of blue, pink, and white Acacia, whose flowers are fragrant and sweet to taste. I used to eat these flowers as a child, first from curiosity and later from hunger. Other trees in the garden covered with edible flowers were mulberry, cherry, and apricot. The mulberry flowers are white and pink. The cherry and apricot blooms are smaller but even more delicious. Then we have

109

catalpa trees with large leaves in the form of a heart. The seeds of the catalpa hang down in long, narrow pods. In the spring, they are lovely, like elegant candles. The large lilac bushes are already blooming, and their perfume is overwhelming. These blessings of nature are thanks to the father of Shura, who, as a medical doctor and national war hero, was awarded posthumously this very special honor of a dacha in Arcadia. How is it possible that I would not appreciate this privilege paid for with his life?

Boys playing in our Arcadian garden

I thought it would be wonderful if we could stay here at our dacha with my parents to enjoy the spring aroma. Cuba has none of these beautiful fragrances; the beach areas have only the strong scent of pine trees, which often cover the coastline together with the palm trees. The ocean around Cuba does not smell of iodine, a rare natural element in the Black Sea.

I could not avoid thinking about how privileged we were to have this modest space in Arcadia, a natural paradise. Very few of the elite people in Odessa could dream about having their own summer property: a room and a garden over the Arcadian beach. Even the super celebrities had to compete for the right to purchase an expensive and usually short stay in the few available state resorts on the Black Sea coastline. The prized Arcadian beach did not have any health resorts built near our dacha yet.

The boys are running downhill to the beach. Ernestico is so amusing in the weird way he runs. He jumps slightly and then moves forward on tiptoes. He always tended to move like this; probably, he will be a dancer like some of his Cuban compatriots. Edik is so different. He always has strong ideas about everything, and he is determined to realize them at any cost. A year earlier, when he was not yet four, he escaped from his daycare center. He went down in the elevator to the street level, then proceeded to the bus stop, boarded the bus when it arrived, and rode on it through Havana to the downtown, where he exited by himself, presumably at the correct stop, and walked to the house of his grand Auntie Laudelina, who had an apartment in downtown Havana.

He rang at her door, and when she opened it, he said: "*Hola* Auntie, I was missing you and came to visit you." She was surprised that he would come without previous notice, and she asked:

"*Dios Santo* (My God!), Edito (Spanish for Edik), where are your parents?"

"They are working."

"With whom did you come?"

"I came on my own. I was with my brother in daycare and wanted to visit you."

"How did you know to find my home?"

"I knew," he answered.

"You are my very crazy child. It is a miracle that you arrived safely. Let me call your Grandmother Maria."

When her sister Maria heard that Edik escaped from the

daycare center, she called me. I went running downstairs from the 7th floor, where I was working, to the 2nd floor, where the daycare was. I found the women in the daycare in a panic because my son Edik was missing. They had searched everywhere but did not find him; they were ready to call for my help. When I told them how Edik escaped and how he arrived on his own by bus to the apartment of his grand-aunt, everybody was convinced that his parents had taken the child there previously. However, neither Eduardo nor I could recall bringing Edik after work by this route to auntie's apartment. Possibly, we did, but we could not recollect it. If his parents could not remember, how could he have remembered how to take a bus, which bus to take, when to exit, and how to find a street and a building with the apartment of his Grand-Auntie Laudelina? Quite incredible; we still do not know how he did it.

So, with this fast runner, one must be careful. I was helping the boys to build sand palaces and could not concentrate on my precarious future because I had to be focused on the children. A fishing boat came ashore with a catch of 'skumbria' (similar to, but larger and more delicate than herring). They make a wonderful meal; pan-fried 'skumbria' is delicious. I negotiated the price in the Odessan jargon with two local fishermen.

"How much do you want for this 'tiulka' (anchovy)?"

"If these are 'tiulka', I am a pygmy! 'Vi shto' (are you stupid), you can't see? Ten 'skumbria' cost 10 rubles."

"I heard you are saying 'skumbria', but the price you are asking is for sturgeon or a dolphin."

"The price is right because they are so fresh. They are still singing!"

"I will pay you five rubles for their singing, which will be a better trade for you than door-to-door 'schlepping' (dragging around). 'Dogovorilis' (agreed)?" I knew it was too early in the season for door-to-door sales, which would require a long trip to find customers.

After buying the fish, we had to return home to clean them. Back at the dacha, I cleaned the fish and started the kerosene burner. A local peasant woman came to sell a few fresh vegetables. Here you go, only in Odessa! After the children had eaten, I put them to sleep and sat down in peace to reflect on my options for the future. It was so nice to be home with my father, where I could breathe the sea air and the fragrance of acacias. Savoring the serenity of the moment, I was inclined to stop wondering and just stay with my parents. Perhaps my father's suggestion is practical; maybe, he could get us transferred to work in Odessa at our Black Sea Institute, where my parents are highly respected because of their 33 years with this institution since its very inception. I will have to look for a daycare center for the children and possibly start discussing our relocation to Odessa with Eduardo.

It was so nice to be home with my father, where I could breathe the sea air and the fragrance of acacias. Savoring the serenity of the moment, I was inclined to stop wondering and just stay with my parents. Perhaps my father's suggestion is practical; maybe, he could get us transferred to work in Odessa at our Black Sea Institute, where my parents are highly respected because of their 33 years with this institution since its very inception. I will have to look for a daycare center for the children and possibly start discussing our relocation to Odessa with Eduardo.

When my parents arrived home from work, I surprised them with a freshly cooked meal. They loved my dinner, never mind that the fish were no longer singing. They told me that so far, no one inquired about me. We may have some respite for a couple of days until people start wondering about the reason my parents were moving to our dacha so early in the season.

I described to them how we spent the day and asked if

they thought it would be possible for me to travel with the children on the tram to the city to order an international telephone call to Eduardo.

My father proudly poses with his rose bush garden in Arcadia

Papa did not think it was dangerous for me to go during working hours to the city because everybody is at work anyway, but he did not like the idea of my placing an international phone call.

"Don't you know that all international calls are recorded and will be used as evidence against you if required?"

"Yes, Papa, I know, but I did not do anything wrong yet. If I decide to stay with you in Odessa, I will never do anything wrong. I need to call Eduardo to tell him that the children and

I arrived home well and sound and that we are enjoying ourselves. I want to discuss with him the alternative which you suggested: coming to live with you and Shura in Odessa."

To myself, I thought that I was not entirely open with my parents because I could not tell them about my recent involvement with the nuclear submarine base in Cienfuegos. To talk about it was dangerous since I had signed the confidentiality agreement. I felt that I was dishonest. My thoughts were cut short when my father reminded me:

"'*Azoy?*' (Really?) '*Yiddisher kop?*' (Smart Jew?) You have forgotten that I sent you photographs in Cuba to make you understand that I was interrogated and instructed to report your arrival immediately to the KGB because they want to meet with you. If you announce with your international calls that you have arrived, I will have to notify the KGB of your arrival as well. Are you ready for that? Also, have you considered the implications? For some reason, they were polite but secretive with me. They would never bother with such good manners if their interest were only local. They probably want you for Cuba and not for Odessa. Also, Boris's accusations about your carelessness might kill your possibilities to work here with the Black Sea Institute, especially if it does not correspond to their plans. Don't you think so?"

"You are right, Papa. Forgive me for suggesting this. I did not think of anything else the whole day except how nice it was to be here with you. You are correct; I need to think realistically of every possibility before we make any move. Thank you for reminding me that my presence here will be discovered soon, and I will be called on the carpet. I'd better smarten up and consider everything; actually, I probably do not have much time. Maybe I have to decide quickly and to take action very soon."

"Don't rush, *Dochenka*. I only want you to know that you and your family always have a home here, where you were born. Whether you want to stay here or to return to Cuba will

115

have to be your decision."

My dearest *'Tateh'* (father) does not know yet about my crazy plan to defect to Canada. Neither does he know about my supremely incompetent attempt to hide in an airport washroom in Gander. Should I tell him about it? How will that affect his heart condition when he learns that the situation is much more serious and complex than he imagined? The effect could be even worse than when I blurted out the terrible incident with Boris.

"*Polinochka*, do not worry," said Shura. "Just stay home with us, and everything will be sorted out. I have so many bright, good-looking, single, and young Russian engineers with promising futures who are directly reporting to me at work. You will never be short of a bridegroom. It will be easy to find you a wonderful and promising Russian husband, even with your two children. You will get a husband who will take care of your situation and settle your problems with Boris. Please stay. It will be the only way to solve all your difficulties."

"You think it will be all right if the prospective husband is your subordinate? No, please, don't waste energy talking like this. I do not want your Russian bridegrooms. My children have their father. We agreed with him that he will do his best to join us in Odessa or anywhere else after we have settled. He always travels abroad; it shouldn't be hard for him."

"You are *meshugenah* (crazy) and never listen. What can I do about you?"

To the true Odessan, for whom pain is a way of life, hard times are good for some humor. I had to answer with our traditional Odessan sarcasm in an attempt to cheer up my parents.

"So, what's new under these skies? Why is it that the Odessa Port is almost 3000 years old, while the City of Odessa itself is only 200 years old?[24] Our professor from the university told us about the history of our city's port, which was called *Ginestra* in ancient times. It was established by the ancient Greeks and later the Romans. The port was used not only for trade but also as the main escape route for women from the entire coastal region of the Black Sea.

These women were seeking refuge from barbaric tribal wars, tyranny, and slavery. Their easiest route of escape from these nightmares was on trading ships departing from Odessa to Europe. I, too, feel persecuted, and I am also ready to escape into the unknown. Let me ask you: who am I to break our local traditions?

Coastal archaeological excavations related to the history of Ginestra

27. Freedom is not Free

Confronting reality, I understood that unless I face the whole issue in its complexity, there will be no place to hide and no peace to live, neither here in Odessa nor in Havana. Shall I comply with the Soviet state instruments of control (KGB) in accordance with my programming from the earliest years in daycare and later in school, at work, and at the university? What I could not understand about our people was their devotion to our Soviet system. Instead of only pretending as I did, they appeared to be sincere.

For example, I will never forget that very special day when one day in early March, I arrived at my school in the morning, and we were not allowed inside the school building. Instead, our teachers rounded us up inside the school courtyard in the rain. It was cold, and we were getting soaked. I could not understand why they were doing it. Normally, after singing together our school's revolutionary song in the courtyard where we were lined up according to our classes, the principal would make the announcements for the day, and we would march in or would be sent back home if classes were canceled for any reason. However, our teachers today were acting strangely as if they had lost their minds. They were crying, and no one explained to us what was happening. We stayed there, wet and confused, until the school principal stood in front of us.

"Dear children, our father and the invincible and undeniable leader of our nation, *Tovarisch Stalin,* died last night," he tearfully announced.

I looked around, and I could not believe my eyes: the girls (our school was for girls only) were in shock. Some of them, seeing their teachers crying, started crying as well. Soon, almost all the girls were crying. Some began to hit their heads against the wall that separated our courtyard from the street.

"Without our dearest father Stalin, we have become helpless orphans, and from the bottom of our hearts, we shall aspire to follow his teachings in all our deeds and thoughts. We will live and behave with dignity as he taught us. Only under the wise guidance of the great Communist Party shall we survive and preserve his inheritance for us. Girls, you may all go home right now, but we will expect you back for the demonstration of farewell to our beloved leader at two o'clock," concluded the principal.

There were tears and mayhem everywhere, especially among the teachers and older students. It was a depressing and desperate crowd. I felt lost, very confused, and just wandered around them, utterly mesmerized. I could not understand why everybody was crying. I thought that if they cried from the happiness I felt, it would be natural, but they were crying from despair. I was disoriented. What I witnessed at the age of eight now was that the people in my school, old and young, appeared to be out of their minds.

A year earlier, at the age of seven, manipulated by my teacher to comment on my father's reflections at home about the extreme danger of being a Jewish doctor in Moscow, I got my father arrested and almost sent him to GULAG. My teacher denounced my father, alleging that he was a direct family relation to the Moscow doctor because I called that doctor Uncle Lionia. Fortunately, she was wrong. The stupid me at that early age, calling all adults by the name of an uncle, but we were not related. My father was released to return home to give me the biggest spanking of my life for my big mouth. This taught me a lesson: never again trust in a system, particularly in the case of being Jewish in the Soviet Union.

Now the bizarre behavior of everyone: they were crying, tearing at their hair, hysterically hanging onto each other, and hitting themselves. It was a total madhouse. The teachers and the students have lost all their brains! Why aren't they happy like me? The majority of them are Jewish, just like me. We were saved from deportation, and they are crying? What is wrong with them! I just turned around, and leaving everyone behind, went home by myself, disgusted and bewildered by all this sobbing. Some of my friends got worried and attempted to call me back, but I was not planning to return to school for any farewell. I was managing to get out of that crazy place all by myself, thank you!

I thought that the teachers and students demonstrated today their utter irrationality. I will ask Papa when he returns home if the death of Stalin will change the deportation orders for Jews. Maybe we will not be deported! Papa came home early and hugged me. Then, later, when he took me to the park where nobody could hear him, he said: "I hope you are right. Nobody else in this country will have the absolute power required to execute such a massive crime. We were saved once again. Nature took Stalin to hell just before he killed all of us. Such miracles make me think that there is a God of the Jews."

"That would be nice, Papa, but why, if God exists, did he permit the mob to kill your mother, and the Germans and the Romanians to kill so many Jews in Odessa? Don't you think, Papa, that deporting any people from their homes is bad? I heard our neighbors say in the kitchen that nobody was safe from the whims of the meat grinder. What meat grinder were they talking about? I was so scared of this meat grinder that I was afraid to ask our neighbors where it was."

"I only hope that the death of Stalin will change the way we live in our country. We shall see what happens next. My true and only little miracle is you, and you were not expected to live when your mother died, but you survived. The doctors did not expect you to live because of severe anemia, but here you are. You are not strong physically, and we would have perished quickly if deported, but Stalin died before it happened. Make good use of this gift and be careful because luck tends to end one day."

After we had hugged each other, I asked him: "What is wrong with all these crying people, everywhere: in my school, on the streets, in our building?"

Papa answered: "When you grow up, I will explain it to you. Now, you are too young to understand. When you grow up, I will try to explain to you all your whys. One day, I will explain to you what I know, but not now. For now, I only need you not to talk with others about what we have spoken about. These are called political matters. Never discuss anything political with others, for the sake of the memory of your mother and your love for me, please."

All this started early in 1952, after several large anti-Jewish campaigns organized by Stalin in Eastern Europe (Poland, Hungary, and Czechoslovakia) failed to produce sufficient results in discrediting the Jews as conspirators with America and Israel, Stalin decided to launch a major campaign of pogroms and to deport the entire Soviet Jewish population to the Far East.

Across the Soviet Union, newspapers spread heavy propaganda accusing Jews of all sorts of crimes and sins. Throughout the nation, except in Odessa, Soviet Jews were forced from their jobs. They were insulted or arrested, or beaten on the streets. Large pogroms were ordered to be instigated across the country thanks to state-sponsored anti-Semitic hysteria. Nikita Khrushchev described in his memoirs the assassination (on Stalin's order) of Solomon Mikhoels.[25] He was a famous and brilliant Soviet actor and leader of the Jewish Anti-fascist Committee. All the members of this Committee, which was created originally by the Soviet Government, were arrested and sentenced to death for international conspiracy.[26] After these executions, Stalin ordered the creation of the Moscow Doctors' Plot and subsequent large-scale pogroms across the USSR as an expression of the Russian peoples' anger against 'the treacherous Jewish cosmopolites'. All Jews across the nation were now labeled cosmopolitans, which, for no rational explanation, suddenly became a state crime contradicting the internationalist tenor of communist ideology.[27]

More details about those events my father told me only when I became older. He always took me to the park and looked for total privacy before he spoke about anything political. Even when he spoke, he would hunch over and hide his face for fear of being overheard or identified by someone nearby. He said that there were many hundreds of unheated cattle trains stationed in each major city on reserve lines to start receiving the deported Jewish population on the pretense of saving them from the scheduled pogroms.[28]

The trains were to be loaded immediately after the public execution by hanging of the 37 Moscow doctors who were falsely accused of a Jewish conspiracy to poison Kremlin leaders. The 37 victims were to be divided into small groups for hanging in different cities of the Soviet Union, starting with Red Square and Manezhnaya Square in Moscow on the 11th of March. At that instant, the indignant Soviet people would start the nationwide pogroms. The Soviet Government would rescue the pogrom survivors by loading them into the cattle trains beginning on the 15th of March. There would be attacks by angry people against the trains, which would reduce the number of deportees to the planned 50% because that was the capacity of the prepared barracks in the Far North. In a communist state, everything should be planned![29]

Later in his memoir, written before he died in 1971, Nikita Khrushchev confessed that Stalin mandated him personally to organize a pogrom at Aviation Factory Number Thirteen, where Stalin ordered the distribution of clubs to workers to beat up the Jews after work. The Jews, frightened by these pogroms, were expected to appeal to the Soviet Government for protection.[30] Soviet State local authorities, on the pretext of safeguarding the Jews and providing a rationale for deportation, were ordered urgently to compile the lists for deportation. The deported were permitted to take with them to the camps in the closed zones only one piece of luggage per person weighing no more than seven kilograms.

The cattle trains, which were already prepared for deportation, were stationed on reserve train lines approaching all the large Soviet cities, including Odessa. According to rumors, these trains were unheated. The wooden barracks in the closed zones had been constructed in a rush to receive the deported Jews and were also unheated.[31] The rumor was that they were built with only one board of thickness and had neither water nor electricity nor communications. These contemporary rumors were later confirmed only after Perestroika, in numerous published revelations by some members of the Politburo, such as Alexander Yakovlev, Anastas Mikoyan, Nikita Khrushchev, and others.

The destiny of those other deported ethnic groups that were thrown into unheated cattle car trains with their old people, young children, and babies was terribly cruel. They were shipped to the subarctic territories of the Russian Far East in Siberia without sufficient food or water provided during their journey. The same transportation method was used in cases of other previously deported groups. When those who survived the journey finally arrived, they were unloaded into unheated wooden barracks where the majority of these people would die. These were the forced labor camps in the so-called 'restricted zones'. The deported adults had to work extremely hard with only hand tools to dig in the frozen permafrost. No communications with the outside world were permitted. Most of those among other minority groups previously deported, especially the old, the children, and the women, died within just a few months.

On the scale that the mass deportations of Jews were to be organized in Odessa, it was not possible to retain a secret. Odessa became ablaze with rumors. There was, at the time, a frenzied daily media campaign in the press and radio accusing Jews of crimes against the state. Everybody in the city knew that state security agencies, local police, regional municipalities, residential registries, workers' organizations, educational institutions, and hospitals were ordered urgently to begin to prepare a full list of Jews and half-Jews (with all personal data, including their addresses and workplaces), effective January 1953.

Our neighbors in the communal kitchen were also speaking of the deportations. They said that it could not possibly be true because we would all die inside those trains from cold, starvation, and thirst even before we arrived at the destination. My father bought on the black market and stored near the exit door of our apartment, two expensive peasant winter coats for him and me: *'dublionki'* (thick sheepskin outside and sheep hair inside the coats), as well as *'valenki'* (thick felt boots) and special winter hats.

"What are these for? They are too hot to wear in Odessa even in the wintertime," I asked him.

Papa invited me to go with him to the park, where he usually talked to me about things he didn't want anybody else to hear.

"We need to be ready," he answered. "This is a very important secret; you can never tell it to anyone. These are not for the Odessan winter, but in case we are deported. As you know, I was in the Navy until your mama died. All military and ex-military Jewish officers will be deported first. They will not allow us anytime for packing up."

"Pack what, Papa? I hate these heavy, horrible, itchy clothes. You will not force me to wear them. Why do the ex-military have to be deported first? Aren't they the heroes of our nation who won the war against Hitler? Don't they deserve to stay in their homes with their families in Odessa?"

"Please, *Dochenka*; it is a very big secret. They deserve to stay, and so does everybody else who will be deported, but the former military personnel are also more dangerous than the others because they might resist and start a fight. Don't tell anyone, please." Papa's voice sounded worried and alarmingly serious.

"I don't want to be deported, Papa. I don't want to go anywhere. I like to live in our city and my home. Is it because of these Moscow doctors again? We are not from Moscow; you are not a doctor; it has nothing to do with us; it is not fair!"

"You are right. It is not fair for any person who is deported. But the security agencies of our country are now discovering such doctors everywhere, including, not so long ago, a group of doctors in Ukraine, allegedly headed by the famous doctor Victor Kogan-Yasny.[32] Suspicion of doctors is now commonplace, so the danger is not restricted to Moscow. Also, many other prestigious Jewish professionals have recently been arrested, so it no longer matters that we have no doctors in our family. Soviet Jews, in general, are now accused of loyalty to Zionism. They are described as the enemies of our country because they are cosmopolitans. I do not want us to be deported either, my dearest. It is very dangerous to talk about it. Please, say no word to anybody. Understand?"

"Fine, Papa, but why are we cosmopolitans? I never heard this from you before. What does it mean?"

"The cosmopolitans are the people who are not nationalists but internationalists. It means that they love all other people in all other countries. It is not rational to accuse us of being cosmopolitans. How can we be cosmopolitans, *Dochenka*, if the Soviet Union is the only country we know? Your grandfather was born in Odessa, I was born in Odessa, and you were born in Odessa. This is why it is completely untrue that we are cosmopolitan. If anyone asks you about this, you should reply that it is false."

"I am still confused, Papa. I don't understand why. The victory of the international proletariat is the main message of the Soviet Communist Party."

"Internationalism is for all other countries, but nationalism is for all our people in our country. In any event, it has nothing to do with us; we are not cosmopolitan."

I did not tell my father that I heard our neighbors talking in Yiddish about their fears of big pogroms because I did not believe in the horrors they were describing. They were saying that pogroms were recently carried out in Kyiv, Kharkiv, and elsewhere in Ukraine and that the deportation of all Jews was imminent.[33] I was frightened by such terrible rumors. I persuaded myself that if I denied them, they would not be true. I was only a kid, and the adults knew better how to help us.

All of us Jews of Odessa, on Stalin' s orders, were now expecting the forthcoming deportation to the Far Eastern regions. Thanks to Stalin's death, our lives could now be spared. Is this something to be happy about or to cry over? Most of our teachers, as well as the students in my school, were Jewish, and many knew that the current hysterical state of anti-Semitism was indeed encouraged and enforced by Stalin. Everyone I met was terrified of Stalin. This is why I was thrown off balance that cold, rainy morning. Was this only a dream, or was it a reality? Was it not good news that he died? Why are these people crying?

The largest group of Stalin's terror victims in Odessa, according to my father, were the "blabbers" - those silly Odessan jokesters who could not keep their mouths shut because they believed that Odessans had an innate privilege to make jokes. What they did not take into account is that Stalin and the KGB had no sense of humor. Many thousands were arrested on this charge (insults or anti-Soviet slander) and sentenced to 12-15 years of forced labor in Gulag camps in the Far East and Siberia. I can still remember how strict my father was about my not listening to any jokes, which could be interpreted as political. It was very difficult to do in Odessa, where one of the few traditions to have survived the social and political upheavals was the talent residents retained to joke about our lives. Sometimes, it seemed that Odessans would prefer to be sent to the Gulag than to stop their silly jokes.

I remember how shocked I was when I overheard one particularly dangerous joke during an outing in the city park in winter. I was playing in the snow when I overheard one of my father's friends, who accompanied him, say: "Hitler would cry bloody hell if he learned that Stalin stole his dream to exterminate Jews". I could not ask my father about its meaning because I was strictly prohibited from overhearing the private chats of adults. Even at this young age, I understood that it was better to forget the remark because it was too dangerous and confusing. Would Hitler be jealous of Stalin?[34] This was contrary to everything we were taught in school.

Our neighbors were whispering in tones of fear and sympathy when new campaigns were announced against the so-called 'nationals'. Those were days when I returned home and reported to my father that all Greek or Polish children had disappeared and never returned to school. It was my first experience with ethnic cleansing. Members of one ethnic group after another were arrested for mass deportations to the Far East, Northern Siberia, or the Arctic regions. Forced deportations were carried out not only in Odessa but also from across the whole Soviet Union.[35] Entire families of those ethnic groups, with their old, their sick, their young, including babies, were arrested and deported. The forebears of these families might have lived for generations in Russia, Poland, Crimea, Caucuses, or the Baltics; now, they were suddenly stigmatized by their ethnic origins. All ethnic groups contributed to their victims.[36]

Once, I overheard a story about some friends of my father who attempted to travel elsewhere within the USSR so they could not be found to be deported. However, the police notified train and bus stations, and agents refused to sell tickets to those on their blacklists, which included Jews and half-Jews. I asked Papa if we too could try to escape somewhere, and he said that it was not possible, that it would be even worse if they located us. He said that we must wait and see what would happen, but he too was very worried. He said it was like living in a fog, an almost mechanical existence when your brain simply has to be switched off. I told Papa that I could not understand why Russian and Ukrainian people became anti-Semites. My childish explanation was that some of them had fallen under the wicked spell of *Baba Yaga* (a fearsome witch in Russian folklore).

"I forbid you to talk about this ever again," said father. "It is *'chaloymis'* (nonsense); there are good and bad people in every nationality. It all depends on their rulers. Good rulers have decent conditions for their people, but the bad rulers keep the majority poor and humiliated. The poor often revolt. Bad rulers want to keep their poor people obedient."

Papa said that many people believe that the vile beast will be kept busy by devouring Jews or other minorities. Becoming satiated with those victims, it will spare their own lives, but they are wrong; one day, their turn will come as well. History has demonstrated this many times, but nobody learns.

Man proposes, but God disposes. Stalin had a stroke and was paralyzed on the first day of March 1953, thus preventing a terrible and shameful crime. Beria immediately issued orders to delay the medical doctors' trial[37] scheduled for March 5th. The trains for deportation were ordered to be removed from Soviet cities[38] despite the deportation plans that continued to hang over the heads of a worried Jewish population for a planned date of March 15th.[39] Only a month later, on April 4th, the arrested Jewish doctors, at least those who had survived their tortures, were declared innocent. The Soviet news agency *TASS* announced that all charges against them were falsified. Each of the survivors was dropped secretly at night at their homes, and the government issued an official communiqué to that effect.[40] It took three additional years to exonerate the rest of their families and other members of the intelligentsia arrested under the same charges. This occurred only after the 20th Party Conference in 1956. The surviving leadership of the communist party decided to keep the plan for Jewish deportation a strict state secret by burning all evidence of preparations made.[41]

When, in the late 1950s, some of the Communist Party members who were imprisoned in Gulag labor camps were released after Khrushchev's revelations at the 20th Party Congress of 1956, they shared their experiences with those whom they trusted. Stories from those Gulag camps conveyed through my street friends were horrible images to visit for a young girl. They shattered any idealism I had left. I felt cheated because racial discrimination and ethnic oppression practiced in our country by our government contradicted the theory of egalitarianism contained in our communist doctrine, as taught and promoted in our school and society. Of course, the works of George Orwell were not accessible to us; they were prohibited. The author describes how in a monolithic state dictatorship like ours, black easily be called white.

The images that came to my mind of the deported Soviet people were those of the ancient Egyptian slaves building the pyramids; the Soviet leadership I imagined as Egyptian Pharaohs. We children, were too young to discuss such frightening and confusing events; these subjects were untouchable and prohibited by our parents. It seemed insane to mingle mentally in this pit of snakes while all we wanted and needed was a stable and secure world where we could play happily forever after and please our parents when and if possible. My only safety was my dear father, whose resourcefulness was our armor.

Odessa was part of the Ukrainian republic of the USSR; however, even being Ukrainian was not safe. They, too, were considered to be dangerous elements by the Soviet Government. The only privileged ethnicity in the multinational Soviet Union was Russian. Starting from the virulent campaign against Jewish cosmopolites in 1948, Soviet Jews lived in constant fear of being dismissed from their work (because all institutions had received orders to fire Jews), and Jewish students worried that they would be expelled from their universities. Those who were dismissed would not be rehired and would starve until arrested for *'tuneyadstvo'* (parasitism). The apartments and houses of those who were arrested or deported were given to the communist Russian workers. Some of the Russians in Odessa were now looking into improving their residences. After they located an attractive dwelling, they would denounce the current owners with the prospect of getting their hands on these accommodations.[42]

Anyway, we still felt lucky to live in Odessa, where, at that time, Jews were the famous and visible majority. To have rounded up all the Jews and half-Jews would have brought the city to a standstill. Everybody in Odessa was living in suspense, anticipating the ax to drop on our necks at any moment. The clocks were ticking, and we were getting used to living in this terrorized emotional state, expecting orders to herd us into the cattle train carriages for deportation.[43]

My father was still holding on to his job at the Black Sea Institute in Odessa. To fire all professional Jews in Odessa would shut down the city. Though the adults around me were acting tense, we children continued playing on the streets as if life would not change. I refused to worry about something which neither my father nor I could influence. As well, deep in my heart, I did not want to believe in something so absurd and awful. In general, all children want to believe in positive emotions and relationships because they are defenseless.

After Perestroika, our historians disclosed that Stalin, like Trotsky, believed he must conquer the whole world and nothing less.[44] In the early 1950s, Stalin was over 70 years old, and he did not want to die without the knowledge that he had in his lifetime accomplished his dream of conquest: to gain a total victory, if not over the whole world, then at least in all of Europe. He was also assured that Soviet nuclear arms would be capable of launching a decisive blow against the United States. This time, he decided not to repeat the mistake he made with Hitler by allowing him to attack the Soviet Union first. This time, he was determined to make the initial strike in the Third World War.[45] Still, he needed a trigger, and he had decided upon the traditional one: anti-Semitism.

Stalin believed that if he deported three million Soviet Jews to the Far East, the European countries and the United States would protest. It would permit him to claim a Jewish conspiracy in those countries and interference in Soviet affairs. Consequently, he would ignite hostilities worldwide and attack opponents, this time with nuclear bombs. He was afraid to die before he fulfilled his mission of world conquest. This was his true destiny and the only vindication for the humiliation he suffered as a child from his father.[46]

We avoided a third world war but continued living in the Soviet "Third Reich". Why were people crying instead of dancing happily when they learned that Stalin had died? In Moscow alone, 500 people were crushed to death by the overwrought crowds during the funeral of Stalin. How many funereal casualties were there in other major Soviet cities? I admit to this perennial personal reflection and sense of wonder about the devotion of crowds to their tyrants.

The cancellation of the deportation of the entire Jewish population[47] (nearly 3 million people) did not stop the flagrant anti-Semitism in my country. Since the times of Ivan the Terrible, except for the period 1922-1949, when anti-Semitism was officially prohibited, it was a habitual attitude deeply ingrained in the national culture and policies. Workplaces were afraid to rehire previously unjustly fired Jewish employees, and the military, KGB, diplomatic, international trade, and political sectors continued a comprehensive prohibition on hiring Jews. The majority of national educational institutions in all sectors prohibited (wholly or with a few exceptions) the admission of Jewish students, except in some sectors considered less important, such as agriculture, food industry, textiles, daycare education, and so on.

The threat of deportation and the growing anti-Semitism changed the attitudes of Jewish people in Odessa. It seems that there was no longer any place for pride in belonging to an ancient, cultured people who brought enlightenment to the medieval West. All the girls in my school spoke about their intention of marrying Russian boys to change their family name and, if possible, their ethnicity. This was necessary, if not for themselves, then for their children. My feelings about it were quite the opposite; I would never change nor attempt to hide my ethnic origin precisely because of principle. Ethnic persecution is utterly vile and insane. Trying to hide by changing my name and ethnicity would be a form of recognizing this violation of our common humanity, cooperating with racists, and paying the price of marriage without romantic love. Lying by marrying to change the ethnicity of my parents was a prostitution of values in my eyes. I rejected such personally degrading ideas from the start.

When I was nearly 14 years old, I argued with my father about my plans to quit my day school to avoid becoming a member of Komsomol. I was under pressure at that time to behave just like the other kids in our school. Everybody, except my close three friends, continued day school and enrolled in Komsomol because it was the norm to which everyone was obligated. I stopped trusting political authorities at the age of seven. That was the time when I was manipulated by my teacher to denounce the careless comments of my father. I regarded all such authorities as false and dangerous.

I have to be honest with myself. I am a rebel from birth who refused to call Stalin my father when I was not yet three years old. I refused to enroll in Komsomol, paying the hard price of having to work on an open construction site, even in winter cold and rain, and studying at night school for three years. I undertook this hardship instead of having the life of an ordinary teen: studying in day school and dancing at night with my friends. I married a romantic Cuban revolutionary, endangering my parents' careers, instead of marrying a "smart" Russian engineer with prospects of an excellent future with a man who would report directly to my stepmother at work. I almost paralyzed my boss and "protector" Boris instead of obliging him and using him to accelerate the promotion of my career in Havana and Odessa, should I choose to live in Odessa.

It would be easier for me now at this stage as well to make everybody happy: my parents, Eduardo, and his parents. All I had to do was not to escape and to return to Cuba or stay in Odessa, complying with the current rules of the game. But it would be a life full of conflict and pain, an act of self-deception, living like the rest of *Homo Sovieticus*. Until now, my life was conflicted between the information from my schooling and the stories my father told me. It was no longer sustainable.

At this point, I had to decide to refuse a life of conflict with my conscience. It was my conscience, which dictated my sense of right and wrong, my natural choice of values. These were the very same values I wanted for my children. Isn't this exactly what we mean when we say that we want to be free? **To be yourself, to live by your values, is the only freedom. This is what freedom is, and freedom is not free.** It requires sacrifice, and I am willing to pay the price. Personal freedom means that I am in control of my destiny. The communist state pretends to take full responsibility for its citizens in exchange for their freedom. This is not only a bad exchange; it is a lie. The returns on the loss of freedom are minimal at best. Too often, the relinquishment of freedom is purchased at the price of life itself, both physically and spiritually. I am willing to assume my responsibilities because they form an important part of my values. Moral life is not possible without freedom of choice. Social systems that remove or dictate choices are, by definition, amoral.

I was fortunate to have a foreign travel passport and a Cuban visa, both of which I could use in an attempt to escape again. This time, I vowed to perform any trick possible to avoid flying with Aeroflot to Cuba. How to accomplish that, I had no idea. But I made my choice to defect: if not for me, then for my children. This was my last chance. I was determined and prepared to pay the consequences.

Paulina Zelitsky, Paul Weinzweig

28. Don't Ask Questions about Fairy Tales[49]

My initial plan was to defect in Gander on our way to Moscow. As a result, I was not prepared for, or willing to face, the KGB in Odessa as they had instructed my father. Nor was it fair for my father to endanger himself by disobeying their orders. How long could I hide in Arcadia? If my understanding of the situation was correct, I could not escape from reality indefinitely. If I chose to stay, I would have asked my father to report on my arrival. Why was I afraid to meet with them? The majority of Soviet people would conform obediently to a request from the KGB, especially considering the offers of future privileges. My problem was that I did not know what they wanted from me, and I believed that it was too dangerous to find out.

The only way to discover what they wanted would be to meet with them, but after that meeting, I most probably would find myself on a short leash. Whenever I thought about this imminent meeting, I knew that I should avoid it at any cost. Once I met with the KGB, I would undermine my only opportunity to leave with a free conscience. I was sure they did not want me to talk with them about seashells, like the new Soviet consul in Havana did. They probably intended to scold me for my careless behavior (the complaint of Boris) and my refusal to provide monthly reports informing my colleagues, or perhaps, they would like me to spy on foreigners they do not trust. If they applied pressure and tried to intimidate me, I was no match for their power. In our country and Cuba, the security services were in absolute control.

I was also concerned about Cuba's cynical nuclear war

games. The Americans would find out sooner or later about the Soviet naval base in Cienfuegos and the Soviet submarines equipped with nuclear weapons. The declarations of the Soviet Government to the contrary were simply a shameless and thinly disguised lie. The Non-Proliferation Treaty, signed in 1968 by the Soviet Union and the United States, was designed to prohibit the installation of any weapons of mass destruction on the ocean floor. The treaty turned out to be more masquerade than reality. What we were doing in Cienfuegos was a clear violation of this international treaty.

Were these not the weapons of mass destruction on the ocean floor prohibited by the Non-Proliferation Treaty? Why was the Soviet Government so anxious to sign the treaty if, at the very same time, they mandated the construction of an offensive nuclear naval base and were successfully operating facilities for weapons of mass destruction on the ocean bottom at the doorstep of America? If all these treaties are only fairy tales, why bother?

Was the purpose of the Treaty to put the enemy to sleep? Is it a game? If so, then we would have to conclude that the Soviet Union won this round. The Americans appeared to be asleep. Was this only an American pretense motivated by temporary political convenience? Or were they complicit in these fairy tales?

Meanwhile, Cuba was becoming increasingly unreliable and dangerous as a Soviet partner. The island had become a tropical nightmare for the Soviet economy. The Soviet and American Governments negotiated the SALT1 Agreement in 1970,[48] but Cuba was excluded from these negotiations and the signing. However, and most importantly, Fidel Castro never believed in peaceful coexistence. Not only did Fidel feel abandoned by the USSR, but he was also resentful and vindictive. As a result, the KGB did not trust him. The commander of the Soviet artillery division stationed in Cuba said to me once that Fidel constantly attempted to create an incident and provoke the start of the war. Fidel did not care about the dangers to the island of a nuclear war. He aspired to manipulate the makings of a conflict because he loved to portray himself as the biggest *macho* of them all. He needed to prove his military prowess, no matter what the consequences or at whose expense.

To fire the first or simultaneous missile - this is the Soviet military strategy. Is America any different? Fidel does not care that Cuba survives; he said as much on countless occasions. The motto of post-Revolutionary Cuba has always been *Patria o Muerte* (my country or death). I did not want to be a party to this criminal madness. I considered all of this absurd and had no desire to allow the omnipotent bureaucrats of the intelligence services to use me, especially in the capacity of the informer, 'swallow or honey trap' for the KGB.[49]

It is the most disgusting form of slavery when the intelligence services are acting as official pimps. I did not know then many of the details I know today, but any prospect of spying was repulsive to me. I would never become an instrument of this hated organization in this treacherous field. I wanted to be free. It would not be possible if I was marked as a spy, never mind for whom and where.

Additionally, I would have to face Boris again, and who knows how he would behave now. Another very serious problem was that I had heard from our Soviet colleagues that the KGB could force me to commit to them in the Soviet Union or Cuba. Once I had signed up, I could never again escape from their embrace. Like others in my generation, I was growing cynical about our official Soviet versions. When the safety of our lives was concerned, we believed mostly in rumors. The official version was: Soviet *razvedchiki* (operatives of security services) are our heroes who would never consider escaping. The rumors were always colored with fear when they had to do with the KGB. These rumors affirmed that defection for those involved with the KGB was a suicidal act because the KGB had a so-called 'wet department' (wet means blood is flowing), which was in charge of the assassinations and kidnapping of defectors. No, I could not afford to meet with the KGB; I could not afford to take such a risk. Never mind how much I loved staying with my parents in Odessa. The KGB would not allow me to stay in Odessa if they needed me for something else in Cuba. I now felt certain that my conflict between two different values could be solved in only one way: by refusing to participate.

I concluded that I had to escape immediately, but how? My immediate priority was to reduce my father's responsibility, who had not reported my arrival to the KGB. The only logical way was to quietly disappear as soon as possible. This would allow Papa to excuse himself later by declaring that everything went by so fast; one minute she was here, the next moment she was gone. No one would believe that he did not have time to report my arrival, but under the recent law reform, he would not be punished on my account because we had not lived together for the last three years. Additionally, I was hoping that since my parents were already at the age of retirement, they could only lose their current employment but not their pensions, which were already awarded.

The next morning, before my parents left for work, I told them that I would investigate how to return to Cuba as soon as possible. Father asked me not to rush with my decision because he wanted to discuss it with me in more detail. Anyway, since today was a Friday, he asked me to wait for my decision until the weekend. I answered that I would wait. Meanwhile, I wanted to investigate the train schedules from Odessa to Moscow and the availability of flights back to Havana. We had the right to purchase Aeroflot tickets back to Havana because we were still the holders of a valid

Soviet foreign passport with permission to travel to Cuba.

Of course, now I was forced to purchase Aeroflot tickets because my special permit for traveling with CSA (Czech Airlines) had been used for the last flight of CSA out of Havana, which we missed. I did not tell my parents about my recent fiasco in Gander when the Aeroflot guards dragged me out of the toilet. I was convinced now, more than ever, that to escape, we needed to fly with a foreign airline without KGB guards. Nobody, not even my father, knew about my current plans. How was I to tell him? His idea for me was that I should not have come home but instead stayed in Cuba. He believed the KGB in Cuba would not attempt to force me into collaborating with them. How naïve! Should I tell him that?

On the other hand, Shura was deceiving herself about my marrying one of her Russian engineers. Could I expect the engineer subordinate to her to shield me from the vengeance of Boris? I was not interested in any Russian husband for the simple reason that the divorce between Eduardo and me was not a fallout romantically, but a protective measure for the sake of Eduardo. The divorce was on paper only; we still loved each other, and we loved our children. Probably, Shura did not understand that, and I must explain it to her. Papa is right. We'd better have a new talk tomorrow about everything, but I must obtain information about available flights to Havana today.

The weather was cloudy, and I decided to take the risk and travel by tram with the children to the city after our breakfast. I would visit the train station and make a call from a public phone to the information desk of Aeroflot International at Sheremetyevo Airport in Moscow to inquire about the next flight to Havana. If I could purchase the Aeroflot flight to Havana, it could at least give me a slim opportunity, once inside the airport, to try to catch in apparent error a different flight with a foreign airline. If I am discovered, I could attempt to claim a misunderstanding and then continue traveling to Cuba as our original Aeroflot tickets indicated. The best foreign airline for my purpose would be CSA (Czech Airlines), from Moscow to Prague. If I could only manage to do that, CSA would have to worry about how to get us to Cuba from Prague. This would permit me to return to my original plan - to escape in Gander from the CSA airline. However, what possibility was there that the CSA flight to Prague and the Aeroflot flight to Havana would coincide with the hour and the day of their departures? I was afraid such a coincidence might be improbable. In such a case, I should consider other foreign airlines for the same purpose. This seemed completely crazy, a thoroughly unrealistic idea. Had I known better the rules for international travel or even had more experience of the functions in Sheremetyevo, I would have discarded this notion immediately as impossible. As an ordinary Soviet citizen, I was sufficiently inexperienced, which permitted me to plan my absurd 'afiora' (mad concoction), attempting to switch to the international airlines by mistake.

You have to be 25 years old to consider anything as bizarre as that. I could not share my *meshugenah* ideas with anyone. Regardless, I was happy to be home because I wanted to see my beloved Odessa at least one last time and record my "Odessa Mama" in my heart. The children were very cheerful; they were traveling by tram for the first time in their lives, and they enjoyed it. There are no streetcars in Cuba, only buses. The opposite in Odessa: we had beautiful old wooden trams crossing the city in all directions.

The tram is so much more fun. It is noisy and runs very slowly, offering a much better chance to see the city than in fast and smooth-running buses. We got out at the public phone station near the city center, from where I called Aeroflot in Sheremetyevo Airport. When the operator answered, I asked for information about the next Aeroflot flight to Havana. She answered,

"Tupolev-114 once per week, on Wednesday, departs at 6 p.m."

"Could you tell me, please, if there are tickets available for next Wednesday?"

She answered: "We have only information about the flight schedules. For the availability of flights and ticket purchases, you must go in person to the Aeroflot sales office in the city. To purchase tickets, you must have a foreign passport and a valid permit from the MVD (Foreign Affairs Ministry) to exit the Soviet Union and to travel to your destination, as well as the corresponding country visa."

"Thank you," I pleaded with her, "clearly, I already know that and have the required permission. All I am asking you, if possible, is the availability of seats for the next flight to Havana."

She became annoyed, "I don't have this information, *'Grazhdanka'* (Citizen), and stop wasting my time. Visit the Aeroflot sales office with the documents I mentioned."

"Yes, thank you."

Aeroflot could provide this information and sell the tickets only in person, and if I visit the Odessa Aeroflot sales office, they will copy my documents and report my request to buy tickets to the KGB. Such is the procedure. This is the same local Odessa KGB that requested a meeting with me. No, I do not want to do it. I will be better off buying my seats with Aeroflot in Moscow, especially if I buy them directly at Sheremetyevo Airport just before our flight. After all, it is the only alternative. This way, the ticket office would not have sufficient time to clear our tickets with the KGB in Moscow and Odessa.

How would I know if there are any seats available for the next flight? Well, I would not know in advance. I would have to take a risk. Anyway, it will make sense because what is important is *'otshvartovatsia'* (to raise the anchors) from Odessa to reduce my father's responsibility. We went to the Odessa train station, where I purchased our first-class tickets for Moscow departing early on Monday. After that, I planned to call Sheremetyevo Airport to ask about a CSA (Czech) flight from Moscow to Prague. To ask for flight information on the phone, I would not have to show permission for a flight to Prague. I hesitated to call the operator in Sheremetyevo just yet; it was too soon, and she might recognize my voice and become suspicious.

**View of the port from Primorsky Boulevard
Odessa is built on a steep hill over the sea.**

**Primorsky Boulevard - Odessan coastal promenade above the port,
ending with a colonnade**

The boys were tired of waiting. It was time to walk, and we had a wonderful stroll around the city despite the cloudy weather: all along the Primorsky Boulevard beside the passenger terminal port area, the one where I participated in the construction during my university studies, and the sugar terminal whose design I was developing for my engineering master's degree.

The Potemkin steps unite the port with the city.

The children were too young to attempt to go up and down the Potemkin steps - our Odessan pyramid. This was a tradition for people strolling along the Primorsky Boulevard. The Potemkin steps were always an outstanding feature of the city, creating its unique image and the myth that the Russian Revolution started on these steps, all thanks to the ingenious film *Battleship Potemkin* by Sergei Eisenstein.

We returned to the public phone office three hours later, and I called information at Sheremetyevo Airport again.

"Could you please tell me when the next CSA flight to Prague is?" I inquired.

"Twice per week: on Wednesdays and Saturdays at 5:40 p.m.," answered the operator.

This is interesting. It is incredible luck, I thought to myself.

143

On Wednesdays, there will be the Aeroflot flight to Havana and the CSA flight to Prague, only 20 minutes earlier on the same day. We returned to Arcadia by tram. It took only 15 minutes by tram and 15 minutes walking uphill. I love it when everything is so near; it is so much easier than in Havana. My parents arrived at the dacha after work, loaded with delicious food from the local delicatessen. I was surprised how they managed to secure such a bounty. Normally, it was difficult, especially after work, to buy anything. Shura explained that she had personal friends working in stores. They would put aside her morning orders - a special survival service to private customers who pay extra for illegally reserved state goods.

Papa announced that he had summoned our only surviving family in the strictest confidence - my Auntie Lina, sister of my deceased Mother Berta, and my Cousin Sveta, who was ten years older than me - to come over the following morning to talk with me. He explained that I was making a very important decision, and he wanted them to advise me as well. I thought that it might not be his idea but Shura's. I answered that it was too late.

"I have already purchased our train tickets to Moscow for this Monday because I decided to return to Cuba as soon as possible."

They looked at each other in puzzlement, unable to understand why my decision had to be so rushed. After walking through the city most of the day, the boys were tired and fell asleep shortly after dinner, allowing us to discuss our situation more freely. Shura complained of not feeling well and went to bed early. She obviously did not want to participate in our discussion because she was afraid of where it might lead. I understood that this was an opportunity to tell my father more about the true situation; otherwise, he might misinterpret it.

"Let's take a walk, Papa; it would be better if we talk outside."

We sat on the bench at the top of our hill overlooking the

sea. This was our preferred place because of the sea breeze at twilight. I felt it was an opportunity to tell him the truth.

"*Papochka*, I know you want me to return to Cuba, but you don't know much about Cuba. The dark sides of Cuba you do not know, besides the fact that at my request, you had to send me a parcel with two ordinary aluminum pails and one hot plate because these essential basic items are unavailable there. I had a new baby and needed to carry water in pails from the port to cook, wash the children, and their diapers. I could not tell you the whole story on the phone or by letter. The reality is that Cuba has beautiful beaches and the historic City of Havana, but it has no pails, no hot plates, nor anything else besides sugar cane for its citizens. I lived a very privileged life there, only because I was working with a Soviet team. Still, the ordinary Cubans have hardly any access to the elementary essentials: water, electricity, nutritious food, or transportation. Even the quality of education and health for almost all Cubans, except for the Cuban elite and foreigners, is appalling. Their Revolution removed all the spoils of wealth they had before. For me to continue even a very modest and decent living standard in Cuba, I would have to work with Boris and possibly with the KGB and/or the GRU."

"*Dochenka*, you never spoke like this about it before. Why haven't you?"

I attempted to explain that our political officers from the Soviet embassy prohibited us from divulging bad news because it would jeopardize the political situation. All letters from abroad are read by the KGB, and everybody knows. The truth about Cuba is that its young leaders are good-looking but incompetent bandits, and they are more *meshugenah* (crazy) than our Soviet bosses.

My father argued that in his mind, our Soviet system was the most abusive in the whole world; after all, the USSR had inflicted more death and misery in our own homeland than in the war against enemies in other countries.

145

I agreed: "Cuban leaders are not as bad for their people as Stalin was for ours, but these Caribbean bandits are more dangerous in their own way. They are unstable, inept, and very aggressive. For example, they decided that the island, which is a tropical paradise, should produce only cane sugar. Everything else has to be purchased from abroad because all other sectors of the national economy were sacrificed to make space, energy, and time for cane sugar. As a result, they have to buy everything from the Soviet Union and its colonies."

Papa was still puzzled: "*Dochenka*, Cuban sugar has never been an attraction for the Soviet Union; we have our sugar made from beets. Do you know that the Soviet Union gave this Cuban sugar as a gift to Vietnam? So why is Cuba so important for the Soviet Union?"

"Why Cuba is important to the Soviet Union is clear: its geographical position," I replied, "Cuba is located only 145 kilometers from the US coastline. We have a navy base in Cuban territorial waters equipped with nuclear weapons. It is a perfect platform with a realistic range to attack the United States, if not from the ground as in 1962, then from under the water using our latest submarines. In 1962, Khrushchev struck a deal with Kennedy to remove Soviet nuclear missiles from Cuban territory in exchange for removing the American missiles from Turkey. The official propaganda was that we removed all those nuclear missiles. Still, this charade did not last for long. Fidel Castro got very upset by the Soviet-American deal, and the Soviet Government promised to return our nuclear missiles to Cuba as soon as possible, but again in secret. I was involved in helping a naval group from Leningrad working on our naval base for submarines operating in Cuba since 1970. This is why I was granted a privileged lifestyle."

Papa was perplexed: "This is incredible. I never thought that you and Boris would be engaged in classified military projects in Cuba. I believed that you were developing a commercial cargo port in Cienfuegos. How did your participation in a classified project become possible without a security clearance?"

"No, Papa, Boris is not involved in the naval project. He was in charge of the commercial part of the project. The Leningrad Naval Design Bureau team is in charge of the design and construction of the Soviet naval base. I got involved only because they decided to stop using their Cuban translator; there were rumors that she was arrested. Anyway, she disappeared. The KGB from the Soviet embassy asked me to assist with translations in exchange for their help with my accommodations. Last year, our base on the south side of Cuba became operational.

"This base is for servicing, maintenance, and repair of our diesel and nuclear-powered submarines equipped with nuclear warheads, ballistic and cruise missiles within range of US territory. The newest subs are amazing. They are undetectable with a minimum of acoustic, magnetic, radar, and visual signatures, and their missiles are launched from 50 meters under the water. Currently, this naval team is designing an ACBP (submerged nuclear submarine base) on the ocean floor. When our Soviet embassy minder informed me that I would have to undergo the clearance procedure to continue working with the naval team, I preferred to get out. I have been replaced by a Soviet Spaniard with the appropriate clearance and was moved back to work full-time with Boris. After the incident with Boris and a verbal spanking at the embassy for not snitching on my colleagues, I lost all my taste for work with the Soviet team. This pact with Doctor Faustus is disgusting to me."

My father began to understand the situation: "Was this then the reason for the KGB interest in you and the investigation they started with me here in Odessa? Are you afraid their interest has to do with that project?"

"Yes and no, this is not everything," I replied, "They now have their translator from Leningrad. I became afraid of them after refusing to write the periodic snitching reports on my colleagues, and because Boris denounced me as careless in security matters. The KGB boss in the Soviet embassy probably wrote a report to the KGB in Odessa suggesting that they teach me a lesson or shut me up, which they probably can do more easily at home and not abroad. Another possible reason is that they might wish to commit me to become an informer or a spy on Soviet colleagues, maybe on Cubans, or other foreigners. I don't know. Still, I detest all of these despicable ventures in snitching and pimping."

My father was shocked: "Really, I have no information about their concerns, and I would be afraid to know. I saw that the situation was dangerous. This is why I wrote to you in code advising not to return."

"Papa, the whole situation in Cuba is dangerous," I continued arguing. "They told me at the embassy that the Soviet Union will not risk war with the United States on Soviet territory. I understand that the Soviet strategy is only to intimidate Americans in world competition for power from a position of military might, but for Cubans, it is different. Fidel Castro is haunted by hatred for Americans and is obsessed with launching a war against the USA. You see, the confrontation with America had become his main justification for maintaining the Cuban totalitarian state. Without the Americans, Cuban leaders would lose their only enemy. They would have a hard time justifying the need for the tyranny of their dictatorship, or the need for arresting dissidents, or the need for financing and training guerrillas around the world. Who will they blame for the economic sabotage of their own country: themselves? They need the USA as the adversary.

Fidel does not play the same game as the Soviets. He does not trust anybody, not even his comrades. He made attempts before, in 1962, to sabotage the Soviet efforts at detente and almost caused a nuclear exchange. The KGB has to watch him and to watch everybody else. I don't want to be involved in that game. This could be the real reason why they needed informers among Soviet projects. They tried to commit me to snitch, but I was evasive. They ignored my reluctance during the time they needed my help with translations, and they were generally nice to me until Boris denounced me for being careless in security matters. They no longer need me for translations, and I am afraid of the moment when they will be ordered to discipline me in their nasty way. This is why I think they instructed the KGB here to tighten the screws on me. Papa, I feel messed up wherever I am - here or in Cuba. I don't want to be a snitch, their spy or informant, nor anybody else's spy."

"*Dochenka*, you probably are exaggerating," said my father. "The KGB does not employ Jews as spies; we are talking here only about informants. Everyone who is allowed to work abroad must also be the informand. This is public knowledge. Most people here who want to survive have to do the same. Why do you think Shura and I have not progressed in our careers as we should have? We would not cooperate with the Soviet authorities. Do you know that all organizations here have minimum quotas for informants, starting with all *dvorniks* (building caretakers); even they have to report on all residents in their buildings."

"No, Papa," I said, "I will not do it. It is disgusting, and you are wrong that they don't employ Jews as spies. They may not employ them for operations in the Soviet Union, but they do for their operations abroad. Our dear government and the KGB are anti-Semites traditionally, but only at home. They will never practice this abroad simply because it is easier to deceive the West's passionate and guilt-ridden utopian Jewish liberals with our phony internationalism. I could give you examples of foreigners I met in Cuba in Havana's Hotel National and Hotel Capri. From some of their personal stories, I understood that these are dangerous and confused people. You have to agree, Cubans will not protect me from the KGB. Quite the opposite, they would simply cooperate in delivering me to the appropriate Soviet authorities. Eduardo and I are no more important to them than the KGB. Apart from that, all these games are scary and insane. Playing games with nuclear toys at the front door of the USA - this is not something I want to participate in."

"Did you speak about this with Eduardo? Does he know what was going on? Does he understand that our *'dybbuk'* (evil spirit) is dangerous?" asked father.

"You mean the KGB or GRU? Yes, that is a good code name for these organizations. Let's keep that name for them. Eduardo knows only in a very limited way because I don't want to screw him up. I signed a confidentiality agreement for my work on the naval submarine base. If I tell him or anybody else, you included, I could be charged under the Soviet criminal code. *Azoy?* (Do I need it?). I am very sorry to have to tell you about my *"tzorres"* (troubles), but I can't help it; at least, you need to know the real facts. Otherwise, you would not appreciate why I am planning to defect, and it could be dangerous for all of us. I cannot lie to you. I have to tell you the truth."

"Thanks, Polinochka," he said, "I had no idea. It sounds like a very dangerous plan. I also do not believe that our homeland is in danger. I do not believe our government is looking for an opportunity to start a nuclear war, but there could be an incident that might spin out of their control. You and the children will be subjected to a big risk in Cuba. I understand. Tell me in more detail how you are planning to defect; where and when?"

"I am planning to start my travel back to Cuba this coming Monday," I responded. "This way, you will be less responsible for not reporting my arrival if they ever find out that I visited you here. If they discover that we visited you, you could answer that I did not spend any time with you because I was in a rush to return to Cuba. Then you could 'spill them the music' (convince them). You could tell them that I planned to have a better time staying in Moscow with some friends of mine. You don't know with whom, and I did not say because we disagreed about that. After all, I am an adult now, and you could not assert your authority over me. We have not lived together for the past three years. It happened suddenly. You were surprised and did not have time to connect with the right officer; something like that."

"I was feeling much better about your stay in Cuba before you described this circus," said father. "Why do you want to take the children on such a dangerous venture? Leave them here with us; at least, we are far away from that Cuban *durdome* (madhouse). After this craziness extinguishes itself, you and Eduardo could decide what you want to do: take the children back to Cuba or come with us here in Odessa. But at least the children will be safe with us here for the time being."

"Thank you, Papa, but that is not possible for me. I have decided and will leave Odessa with the children on Monday. The die has been cast."

"You have decided. *Mazel tov*. (Congratulations/Good luck). How are you going to travel on Monday? To where?" asked the father.

"We will take the train on Monday to Moscow," I replied. "We will arrive in Moscow on Wednesday by noon and take a taxi directly to Sheremetyevo. We will purchase a flight to Havana with Aeroflot in Sheremetyevo, just two hours before the flight at 6 p.m. This is my plan."

"Why go by train?" Papa wandered. "Why don't you fly? Why don't you try to purchase your tickets with Aeroflot in Odessa? What are you going to do if, after you arrive at Sheremetyevo, there are no vacant seats on your flight?"

"I don't want to leave a trail," I explained. "Aeroflot records names, but the train service does not. If I purchase my foreign flight from the Odessa office of Aeroflot, they will ask approval from MID (Foreign Affairs Ministry), and MID will inform the KGB in Odessa, and I don't want them to know that I was visiting you."

"Hold your horses, my big talker, not so fast," Papa said.

"Do you know if this flight has any available seats? You will need three seats."

"I don't know, but it will be worthwhile to try," I suggested. "If they don't have the seats, I will be forced to purchase our tickets for the next available flight. Meanwhile, we will stay in Moscow."

"Where in Moscow can you stay with two small children?" asked father. "Are you such a *macher* (big shot) that the Moscow hotels will let you stay without checking with MVD (internal security police)? This is the first thing they will do."

"I might be able to fix the electricity at the cabin in Lesnoy and purchase the bedsheets to sleep, if necessary," I guessed. "If everything fails, then I will ask for advice from your cousin Raya to help us with some temporary accommodations. I should try the cabin in Lesnoy first; it just might work."

"Still, it doesn't solve your problem with Boris in Cuba and, as I understood from your story, the cat and mouse nuclear game with the Americans is dangerous and unpredictable," said father.

"Yes, Papa, you are right," I admitted. "The truth is, I am hoping to defect in Gander, Canada, on our way to Havana. You see, the Aeroflot flight is direct Moscow-Havana, but it has refueling stops, usually around 40 minutes: one in Shannon, Ireland, and another in Gander, Canada. I want to defect in Gander. If we fail to escape in Gander, we will continue to Cuba. This is my plan."

"Gander, Canada? Are you sure? Who will be waiting for you in Gander? What do you know about Gander?" Papa became agitated. I thought that our discussion was dangerous for his heart condition and his high blood pressure.

"Papa, I have everything arranged. I cannot tell you how or who is waiting for me in Gander because too much information will be only a burden on you. I am sorry that I have to tell you the truth while knowing how delicate your blood pressure is. The less you know, the better when the KGB questions you afterward about my plans. They mustn't learn of my visit with you in Odessa. This is why no one else besides you must know of my plans. Please make sure that Shura and my relatives do not talk about my visit to Odessa and do not share our discussions with Shura or the others. Otherwise, they will become implicated as well."

"Thank you, *Dochenka,* for telling me the truth. I feel much better and confident knowing the whole story. You do not have to worry. If you can pull it off, it is a unique opportunity. I approve. Does Eduardo know?"

"No, Papa, he does not," I said, "but we agreed that if either of us has the chance to defect, the other will join him at a later opportunity. He does not know any details yet, for the same reason that I do not want to burden you with more detailed knowledge. Still, I want you to understand that what I am planning to do is very serious, and you must be extremely careful discussing my plan with anyone, including Shura and all of our relatives and friends. The less they know, the easier it will be for them. Remember, none of them should ever admit that they met with the children and me. I never came to Odessa. *Dogovorilis* (agreed)?"

"Polinochka, I only worry about your well-being and happiness," he concluded.

"Don't worry, *Tateh*. If we can defect, we will make a free life in a free country. If we don't, then we will return to Cuba. Eduardo knows that."

Paulina Zelitsky, Paul Weinzweig

29. With the sad whisper of lowered flags[52]

The next morning, we had visitors: my Auntie Lina (sister of my deceased mother, Berta), my cousin Sveta (daughter of Fania, the deceased sister of my father), and her husband. They had come to see the children and me in a last attempt to convince me to stay in Odessa. All the ladies, including Shura, were sad; they were weeping, as women often do. Papa left me alone with them and went to comfort Shura, who, using the excuse of preparing our lunch, went outside to sit 'na shucher' (to guard for our safety). Papa agreed with me not to disclose my plan to escape, even to Shura.

My relatives were elated to see children grown and handsome, but their main focus was convincing me to stay in Odessa. I suspected that it was an idea of Shura because she still hoped that they might convince me to stay. It was obvious to me that Papa and Shura were divided in their opinion about what was better for me to do. My father favored my return to Cuba, hoping that I would be safe in Cuba from the pressures of the Odessan KGB, while Shura would prefer our moving back home to Odessa and fitting into Soviet society. Neither Shura nor my relatives knew anything about my father's meetings with the KGB and their request to inform them of my arrival. Papa was warned by the KGB to keep these meetings secret.

My Cousin Sveta was married and had a six-year-old son. She lived with her family in an apartment (one large room), which my father got for her in our building, and she often visited my parents. I was not close to her because, being ten years older, she looked down on me. She often patronized me by zealously arguing that I do not appreciate my good luck at being born into such a well-established family, living in such privileged conditions, meaning our centrally located apartment and our dacha in Arcadia. Now, sitting across from me with her husband, she began her inquisition. She told me that, with my parents and my profession, I was guaranteed to have a good life in Odessa. Anybody in Odessa would consider my situation to be the best of all possible worlds! How could I leave such privileges, and what would happen to my parents? Is it fair? Why am I so egotistical?

She told me that I was immature, spoiled, and *meshugenah* (crazy). She showered me with guilt for not looking after my parents when they approached their old age. I knew that she was telling me the truth, but I was not listening since I had already made up my mind not to trade the slightest possibility of escaping to freedom for a good life in Odessa. I felt quite annoyed that my parents had resorted to such manipulative intervention. Her husband, Grigoriy, passively supported his wife in everything she said, convinced that she understood my reality better than I did. There was something in her and her husband that I never cared for; probably, their conviction that they knew better about everything.

My Auntie Lina (sister of my deceased mother) acted and spoke differently. She was very careful and did not attack or criticize me, but rather suggested that if the children and I preferred to stay with her and her family to think about my future, we would be very welcome to stay with them for as long as we wanted. When I told her that I was grateful for the offer but determined to return to Cuba, she gave me an imported and probably expensive gift to take with me as a remembrance of her.

She was not as pushy and offensive as Sveta, but I suspected the offer to stay with her was motivated by the continuing traditional competition with my father in their old dispute about which family (his or my deceased mother's sister) I should live with. I thought that it was rather unfair because my father trusted her, but she could not resist her possessive nature and used this as an opportunity to compete with my father. My loyalties were always with Papa, and I was annoyed with what I interpreted as a display of their rivalry at such a difficult time. Instead of being a stabilizing experience, their visit made me even more defensive and sad, especially considering that none of them, including Shura, knew my real situation, which I had confided only to my father. Nobody but my father could be trusted with something so subversive.

I could not help but remind them that we had a very short time to enjoy one another, so let us not spoil it. Instead, we should take pleasure in the company of the children whom they would probably not see again for a long time. Despite everything they said, I reminded them that I was determined to return to Cuba, and nothing they said would change my resolve.

They left after lunch because it was clear that their efforts were futile. I was not listening. They looked anxious when my father warned them to keep my stay in Odessa and our meeting secret. There was no need to explain the reasons. All of us were aware that any contact with those who reside abroad is dangerous. It was safer for them not to ask much and to know even less should they be interrogated by the KGB. I appreciated that Shura was trying her best to convince me to stay and protect me, risking her exposure to my relatives, who were her rivals and were traditionally opposed to her actions. All this effort was her only recourse to keep me at home, but I was known for my independence of mind and was never easily manipulated. A wasted effort! When they left, I felt relieved to get rid of my relatives, whom I always considered 'nudniks' (annoying people), especially now that I wanted to enjoy every second remaining before we departed from Odessa. I knew that it was our last time and needed to engrave the images of my parents and the surroundings from my happy childhood in every cell of my memory.

During these two days, the children were introduced to our traditional Odessan dishes served by Shura: bagels with lox and the best spicy vegetarian Odessan borscht, which is so different from the Russian or Ukrainian meat-based versions. There was gefilte fish, vinaigrette (spicy, red, cold salad with a base of beets and pickles), chicken liver pâté, eggplant caviar pâté, and fantastic cherry strudel. Nothing is more delicious than these authentic Mediterranean Jewish dishes. The best part is that Shura did not have to cook them by herself. This traditional Odessan food had been available, lately and inexpensively, from the numerous Odessan delicatessens where Shura was accustomed to shopping after work (nowhere else in the Soviet Union, only in Odessa). It was a real feast, especially when combined with local fresh fried fish, such as 'kambala' (flounder).

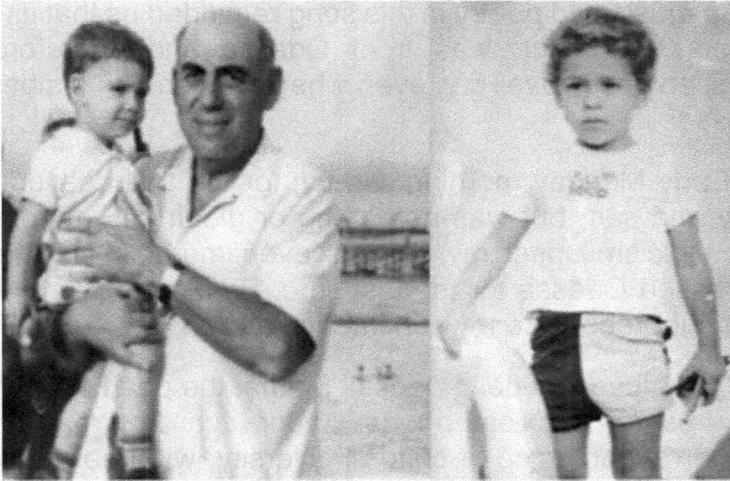
My father and the boys are having a wonderful time together in Arcadia.

For two days, we ate well and relaxed by strolling along the deserted early-season seacoast promenade with fragrant trees on the hillside above the coastline on one side and the open sea on the other. After all, who can resist the fragrance of acacia trees in full flower and the Black Sea breeze? We enjoyed walking in this warm spring weather before the summer heat, the children running and playing along the way, my parents and I laughing at them. It was a peaceful and happy moment, allowing us to forget the realities and worries

Paulina Zelitsky, Paul Weinzweig

about the unknown future and its dangers.

Papa played his record of the revered Soviet singer and actor Leonid Utyosov singing the Odessan wartime song called *Odessit Mishka*. The lyrics drifted into our hearts:

"With the sad whisper of lowered flags and in deep silence

Without pipes and drums, the last battalion leaves Odessa.

You are the Odessan Mishka, and the Odessans never cry!"

The music and poetry in this song reminded us that its hero, Mishka the Sailor, was from Odessa and, therefore, an Odessan shall never cry, even when abandoning his beloved Odessa.

Early Monday morning, we left for the train station. I felt sorry and sad, but was not crying or gloomy in my outlook. This stoicism upset my parents even more. In my heart, I addressed Odessa for the last time. Emigrants from this fair city might recognize my sentimental mood:

"Goodbye, my dear Odessa Mama, the pearl of my heart. You have intoxicated us, your children, with the Mediterranean spice of cultural diversity, with the agility and liberality of your commerce, and with European enlightenment that made us more resilient to the savagery enforced throughout a long history of unwelcome invaders. Your beauty and your climate, together with our humor, irony, and music, created a hospitable oasis in the Russian desert of dread and drudgery. You, my dear Odessa Mama, have struggled to survive and will one day win simply by laughing and seducing with your talent, your charm, and your ingenuity, but I cannot wait for this moment and must leave. Farewell forever. I will never forget you. I will keep you always in my heart as long as I live."

The Sea is Only Knee Deep

My parents came with us to the train station to take a sit-down in our own compartment in the first-class soft (sleeping) carriage. It is a Russian tradition: to sit together before the departure and to wish a good voyage. Shura fought with her tears, and Papa was grim. So far, we were very lucky - nobody appeared out of the blue to drag me away, and nothing disturbed our farewell. That alone was a good omen. It suggested that today's KGB was sloppy, not the same vigilant outfit from earlier times. It did not appear as if they were informed about my presence. Actually, I spent nearly four days undetected in Odessa. Our good fortune was holding. I arrived invisibly in Odessa at night and departed unnoticed in the late morning.

Farewell, Odessa Mama! A sculptural façade on a building overlooking the port

Speaking in a low voice, I said, "Papa, please remember, if I can't purchase a flight to Havana for the same day as we arrive in Moscow, I will send you a telegram or will call. If I manage to purchase our flight for the same day to Havana, I will not be able to let you know because we will be on our way. In that case, I will call you after we arrive in Havana. If I did not call, please wait for a week and then call Eduardo only to inquire if he had any news from me. To answer his questions about us, just say that you have not heard from me and that you know how stubborn I can be. Eduardo will understand what you mean."

Papa solemnly nodded his head in agreement. He said only that he and Shura would be returning to their city apartment. If there is an emergency, I could call them at work. He did not want me to notice how sad he felt, so he put on a brave face:

"'*Ne drefuy*' (Don't be afraid), '*Mazel tov!*' (Good luck!)," were his last words to me.

The only way to contact was to send a telegram or call at work, which was not desirable because the phones at work might be monitored. Tearfully, we kissed and hugged until the train stewardess came to check the tickets and demanded that my parents leave the carriage. They stood on the station platform beside our window, and we kept looking at each other until the train slowly began to move. We were throwing kisses, all the time thinking that at this moment, we probably were separating for a very long time. No, we could not believe in separation forever.

"CHU, CHU," shouted the excited children and attempted to open the cabin doors. I did not move to help them because I was quietly crying.

"Poli, why are you crying?" asked a surprised Edik.

I answered: "I didn't want Grandpa to see me crying because he has a delicate heart, and I should not upset him. You are right. I am Odessan too and shall never cry."

Who could hold these two little boys behind the closed doors of our small compartment? Half an hour later, I was already chasing after them along the train corridors into the common hard wagons (equipped with wooden stacked benches with no mattresses or lining). They were overcrowded, with peasants hauling bags with some products for sale in local markets. The common carriage is much cheaper; they are equipped with two levels of hard, naked benches along the whole length of the carriage without any separation. The air was thick with the strong smell of cheap tobacco, vodka, salted fish, and many unwashed human bodies. This did not stop the children from approaching everybody and becoming familiar with those who spoke to them. I had a hard time returning the kids to our compartment. Two other passengers who boarded the train at a remote intermediate station were brought into our compartment a few hours later. An attendant brought us hot tea, and we unwrapped the food that we carried from home to share it and to chat with our new neighbors. Such was the traditional train custom. It was not hard to break the ice with the kids and me. They asked where we came from since the boys did not look Russian and spoke little of the language.

"These kids are *'polovinka'* (mixed)," I explained, adding that we were returning to their father in Cuba.

Our compartment neighbors, Valery and Milochka, said that the sight of my children made them happy. Their experience with their own child was traumatic. They were a married couple, but lost their only child when both of them were arrested in Odessa in 1949. Their story was typical: they were only teenagers when they got married after they met at the front during the war. They thought that they were lucky when they were awarded a large room at a prestigious Odessan address, but that was the beginning of their downfall. When their baby boy was six months old, one of their neighbors falsely denounced the young couple for hiding information, allegedly about some intended industrial sabotage. The accuser simply wanted their room because of its distinguished address. The couple was arrested and held in prison with their baby. The investigator was not interested in any evidence of their crime or their protests about false charges. They were sentenced to eight years of forced labor

161

in Kolima in the Far North. Horrible conditions and starvation killed their baby in the labor camp. Milochka lost the ability to have more children.

They were released in 1956 but were not allowed to return to Odessa. Instead, they were restricted to living in remote communities, far from industrial cities. Now they were traveling to Moscow to appeal this residential decision. They wanted the court to recognize that they had been the victims of false accusations and were repressed unjustly. They lost their only child and their apartment in Odessa, which was now occupied by the person who falsely denounced them. All of their possessions were expropriated by the state and then offered for sale in special stores called Sales of Incidental Goods. These outlets offered the secret police and Communist Party members first pick, and they were not required to pay. The couple felt that rebuilding their lives in the misery of the village where they were permitted to reside was impossible.

Milochka was very ill after Kolima, and Valery's health was damaged. During the past four years, they struggled to survive on the miserable income from their menial jobs in the remote community where they lived. During this time, they were appealing to the court in Moscow by mail to grant their right to reside in Odessa and to return their room to them. It was all to no avail. Everybody told them that they were wasting their efforts, that the appeal would not bring back their son, their apartment, or their family possessions. Still, they persisted, unable to imagine how to continue their present lives. They were not resentful about their destiny because, as they said, "You see, those were very bad times, almost as bad as the 1930s.

To fall victim during those times, you could simply walk down the street at the wrong moment when the police quotas for arrests by the local MGB (Ministry for State Security) department were not yet fulfilled for that week. To fill these quotas, they would sweep the streets and arrest innocent passers-by. They would hold those arrested without charges until they invented false charges against these innocent citizens. Those were very bad times; the principles of communist ideology were completely ignored by some of Stalin's people."

Such stories reminded me of my history classes in school about the awful behavior of *Oprichniki* (security police) of Ivan the Terrible in 16th-century Russia. So what had changed for those who lived on lands occupied by Russia over the centuries? The story of Valery and Milochka fits perfectly within this despotic imperial tradition. The lawless, tyrannical state security went about their business as they pleased by intimidating and punishing innocent citizens instead of pursuing real enemies. Such practices were prevalent throughout Russian history.

I should have controlled my indignation, but suddenly, surprising myself, my anger rose against Milochka's passive acceptance of their suffering and of the abuse the state committed against her and her husband:

"I think you are wrong, dear. Let me cite Lenin for you; his famous phrase everyone knows: 'There are no morals in politics, there is only expedience. A scoundrel may be of use to us just because he is a scoundrel.[50] What could we expect from such political ethics? This was the true culprit and not your bad luck."

Immediately after this explosion, with such a strong accusation against the Soviet state, I was overcome with fear. Looking at my neighbors' shocked faces, I was struck by the idea that they could report me if they wanted. I was stupid. What was wrong with me to open myself so dangerously to people unknown to me? What if they were provocateurs who were sent intentionally to take seats in our compartment to bring me into this dangerous conversation?

Valery and Milochka looked at each other in disbelief. Valery said, "Don't talk like this in front of us, please. It is very

163

dangerous, especially for us."

I realized that my fears were false; these people were not provocateurs, only innocent but terrorized victims. These humble people blamed bad luck and not the state that converted all of us into slaves and prisoners. Still, they prefer not to torture themselves with the idea that they were deceived all of their lives and that their suffering was for nothing. Valery and Milochka, like most other Soviets, neglected to question either the sanity or the morality of their leaders. I wonder today if they would change their minds during the perestroika after learning that Vladimir Ulyanov (alias Lenin)[51], as well as a majority of the Bolshevik leadership, were German spies hired by the *Wehrmacht* (German military) and financed to start the Russian Revolution to enable Germany to win the war.[52] The so-called father of our nation, Joseph Dzhugashvili (alias Stalin), was an agent of the Tsarist Secret Service (*Ochrana*) hired and financed for 14 years as a provocateur by *Ochrana* to expose and to exterminate Russian revolutionaries. In other words, our most venerated ideological leaders and their close associates were hired subversive agents on the payroll of secret intelligence agencies of the enemies of the Soviet Union. When, eventually, after the dissolution of the Soviet Union, this information was revealed, many communists categorically refused to believe it.[53]

The Soviet leaders and many of their entrusted lieutenants pretended to act in the name of the ideology of the Revolution, to which end they committed monstrous crimes, ordering mass murders of their citizens. Their motivation for genocide arose solely from their desire to achieve absolute power and to prevent leakage about their association with the enemies. Terror was the tool used to create the cheapest slave labor to build a huge and powerful military industry designed to gain control of the world. All of this was staged in the extreme conditions of the northeastern climate in an isolated land rich in resources but inimical to human survival. No freely hired labor could be lured for physical work in such conditions.

Then, I remembered my mother and my uncle, who also died as young victims of this deception. At that moment, I, too, felt humiliated, embarrassed, and impotent, for I could not have done anything to prevent it. Quickly, I overcame these feelings and decided to think only positive thoughts. Life's importance is not in the past; it is in the future!

I advised Valery and Milochka that, in their place, it would be more practical to concentrate on relentless appeals for permission to move to Odessa, justifying it by the better use of their professional backgrounds because of the job opportunities in Odessa. I think it is much more important to fight for the future than to look back at the past, but all people are different, and I hoped they would not interpret my remarks as patronizing.

The train attendant brought tea, and we shared a meal again. Our window was completely dark now. The children were put on lower bunks to sleep. Valery and Milochka took their upper bunks, but I continued drinking more tea. It was sweet and strong. Finally, I was able to think in peace about how to handle the expected supervision by the Aeroflot guards. I could not hide in a toilet again. We would have to change tactics. This time, we would need to run, and our running should be faster than the Aeroflot security agents. How funny it would look if, with two small children, I managed to run faster than the KGB guards.

No, this sounds implausible, if not impossible. I had already anticipated this absurdity, which is why I was interested to learn more about the CSA flights from Moscow to Prague. The direct flights from Moscow to Havana on CSA are no longer available; only by Aeroflot. I had no special permission to purchase a CSA flight instead of Aeroflot, nor did I have permission to purchase any flights to Prague as a destination. Our Soviet passports, by the unwritten rules of MVD (Internal Affairs), permitted us, as Soviet citizens, to purchase a flight to Havana by Aeroflot only. The special permit, which I obtained earlier in Havana from the new Soviet consul, was already wasted when I purchased our tickets originally with CSA and missed that flight. However, my mind continued to dwell on the advantages of Czech Airlines compared to Aeroflot with its KGB guards. Czechoslovakian guards were concentrating on Czech passengers. I was hoping that Soviet passengers were beyond their suspicion, and this could be an opportunity. When I called Sheremetyevo Airport and was told that there would be a flight to Prague by CSA at approximately the same time as the direct flight on Aeroflot to Havana, it was a happy coincidence, perhaps an omen. Still, what I imagined and what was possible could not be reconciled in my mind, only in the real situation and at the moment. At the moment, I did not have a clue how it might play out.

A new idea began crystallizing in my mind. Edik is a natural runner; the way he was running from us on the beach in Arcadia, I could not catch him. Who could suspect this darling, angelic-looking five-year-old of escaping? However, Ernestico was still too young to run fast over a longer distance. Eduardo and I used to laugh at his bouncing because of his habit of jumping on tiptoe while running. He was still only learning how to run normally. I would have to run with him in my arms after the much faster Edik. It would not be easy to carry Ernestico and run. I would need to use both my arms and hands to hold him and make sure to wear flat shoes instead of my usual high heels. I decided to experiment by running while carrying Ernestico in my arms. Tomorrow, I will see if it works. I lay down carefully beside Ernestico, who was sleeping in the middle of the bottom bunk. Moving him to the wall is safer because my body would prevent him from rolling over the edge onto the floor in the middle of the night when the train brakes suddenly.

I had a hard time trying to fall asleep, afraid to move on this narrow bunk in order not to squash my child, and there was not enough air. With three adults and two children in such a small compartment, the atmosphere was stuffy. Despite being so very tired, sleep remained elusive. Whenever I did manage to drift off, the train's frequent station stops brought me back to a restless consciousness.

30. Necessity Breaks Iron[57]

The sudden jolt of the train as it stopped at another intermediate station brought me to my senses. The train attendant opened the door of our compartment and left glasses with hot tea on the small table beside the window. While the others continued to sleep, I sipped the hot tea and wondered whether it was reasonable to take such an ultimate risk with two small children. My plan to outrun Soviet security agents and seek asylum with Canadian authorities while carrying Ernestico in my arms was looking less realistic. Eduardo was right when he said that our chances of escaping with Ernestico would be ridiculously low, especially with Aeroflot. If they catch me a second time, I will get a tough sentence, meaning the Gulag camp for sure. Maybe I should stop trying to invent impossible defections and prepare myself mentally for returning to Cuba, whereby obeying the orders of my superiors, I could still make a privileged career. Boris had become less of a monster in my receding memory, particularly after sharing the trauma with my parents. And, who knows, perhaps things might change at some later date, and we would have another opportunity to travel and defect with the Czech airline. My main obstacle was my rejection of any involvement with the KGB, which clearly conflicted with any career prospects. I felt trapped at the edge of the abyss, not in the best state of mind.

The rhythmic movement of the train reminded me of a song which we had to sing every morning in school: "We are the children of those who attacked. Our locomotive flies forward."

Every school morning, we children were required to sing the national anthem before we would be allowed into the school building to start our classes (in my case, daily from the age of six to thirteen). It is interesting how I never noticed that its lyrics were not so sweet. The words are a cold, cruel call to extreme violence - a bizarre and dangerous message for young minds. The rhythmic movement of the train that night and my current fears made me think about the meaning of this song. When I was a child, I liked its spirited, aggressive tones because they would invigorate our sleepy early mornings. Growing up, I never gave it any practical meaning because we were so accustomed to being saturated with the artistic expressions of Soviet propaganda based largely on hatred and vengefulness.

For the first time in my life, it dawned on me how the final words of this song were so cruel and crude: "We have the guns in our hands, Burning all with a vengeance." It was a message designed for the vicious and criminal brainwashing of children. Why is it that I did not see sooner how barbaric it was? And to where have I arrived now? To plan how to join the enemy and abandon the Soviet train? Only to be attacked by my compatriots?

I was not fit to adapt to a Soviet political system when I categorically refused to accept Stalin as my father, even by the age of three. It just meant that my own father's parental authority continued supreme over all those phony fathers enforced by my teachers. I was appalled when they attempted to manipulate us with the Pavlik Morozov story to convert us into snitches on our parents.[54] Most children developed the habit of obeying their teachers, a habit inbred in us since birth. None of us even noticed how we were becoming indoctrinated with hatred and aggression through the instruments of culture, force-fed everywhere and constantly. *Homo Sovieticus* did not think for themselves; they were not trained to question the official information - they implicitly trusted it. They readily acted on orders from the authorities. By adopting the lie, they are avoiding any suffering from personal guilt or embarrassment for their actions. They convinced themselves that the dictatorial system was moral when it originated from the state. In this way, they avoided the experience of psychological pain.

Sooner or later, I would clash with this system. Pretending to be obedient was only a temporary tactic to escape punishment, but, in the long run, I would reveal my disobedience. It is a terrible burden to live a false life. The same applies to my children, who would be subjected to the aggressive propaganda of hatred and violence against the enemy. They would be exploited at the will and whim of the government.

I did not want my children to become *Homo Sovieticus* and be forced, like I was, to sing poisonous songs of hostile propaganda. I gave life to my children, and this made me responsible for delivering them to freedom. If I delayed their freedom, it would take much longer to develop them into their natural human state, if at all possible. Moses had to keep the Jewish tribes in the desert for 40 years to retrain them to become responsible free people following their escape from Egyptian slavery.

Later in the morning, after the children were up and had some breakfast, I took them to play with me in the train's narrow corridors. I needed to experiment with my running scenario while carrying Ernestico in my arms. There would not be any other opportunity for such practice after we arrived in Moscow. Stupid me, I should have rehearsed this in Arcadia, where we had plenty of space and opportunity.

We stood at one end of the long corridor, aiming at the other end. I gave instructions to the oldest:

"Edik, we will play the game of who will run the fastest. I will point with my thumb in the direction we will need to run: right or left. I will give you a secret signal - only for you and me - and you will watch for my signal showing you where to run. I know the conditions for your running against me are not equal: you are the little boy, and I am the big mother. To make it fair for you, I would carry Ernestico in my arms while running.

If you want to win, don't stop running even when you hear my shouts for you to stop or if you bump into people who might try to block your way. You must reach the end of the corridor first before stopping if you want to win this game. The winner gets to eat the chocolate that Grandpa gave us."

"Poli, if you win, can I get to eat your chocolate too?" asked Edik.

"No, my sweet, it is a tough game; if you get to eat the chocolate regardless of who wins, what incentive is there for you to try hard to win?"

"Ernestico, I can't run when you are sitting like a lump in my arms. I will need your help if you want to win. Please wrap your legs around my waist and hold onto me very tight to help me keep my balance. Ready?"

I was feeling guilty about all those passengers whose passage we would interrupt while they tried to pass through the corridor.

Holding Ernestico, with his crossed legs around my waist and his hands locked behind my neck, like a Cuban peasant boy climbing a palm tree for coconuts, we walked to the far end of the long, narrow train corridor. With my hands still locked under Ernestico, I pointed with my thumb to the right. After a moment of doubt and hesitation, Edik sprinted happily down the empty corridor, indifferent to the rocking movement of the train. I followed him, shouting, "Stop! Stop!" But he did not stop. On his way, he bumped into a man emerging from the lavatory, but the incident did not deter him. I was trying to follow, but I was too clumsy with the child hanging on my neck while the train was swaying and jolting. I was too slow; there was nothing I could do about it. It was not possible to run with a child in your arms. At least, Ernestico just loved this game, and he held on to me with the Cuban skill of a palm climber, as if I was a running tree trunk. We reached the end of the corridor, knocking into passersby on our way. Edik announced that he won and demanded his reward immediately. I was losing my balance from the rollicking movements of the train and needed to steady myself against the sides of the coach just to answer him:

"Not yet; we should try the opposite way. Ready?"

Edik rocketed toward the opposite direction while I dragged my feet after him again. I shouted, "Stop, stop." Edik did not stop. He was now too excited to quit. This time, our noise brought the steward, who grabbed Edik before he could reach his destination.

"*Grazhdanka* (Citizen), you are disturbing the order. Your child is misbehaving. He is running along the corridors. Immediately remove him inside your compartment," said the steward.

"Sorry, *Tovarisch* steward, thank you. It is just too hard for a small boy to stay still for a long time, but I promise you he will behave," I apologized.

With that answer, I brought the children back into our compartment and stopped our experiment before we could be evicted from the train by the police. Nevertheless, I had already drawn some conclusions about the feasibility of our running exercise. The boys were learning to play this game and were cheerfully collaborating with me. Theoretically, it was possible. Both of them were doing a really good job. I needed to be stronger.

"Poli, you should give me both chocolates to eat, mine and Ernestico's. I won because it wasn't my fault that the man grabbed me."

"No, Edik, you get only one chocolate. The other one is for Ernestico because the rules of the game were that you couldn't allow anyone to stop you until you reached the end of the corridor. I hope you learned that and do not forget for the next time when we play 'the running and no stopping' game. But for now, let's play again 'yolky-palky' (a game of clapping hands) like we did yesterday with Valery."

Later, Valery and Milochka began teaching the boys to play more games, and the time flew by quickly. We arrived at *Kievskaya* Station in Moscow at noon. Valery and Milochka helped me with the children to the taxi station and kissed each of us goodbye. I needed that hug from good people who had no idea about my intentions. They would be the last human beings to express warmth and loving attention towards us before my planned plunge into the abyss.

It was after 2 p.m. when we arrived at Sheremetyevo-1. The flight to Havana by Aeroflot was at 6 p.m., and I was extremely worried about the availability of seats for this flight. We would have to spend a whole week in Moscow if the seats for that day were not available. I could not just walk into a Moscow hotel and purchase a week's stay before the next flight. Before a hotel could rent a room to any Soviet citizen, the hotel was obliged to send this person's passport for approval by the MVD state security police (actually, by the KGB). Since I wanted to avoid the KGB at all costs, I would have to depend on Autie Raya, who was living outside of Moscow in New Cheremushki. I was hoping that she would accept our stay with her family in their small one-bedroom apartment. I was not close to her and was not sure if she would invite us to stay with them. The cabin in the village of Lesnoy, that was lacking amenities and electricity, would have to become our shelter until the next flight, for which we hoped to purchase tickets.

At the airport, we spent an hour in line at the Aeroflot ticket sales counter until the airline sales staff accepted our Soviet foreign passport, permitting its holder to travel abroad to a specific country: in my case, Cuba. This so-called foreign passport had none of the personal identifiers listed in my internal passport, only my name and the names of children dependent on me, the date and place of birth for each of us, as well as the countries to which we could travel.

"Could you tell me, please, if there are seats available for the flight to Havana tonight? I need three seats: for my two children who are listed in my passports and for me."

I was waiting for an answer from the sales clerk with heightened anxiety. My heart seemed to stop beating, and I could barely breathe while the sales clerk was checking the lists for tonight's flight. After going through the list, she took another look at our passports:

"Where are the children? How old are they?"

I realized that she would ask these questions only if seats were available. I felt relieved. "Here is Eduard (Edik), just turned five, and Ernesto (Ernestico) recently turned three."

"You are lucky; some seats on this flight are still available, and your foreign passport is up to date, but I will need to see your internal passport and obtain the approval for the sale of your tickets from the representative of MVD (internal state security)."

Reluctantly, I handed over my internal Soviet passport. It specified my name, date, and place of birth, ethnicity, approved residence address, changes to the resident address (the residence address can be changed only on approval by MVD), previous convictions, previous citizenship, marriage status, blood type, right to have a radio station, right to come nearer than 101 kilometers to the 'rezhimniy punct' (cities with military-industrial complex), and the permanent residence address of the passport holder (original address at birth). I did not want MVD to pin down my Soviet residence address and inform the KGB in Odessa that I was attempting to exit the country. That would kill all my hopes of avoiding a meeting with the KGB.

Please, wait behind the railing. I will call you after we receive this approval."

"It is already three p.m. You said that my passport is valid. Please expedite their approval if you can, because I am extremely worried that it might delay our departure, and we will miss our flight to Havana. It would force us to wait in Moscow." I was pushing, trying my luck with the sales staff to avoid MVD altogether.

"' *Grazhdanka*', this is what we have to do. Don't argue and wait behind the railing," she answered angrily. Oops, it would be better not to push too hard, and I retreated behind the railing. After more than an hour of waiting, I was feeling increasingly anxious, worried that we would miss our flight. My nerves were fraying as I repeatedly chased the children who were getting restless in a restricted area while I attempted to keep watch over our luggage.

The problem was that each sale of an international flight by Aeroflot had to be approved by the MVD (Ministry of Foreign Affairs) passport department in Moscow, which in turn would send it to the KGB travel department for approval. Only after MVD in Moscow received approval from the KGB, including the KGB in Odessa, the city of my residence, would they permit their officer at Sheremetyevo Airport to approve the purchase of our tickets. Our documents were in order, but in my strategy to avoid the review of them by the KGB, I pushed the schedule of approval to the extreme by arriving late and pestering the agent. There was nothing left to do except to beg the airline sales clerk to expedite the purchase of our flight.

The sales clerk, seeing my distress, asked me to wait to the side while she sought the MVD officer personally for approval. I was nervous because I did not know what to expect. Maybe MVD had instructions to prevent me from leaving the country. When, finally, the sales lady returned with my passport in her hands, instead of calling me, she continued consulting with her colleagues in the glassed room behind the counter. Finally, she emerged and called me to the counter:

"I asked the MVD officer to expedite your approval because you have young children and might miss your flight. Meanwhile, you will save time by paying for one full adult fare and two children at half price. Unfortunately, the back seats are the only ones available." Her voice was low and sounded sympathetic.

"I am grateful to you from the bottom of my heart. Thank you, the back seats will be fine."

I felt relieved but still cautious. I paid for the tickets and checked our suitcase. Only our foreign Soviet passport was returned to me to travel; my internal Soviet passport was kept by the office of the MVD; I could reclaim it on my return to the Soviet Union. I didn't care about it any longer. To leave, to depart at any cost, was my sole intention.

We still had to line up for immigration and security. It usually takes quite a while, and we had less than an hour and a half left before our flight. I was worried, but my restless little boys seemingly eased the immigration procedure because they let us through without major delay. We rushed towards the gate, Ernestico bouncing in my arms and Edik holding onto my skirt. It must have looked comical. It seemed too slow. By the time we reached our gate, all the other passengers had already exited the gate and were walking on the tarmac towards the aircraft with the Aeroflot name on its side. The airline guards accompanied the passengers, and the agent was annoyed with our delay when we arrived late at the gate desk. The airline desk agent checked our documents, indicated the exit, and told me in an irritated voice to catch up with the rest of the passengers on the tarmac. When we finally exited onto the tarmac, instead of following the other passengers for Havana walking towards the Aeroflot plane, I stopped and lowered Ernestico down to the ground, pretending that he was too heavy for me to carry him. This allowed me to increase the distance from the group walking ahead and to look around the tarmac for the CSA aircraft. Immediately, I noticed another group of passengers lining up at the aircraft ladder with the plane's CSA name printed on its side. I figured out that it must be the CSA flight to Prague, the flight of which I had dreamed.

This was a unique opportunity. The security guards were following the rest of the Aeroflot passengers and failed to notice my fussing with the boys and my falling behind their pace. I needed to get into the CSA aircraft fast before anyone realized my transgression. How? I was holding Aeroflot tickets to Havana and not CSA tickets to Prague. The CSA attendants scrutinized the tickets of all passengers before they were allowed to climb the aircraft ladder. My only option, if caught, was to pretend that I was confused and got into the wrong passenger line of the wrong aircraft by mistake. In such a case, I should hide my Aeroflot tickets to Havana, which I was still holding in my hand. I dropped them into my purse. Grabbing the children, I walked fast and decisively toward the passengers lined up at the CSA aircraft. I thought that in the worst case, if I was discovered, I would pretend to be disoriented, a stupid young provincial mother. But how to climb the ladder? The CSA flight attendants on the tarmac were asking passengers for their tickets and passports before they were allowed to climb the ladder.

I slowed down. I could not show our Aeroflot tickets because they would simply redirect us to the Aeroflot plane nearby and possibly even send a security guard along with me to make sure that we did not get lost again. Uncertain about what to do, I simply kept waiting at the tail end of the passenger line at the bottom of the ladder. Suddenly, our luck turned golden. With only a few passengers left on the tarmac, the flight attendants were called up the ladder. Then, after speaking with the crew, they indicated to the few remaining passengers, ourselves included, to proceed to the top of the ladder. I thought that this could be a game-changer. I was still fearful of a possible alarm call from the airport authorities inquiring about us in case the airport security noticed that we got lost on the tarmac. Yet, I was heartened by this abrupt opportunity to get so close to the aircraft's entrance. Quickly, I climbed with the children to the top of the ladder. We were made to wait on the outside platform with a few other passengers still left to be inspected.

The Czechoslovakian attendant, a young and tense-looking man who met us at the top of the ladder, was in an obvious hurry when he asked for our tickets. When my turn came to show documents and tickets, I displayed my Soviet foreign passport and spoke to him in Russian in an agitated and nervously shrill voice about my husband, who was already inside the craft and was holding our tickets. While the flight attendant was trying to understand what I was saying, I instructed Edik in Russian: "Run inside the cabin to find your father and tell him that we are coming behind." Edik, excited by the possibility of his father being inside the aircraft, flew under the flight attendant's hand and dived through the passenger entrance, past the line-up of standing passengers waiting for their seats, and sneaked into the passenger cabin looking for his father. Absorbed in his quest, he completely ignored protests from the flight attendants. At this moment, I took advantage of the temporary indecision of the attendants who did not know how to react in such a strange circumstance. After all, we were Soviet citizens and maybe the family of an important Soviet boss. Following such paranoid reasoning, they would not dare to harass us. After Edik suddenly disappeared inside the cabin, I turned to the attendant and apologized in Russian:

"Sorry, my child is flustered and afraid he will lose his father because we got separated on the tarmac. My husband has our tickets. He is already inside the cabin, waiting for us. My son is looking for him, and I will sit my child down as soon as we take our seats, which my husband is holding for us."

Now I had crossed the Rubicon and was playing a very high-stakes game. If the attendant insisted on seeing my husband, he would discover there was no such person inside the cabin with our tickets. I had no idea if there were vacant seats to claim. In case my ruse was discovered, the attendants would call airport security. They would recognize immediately that my story about the husband with the tickets was a lie. Normally, the flight attendants would do exactly that, but in this case, they were too much in a hurry since our flight was already late and the Aeroflot flight to Havana was waiting for the CSA flight to Prague to take off first.

We won the lottery at this point. The attendant allowed me to follow Edik inside the cabin. I found Edik at the back in utter disappointment because his father was not to be found anywhere. I dragged him into taking a vacant seat beside me (with Ernestico on my knee) and a young Russian male passenger in the third seat. It was our very good fortune to find vacant seats beside a passenger who might appear to the attendants to be that very husband whom I was claiming.

Surprisingly and inexplicably, this impromptu strategy worked. This was a miracle. My papa would often tell me when I was a kid that I should not be afraid of scary moments because my deceased mother, Berta, would safeguard me in perilous situations. I thought to myself that surely, this was such a moment, and she was protecting us. I felt extremely grateful to her.

The Czechoslovakian attendants could not imagine a young Soviet woman with two small children defecting from Moscow to Prague. It was absurd from anybody's point of view. What Soviet citizen could be that mad as to attempt to defect to Prague, which was controlled by the Soviet KGB? There was another good reason why I got away with something as preposterous as traveling on an international airline from Moscow without airline tickets. Czechoslovakian security guards, trained by the KGB to prevent defections, were not present during the flight from Moscow to Prague. The route Moscow-Prague was considered a no-brainer; it was completely safe. Nobody, in their right mind, would attempt to defect from Moscow to Prague after the invasion of Czechoslovakia by the Soviet Union. It would be like jumping out of the proverbial frying pan and into the fire.

The flight attendant probably allowed us to sneak in and to take vacant seats beside another Soviet male passenger without insisting on seeing our tickets because, in his eyes, it was inconceivable that a Soviet mother with small children was capable of getting through Moscow airport security without proper tickets.

Our neighbor in the seat beside was an affable and surprisingly well-read Soviet passenger in his early thirties. He asked me where we were going, and I told him to meet with my husband. To stop him from asking any more questions about where and why, I went on a counter-attack and asked him where he was going. He replied that he was returning to Prague, where he was working for the Soviet trade mission. I thought he probably was a KGB operative because all employees in Soviet trade missions around the world were with the KGB. I got him interested in talking to me about the latest Czechoslovakian publications in the Russian language and where I could find them.

So, here I was, looking like the privileged wife of some important Soviet bureaucrat, dressed in expensive attire from London gifted to me by my penniless Cuban husband Eduardo, while desperately fleeing the KGB, and casually sitting beside a KGB agent who was unintentionally a stand-in for my husband and was inadvertently protecting me from the suspicions of Czech security, as we chatted peacefully in Russian about world literature.

Time passed quickly. It was a reasonably short and comfortable three-hour flight. No one asked me about our tickets again. I now remembered our suitcase and secretly bid it farewell. Probably, it has already left Moscow on Aeroflot for Havana. Everything I owned to date was suddenly gone. So what? I should not cry over the loss of our beautiful imported dresses and shoes purchased by Eduardo for us in London. Any Soviet or Cuban woman would dearly regret losing such personal valuables, but I had to worry about more serious consequences of our flight to Prague.

31. My Metamorphosis in the City of Franz Kafka

Israeli poster for the Franz Kafka play The Metamorphosis

Prague was a temporary refuge. The city also had a special meaning for me because it was the home of Franz Kafka, whom I considered one of the most ingenious writers of the 20th Century. While my son Edik was in a Cuban hospital for a tonsillectomy, Dr. Nader, my Jewish Czechoslovakian friend in Havana, and I had a chance to talk. Dr. Nader gave me a book banned in the Soviet Union and, therefore, previously unknown to me. *The Metamorphosis* is a short story by Franz Kafka about Gregor Samsa, a traveling salesman, who awakens one morning to find himself transformed inexplicably into a monstrous beetle, after which his life becomes a nightmare of persecution and beatings from family members and others, from which he eventually dies, utterly alienated from his former humanity.

I was stunned by the imagery of this story. This moral tale

of human fear and loathing, hatred and cruelty, abandonment and estrangement struck a sympathetic chord in my imagination. Was our Soviet life so different? Were we not all bugs in the eyes of the state, beaten and humiliated in the name of some abstract higher power? Every Soviet citizen was, like Gregor Samsa, born human but defined as vermin. I, too, had become a bug because I did not adapt obediently to my totalitarian environment, expected from every *Sovok* (*Homo Sovieticus*). I was forced to survive as a chameleon, changing colors in each new environment, disclosing no opinions of my own to outsiders; otherwise, I would perish. Being a chameleon was hardly a choice; it was merely a technique for survival. Only free people have a truly free choice - slaves do not. Still, my inborn anarchistic nature refused to cooperate with this bureaucratic abuse of power. I could not help but think independently. Refusing to become a bug to be stepped upon, I tested the limits of good luck and found myself and my children in the Prague airport, in the land of Kafka, my literary hero. Now, where was I to go from here?

The flight to Prague was short compared with the trips I used to take when flying to Havana. Just a few hours and we were arriving. The journey was almost too short since I would prefer to extend this respite in the insulated aircraft cabin before confronting new and unknown challenges that were awaiting me. I could not prolong the flight; it landed on time. The children and I were led, with the rest of the passengers, into the terminal building to immigration. It was clear that I would have to be persuasively artful with Czechoslovakian immigration to account for our landing in Prague without visas or tickets.

When we were brought in front of Prague immigration, I handed over my passport and said in Russian that we were a Soviet family separated on the tarmac in Moscow while waiting to board an Aeroflot flight to Havana, where my husband works in a Cuban Ministry. I tried, as convincingly as I could, to explain our predicament.

"My children and I became separated from my husband and our group of passengers in Sheremetyevo Airport while we were boarding. It happened because I chased my child, who ran across the airport tarmac. After I caught him and rushed back to where we left my husband, I could not find him. I assumed that he did not wait for me because he was mad at our child's misbehavior and the arguments we recently had about our son. I thought that he was already inside the aircraft. In an attempt to find my husband, who was holding our tickets, we also boarded the aircraft. Only when the plane was already in the air, and I had an opportunity to search the cabin, did I realize that my husband was nowhere to be found. It was at that moment that I understood my mistake: we got onto the wrong flight, CSA to Prague instead of Aeroflot to Havana. However, there was nothing I could do to stop this flight, which was already high in the air. I kept quiet because I was afraid that the flight attendants would become angry with me for pushing my way onto the wrong flight."

The immigration officials brought us aside to the CSA airport office. None of them could believe what they were seeing or hearing. They were surprised, to say the least. This situation had never occurred before. Looking at their amused faces, I imagined they were making cynical remarks about a stupid Russian woman whose bewildered husband is probably tired of her hysteria, despite her pretty appearance, and was only too happy to leave her to deal with her crazy kid on her own. Still, there was palpable disbelief as to how we managed to arrive in Prague without tickets or visas.

I suggested, "You can check with Aeroflot about our flight, which we missed. I am sure they will confirm that we are the lost passengers from their Havana flight."

The immigration officer and CSA manager left us sitting in the room. I assumed they went to talk with Aeroflot officials and ask for their confirmation that the female passenger and two children were missing from the Aeroflot flight to Havana. Aeroflot should confirm that the boys and I were indeed missing but that our luggage was already on its way to Cuba. The CSA manager would inform Aeroflot that we got on the wrong flight and arrived in Prague instead. No doubt, all of them were puzzled. In this case, they should think that everybody was guilty: it was my fault for being stupid, it was the fault of Aeroflot that their passengers got lost on the tarmac in Sheremetyevo, and it was the fault of CSA that permitted us to board the CSA aircraft without proper documents. They must have marveled over how this entire crazy incident was possible and how this brainless Soviet woman could confuse the airlines and their destinations in such a flagrant fashion. We were vindicated when the immigration official and the CSA manager returned to inform us that Aeroflot confirmed that we were their lost passengers. The airport manager would discuss with the airline how to assist us; however, we will have to wait at the airport departures area until a decision is reached. Because we had no visas for Czechoslovakia, immigration would not let us go free.

Not to be outdone by the bureaucratic enemies of Franz Kafka, I made a presumptuous, but to my mind, logical proposal:

"The only solution in our situation would be for CSA to issue our tickets for their next flight from Prague to Havana, where my husband and our luggage will be waiting for our children and me. Of course, Aeroflot would reimburse CSA for the price of our flight."

I felt relieved that so far, no one suspected a young Soviet woman with her small children trying to defect to Prague. Up until this point, we were treated humanely by the Czech authorities. We were asked to take a seat in the waiting room of the airport until there was a CSA decision regarding when and how they could get rid of us. Another long wait; only this time, there was some hope. To cheer up, I recalled the famous lines of the exiled Russian classical poet Mikhail Lermontov. I turned them over and over in my mind as an expression of my secret longing for freedom.

Farewell, farewell, unwashed Russia,
The land of slaves, the land of lords,
And you, blue uniforms of gendarmes,
And you, people, obedient to them.
Perhaps beyond the Caucasian mountains
I will hide from your pashas,
From their all-seeing eye,
From their all-hearing ears.

While quietly celebrating my temporary advantage with Czechoslovakian immigration and feeding the children with another chocolate bar Papa had stuffed into my purse in Odessa, a female Czech security agent came to ask me about the details of our incomprehensible story. She was middle-aged, stark gray in complexion, old-fashioned, but not rude in the way Soviet security typically was. I was only anxious that she might start asking me about my mysterious husband, from whom we fictitiously separated in Sheremetyevo. However, before her interrogation began, we noticed that Edik had disappeared. Only a moment ago, he was standing beside me, holding onto my skirt and chewing his chocolate, but when the security lady began talking to me, he had disappeared. Everybody was now alarmed: security, airport administrators, guards, the translator, and me, with Ernestico in my arms. All of us were forced to interrupt what we were doing and start a search of the airport building for my lost son. Finally, he was found; he was playing with somebody's puppy outside the arrivals area, near the exit door of the airport building. This kid was a genius in the way he could frighten adults with his disappearing acts.

There was a benefit from this incident: Edik gave everyone an essential and timely demonstration of how easily a child could be lost in an airport terminal. Even the immigration officials did not notice him. He could have left the airport building and gotten truly lost in a foreign country. No further questions were asked after we returned to the waiting room. I used this moment to push forward their decision about what to do with us by raising a fuss over my fear of losing my child again if kept too long in the airport's international departures area. I complained that the three of us were tired of sitting in the same place without a chance to go anywhere because we lacked a visa to enter the country. I also expressed my fear that a long wait in these conditions would make my children sick, and that would become the responsibility of the airport authorities. I tried to convince them to send us by a CSA flight to our original destination to catch up with my husband in Havana, impressing them that this would be the fastest way to get rid of us.

They told us to sit down again and wait for their solution to the problem. After an animated discussion that lasted for about an hour, which I observed on the other side of their walled glass office, they conveyed to me their positive decision: I was allowed to purchase CSA tickets to Havana. This was exactly what I wanted, except that in Prague I could only pay for our tickets in the Czech currency. However, I had no legal permission to exchange currency. This was a problem. I did not have any Czech currency with me because currency purchase without a visa, a booked flight, and a permit from MID (Soviet Foreign Affairs) was illegal in the Soviet Union and Cuba. We did not have such a permit to purchase currency at the airport, and consequently, CSA could not sell me the tickets.

I asked: "What happened about Aeroflot redeeming our unused flight to Havana? Did you ask them about it?"

"Aeroflot refused to redeem your tickets," was their answer. "Aeroflot said that as far as they are concerned, you have already used your Aeroflot tickets because it wasn't their fault that you missed the flight. Your luggage has been flown to Havana, which demonstrates that they fulfilled their responsibility."

Now, I was amused. This was a typical Kafkaesque drama: absurd, self-defeating bureaucracy in the airport.[55] I asked if, in Havana, we could repay the CSA flight with Cuban currency. They answered that so far, nothing was clear. This looked promising. They would have to check with Havana airport. As for myself, I knew that there was no other solution except for CSA donating the flight to us at its own cost. Shortly, another CSA administrator, a bald, middle-aged, and soft-spoken gentleman wearing a tired face, came back with another negative answer.

To repay the CSA tickets in Havana, we needed the approval of the Cuban MINREX (Foreign Affairs Ministry). I replied that I could not possibly get it for the reason that I was not a Cuban citizen. My answer sent the poor, puzzled CSA administrator into the glassed back room once again, where he had another lengthy consultation by phone with somebody. When he finally exited, he told me that they were going to send us back to Moscow with the next CSA flight. Meanwhile, we would have to wait in the departures area because we had no visa for Czechoslovakia.

Understandably, I became deeply distressed by this decision and kept insisting that they should send us to Havana if they wanted me to repay the flight. I persisted in explaining that there was nobody in Moscow to assist us because, as Aeroflot informed them, all of our possessions were already on their way to Havana. I even began quietly crying out of desperation. Watching me break down, the children became frightened and very moody. The administrator returned to the backroom to consult with somebody in charge.

Now, the children were hungry. All I had to feed them were the last two large chocolate bars given to us by my father before we left. Of course, this was too much chocolate for small children, and they became hyperactive from the sugar overload, chasing each other, shouting, and disturbing the public order in the waiting area. I was extremely tired and hungry as well, but the chocolate was reserved for the children. I was terribly frustrated and increasingly depressed by the fact that our salvation was so close: the CSA permitted me to purchase a flight to Havana. However, without Czech currency or Soviet Ministry authorization to use rubles abroad, this apparent last opportunity slipped agonizingly away. This new obstacle persuaded the administrator to send us back to Moscow, a scenario I needed to avoid at any cost. The KGB in Moscow would take a special interest in my fairy tale Soviet husband, with whom I was presumably separated while en route to Havana. There would be no need for a superior brain to unravel my real intentions, especially if they discovered my earlier attempt to hide in the washroom at Gander Airport during our flight from Havana to Moscow. The speculative drama played out in my stressed imagination. I would be taken into custody. My children, who have Soviet citizenship, would probably be sent to my parents in Odessa. I knew that Eduardo would help my parents to raise our boys. I will be arrested and charged with attempted defection, which is equivalent to treason in my homeland—Kafkaesque tragedy at its finest.

The most important part of such a scenario was to make sure that my visit to my parents in Odessa was not revealed. I needed an address in Moscow where the KGB could confirm that I stayed the entire last week on my own without anyone's knowledge or help. I was glad to have the address of the cabin in Lesnoy near Moscow and relieved that I had left it in disarray to prove our occupancy. Nobody in Odessa, except my parents and my nearest relatives, knew of my coming to Odessa. None of them would admit that they met me because, if they did, they could be arrested as well and sentenced to labor camps for not informing the authorities. This is what was going to happen in the worst case. Still, I felt frustrated to be marooned only by the absurd requirement for Czechoslovakian currency. On account of this insignificant detail, my plan lay in ruins, and our lives were wasted. Like Gregor Samsa, I had metamorphosed, at that moment, into a despised insect.

In my mind, all this was unfair. I was not a criminal, not a traitor in the eyes of civilized people, not an enemy of the

Soviet people. I had simply chosen not to cooperate with the secret services and not to enslave the rest of our lives at the hands of these indifferent bureaucrats. This should not merit arrest and torture, the confiscation of all possessions (even though our sole possession was a suitcase which was on the Aeroflot flight to Havana), a sentence of 10-15 years in a forced labor camp in the Far North, or possibly, even execution. These were the standard punishments under Soviet law in effect until 1997. I felt miserable.

I thought that we were not even valued as slaves. Normally, slaves belong to the owners who would have an economic interest to protect their value. In the case of Soviet citizens, the owner was the state (an entity without a face or personality), and it did not care about the value of its slaves. I was deeply discouraged both for my family and for myself. The pressures were overwhelming. I was soaked with sadness, sitting in a desolate state on a hard bench. My tired and hungry children had finally fallen asleep on these wooden benches. Suddenly, somebody poked my shoulder. It was the translator. In a soft voice, she said, "Please, take your children and come with me to the administrator's office."

It took me a little while to gather my weary mind and body and the sleeping boys. I no longer expected a sympathetic reception. I was sure that we would be put on the Aeroflot flight back to Moscow. I picked up Ernestico, still asleep, and carried him solemnly in my arms. It was more difficult to persuade Edik to wake up and walk with me. When we arrived at the office, the administrator was seated at his desk. I observed his tired, melancholy face. It was too late at night; obviously, he needed to go home, but my defeated posture and my children sleeping on the bench of a brightly lit terminal building must have made him feel either guilty or compassionate. He wanted to help before he retired for the day.

"We managed to arrange seats for you and your children on a joint CSA-Cubana flight to Havana. The IL-62M aircraft is going to depart at two p.m. the day after tomorrow. Here are your tickets. No, we will not insist on reimbursement when you arrive in Havana. Your costs will be covered by our airline."

"I am grateful to you from the very bottom of my heart." That was all I could say in my half-dead state. I just stood there, astonished by this revelation, bewildered by fatigue, and relieved that my death sentence was suddenly lifted.

"It is not all; meanwhile, you can use the airport guest room, where you will be able to rest with your children for tonight and tomorrow night, because the next flight to Havana is only two days from now. I have also arranged for your temporary Czechoslovakian visa for these two days to allow you to move around the city with the children."

"Thank you for your thoughtfulness and kindness. My children and I appreciate your care for us."

Then, the translator invited us to follow her to the terminal's vacant staff restroom, where there was a double bed and a shower. I felt elated but too tired to express further gratitude. She explained to me that we could rest at night and even take the bus to see the city of Prague tomorrow during the daytime. She warned me not to get lost in the city.

"Oh yes! You can be assured that we will be on time for the flight. Thank you for all your help." Thoroughly fatigued, I managed to murmur these last words as she departed. This time, having been granted a reprieve to live again, I had no energy for celebrating or remembering Russian poetry. At last, I could relax, knowing that our tickets to Havana with CSA were assured. We collapsed on the bed and fell asleep.

When we got up in the late morning, we dressed and took the free airport shuttle to the city. We walked the entire historical center of Prague for hours. With every pore of my body, I was inhaling this truly European culture. In Russia, the 350 years of Mongol rule from the 13th to the 17th Centuries deeply affected Russian culture and was the cause; it has been argued for Russia's retardation in art and architecture and its difficulty in keeping pace with the development of Europe.[56] Few Russians admit that there is still a deep cultural chasm with Europe.

The center of Prague was spacious and old European with Gothic architecture. We walked for many hours along the beautiful cobblestone streets of the old part of Prague. This was where Franz Kafka was born, raised, and worked. We even went to take a look at the old synagogue where Franz Kafka's Bar Mitzvah was held.

On the west wall of the main synagogue hall, there is a glass case shaped like the two stone tablets Moses brought down from the mountain with the Ten Commandments. Tiny light bulbs fill the case, lighting up on the anniversary of someone's death. One of the lights is dedicated to Franz Kafka. The Old Town Square has numerous cafés, restaurants, and architectural gems. Franz Kafka went to school here in the 1890s. It is located between Wenceslas Square and the Charles Bridge, crossing the Vltava River in Prague's Old Town Square, founded in the 12th Century. It is a jewel of European architecture, including Gothic and Baroque styles. The square also has an astronomical clock installed in 1410, which was still working. I was greatly impressed with the architectural beauty of the bridges, adorned with sculptures, crossing the Vltava River. It seemed logical that such a talented genius as Franz Kafka should have developed in this beautiful city.

I could walk the whole day enjoying the atmosphere of European culture, but my small children were tired and hungry. My problem was that I did not have any Czechoslovakian currency. I found a modest restaurant where I hoped to be able to exchange some of my Russian rubles (illegally, of course, because I did not have a permit from Soviet Foreign Affairs for currency exchange). I spoke in German and in Russian to the waiter, offering him my rubles. The hungry eyes of my children proved to be an even better translator. The manager of the restaurant, an older gentleman with a mustache, told the waiter to bring us to one of the tables. They fed us a complete large meal but refused to accept Russian rubles as payment. The manager was uninterested in my rubles but gracious and generous in feeding a hungry mother with two small children from a foreign land. A caring and protective attitude is one of the hallmarks of civilized people.

We returned to the international airport terminal when it was almost dark, with some bread in my purse for our breakfast the next morning. I put the children to bed and marveled at how kind, considerate, and courteous the Czechoslovakian people had shown themselves to be in only the last 24 hours. I had trouble imagining a Soviet airport administrator who would bother arranging for a free flight and a free room to accommodate a mother with two small children. The Czechs did not have to help me. Truly, their obligations were limited to calling the KGB and returning me to Moscow. The airport manager did not do that. I wondered why.

Only two explanations were possible: one is that Czechs are more compassionate because they are more cultured people who experienced the brutalities of German and Soviet occupations. Still, another explanation is that they subconsciously resisted Soviet oppression by helping its victims out of purely human sympathy. Czechoslovakians were not yet converted into *Homo Sovieticus*. The Soviet occupation was too recent. They retained the spirit of a civilized people. It appeared that the more educated and the more developed the culture was, the more difficult it was to transform the population into *Sovki,* who lacked any individuality. I was right in my plans to defect with the Czechoslovakian airline and not with Aeroflot! Unfortunately, we could not return to visit the city again. The next day, we will be boarding the CSA flight early in the afternoon, and I cannot risk being late for this flight. It would be better if we woke up later in the morning, catching additional rest, before that very long and important journey. The hours of walking and fresh air had reinvigorated us. That night, unlike many previous nights, we fell into a deep and restful sleep.

Full of energy in the morning, the children began running inside our small room. I had no idea what time it was. My hand-wound watch had stopped that morning, and our small room had no window. I needed to ask somebody outside about the precise time, but I did not want the boys to run outside the room, provoking unnecessary attention to ourselves. Probably, we still had a few hours before our flight. I dressed the children, and while I was dressing myself, Edik was playing with his brother, who locked himself in the washroom. I asked him to open the door. Ernestico was standing beside me, puzzled by the game his older brother was playing.

Suddenly, I heard a terrible cry from Ernestico. I turned around. What happened? Ernestico was holding his little hand in the door frame of the washroom and screaming in unbearable pain. As soon as I ran to the door, I understood that his little finger was caught between the door and the frame. What happened was that Edik opened the door on my orders, but as soon as his younger brother tried to hold onto the door, Edik shut it again and caught his brother's little finger. He got scared or could not understand what he had done, and continued to keep the door closed with Ernestico's little fingertip caught in it.

I shouted in anguish for Edik to open the door. Ernestico was bleeding badly from the tip of his finger, which was now sliced off. He was screaming from the pain. I lifted him in my arms and told Edik to follow me by holding my skirt. Nearly losing my mind, I ran with the bleeding, crying child into the street to catch a taxi to the hospital. I shouted to the taxi driver to take us straight to the nearest hospital or clinic. He drove us to a hospital near the airport. Worried about the finger of Ernestico, I did not care any longer about our flight. Ernestico's blood was now covering both of us. As soon as we arrived, I jumped with the bleeding child out of the taxi and failed to notice that the taxi driver did not ask me about the fare. I guess he was overwhelmed as well. Edik, feeling very guilty, was holding tightly to my skirt and following, running behind me. With my face contorted in horror and my child crying and bleeding, our appearance could shock anyone.

On arrival at the hospital, the emergency doctors took us immediately into the examination room. They gave Ernestico an injection against the pain, washed and examined the wound, made an X-ray of the finger, disinfected it, and stitched together the open wound. They said that he was lucky to slice off only the tip of his finger. X-rays of the finger demonstrated that his finger bone was intact.

So, he was very lucky. If his finger had been introduced deeper into the frame of the door, the finger bone could be crushed. This would require a much more serious operation. Ernestico had now calmed down. The injection removed his pain, and according to the doctor, he was in a condition to travel on a plane. The nurse called a taxi, which took us directly to the airport. With splotches of blood on our clothes, we arrived at our gate just 30 minutes before flight departure.

Czech and Cuban attendants and plain-clothed security guards were cordial and accommodating to the passengers, including the children and me, despite our arrival so close to the flight departure. When I told the attendant that my children did not have milk for breakfast, only a little bread with water, he placed us in the front seats and made sure that the children had milk before our flight departed. I thought again that it was clear why the Soviets were not allowed to take flights by any airline other than Aeroflot. Sure, the Soviet Government would prefer none of us to experience friendly, humane treatment by foreign airlines because, after that experience, we might expect better Soviet treatment of passengers. This is apart from preventing possible defections. Mean-spirited treatment of slaves helps to maintain slavery.

I was sad to be leaving Prague. Silently, I said my farewells to the beautiful city with its kind citizens and its brilliant literary saint. Viva Franz Kafka!

Ernestico drank his milk and fell asleep; the injection at the hospital made him drowsy. It was important now to prepare Edik to fulfill his part in our forthcoming mission, which was approaching. I felt much more determined and confident. There was no space or time left for any doubts. All our actions, from this moment on, were final. When the plane's attendants and passengers were busy with their meals and after assuring myself that nobody could hear us, I spoke to Edik in a whispered voice:

"Edik, I understand that you want to play, but when we are traveling, it is only safe to play when I tell you so. What happened to Ernestico's finger was an accident. It was not your fault, but this accident happened only because you disobeyed my order."

"I did not want Ernestico to slice his finger."

"Yes, my love, I know. Still, you have to learn to listen to your mother. Only on condition of obeying my rules will we make this difficult voyage. You must obey my instructions while we are traveling, or all of us will be punished; maybe, even worse than we already have when your brother's finger was caught in the door. You must change your attitude from misbehaving to listening to your mother, and I promise that you and your brother will be given toys as a reward. Then, you can play and have a very good time. Agreed?"

"I am sorry. I will be good. When do we get the toys?"

"Edik, you are such a smart boy. Remember the game of who can run faster we were playing while on the train, the game of running and not stopping until I showed you with my thumb?"

"Yes, I remember. But when do we get new toys?"

"Darling, you will get them after you win. To get the toys, you will have to win our game. In a few hours, our plane will stop at another airport. We will spend some time there to play, but only on my instructions. The rules of the game are these: you will always walk beside me, holding tight to my skirt until the moment when I tell you that we must start playing the game of running, one we played on the train.

When I tell you 'GAME,' you know it is a signal to watch the thumb of my right hand. I will point this thumb in the direction I want you to run, just like we did on the train when we traveled back from Odessa to Moscow. When you see my thumb indicating which side to run, you must start running hard in that direction. I will follow you with Ernestico in my arms, trying to catch you, just like we played before on the train. I will shout 'STOP', but you will not stop; instead, you will run even faster until I shout to you, 'HERE'. When I shout 'HERE', you stop right away, wait for me, and then give me your hand. These are the rules of the game. The winner of this game will get new toys, I promise."

"Yes, I will look at your thumb after you say 'GAME' and will run where your thumb will show. I will not stop even when you say 'STOP', but I will stop when you say 'HERE'. Is this correct? Now, can I have the toys you promised?"

"Not yet, love. You are a very smart boy, but first, you have to win the game!"

32. Parting the Red Sea

Ernestico displayed a healthy appetite after he awoke. He did not complain much about his bandaged baby finger and even began playing with his older brother. Happily, children have short memories of terrifying moments. I was not so fortunate. I felt tense and could not rest, even after the meal, when both children fell asleep. It allowed me to escape into the lavatory of the aircraft in a pathetic attempt to wash, the best I could, my dress marked with blood from the finger of Ernestico.

I was thinking about what I must say to Canadian authorities. My English was self-taught, learned simply by memorizing written words from a dictionary. We had no access to any English-language literature, films, or TV programming. In Odessa, the traditional foreign language learned in school was German or French. In my school, it was German. The new interest of Odessans to learn English as a foreign language began in the late 1970s with the beginning of Jewish immigration to Israel.[57] One of the consequences of learning English on my own was my awkward and often incomprehensible pronunciation. I was using my German-speaking skills in the pronunciation of English and stubbornly attempted to pronounce English words as they were written rather than as they should sound. It was a good thing that I was still blissfully ignorant of defects in my spoken English; otherwise, I would be afraid even to open my mouth, which would be much worse for the Gander drama on the near horizon.

A few hours into our flight, there was a surprise announcement that there would be a refueling stop in Shannon, Ireland. This news alarmed me. How is it possible

197

that, instead of Gander, the refueling stop will be in Shannon? What to do now? Then, the CSA attendant announced that passengers must not carry any hand baggage because the stop is only 20 minutes, and the passengers would not be taken into the airport but would be waiting in a secure enclosure on the tarmac. I felt desperate. This change in refueling at Shannon airport would kill our last chance. I inquired in Russian: "My children are very tired. How soon until we reach Havana?"

"The next stop will be to refuel in Gander, Canada, before we continue our flight to Havana. Don't worry, this stop in Shannon is very brief, and the one in Gander is not much longer," replied the attendant who spoke poor Russian.

The news was getting better again. Our aircraft, a Bristol Britannia turboprop, needed to refuel twice on the way from Prague to Havana. After all, we would have another opportunity. I calmed down, and we boarded the flight again. A few hours later, we heard the announcement from the pilot that the plane was approaching Gander Airport in Newfoundland, Canada, where the aircraft would be refueled once again. As a safety precaution, just as in Shannon, the passengers would not be allowed to stay inside the craft during refueling. The CSA crew will guide the passengers to the terminal building, where a special isolated area is prepared and refreshments served. This will take approximately 40 minutes. Passengers should carry only their passports and boarding passes. They are not allowed to take with them any carry-on luggage. Now, I realized that since we were occupying the front seats in the cabin, we should be the first to exit from the plane. I did not want to be at the front of the line of passengers, so I decided to delay our departure by locking myself with the children in the washroom at the back of the plane. This was what I did at the very last moment when the craft came to a full stop on the runway. It was not so easy to walk back with two children against the forward flow of passengers, but we managed. Once we were locked in the washroom, I reminded Edik about our running game, which we will be playing when we step onto the tarmac. He remembered that the keyword to start is "game" and declared himself willing and ready. Now, we were the last passengers leaving the aircraft. Our passports and tickets were in my hands, and all of our original documents and most precious personal family photographs were inside my bra. There was no way that I could avoid carrying Ernestico in my arms while running; after his finger injury, he was not in the best of shape. I needed to direct all my efforts to hold him tight in my arms because, after the recent trauma, his grip might have weakened.

Gander International Airport

We climbed down the ladder. After presenting our tickets and passports, I looked around to make sure that nobody was watching me. Satisfied that we were more or less inconspicuous, I placed my passport and our tickets into my self-made document storage compartment inside my brassiere to free both my hands while carrying Ernestico in my arms. The passengers were lined up to walk across the tarmac with Czech guards and flight attendants prepared to walk on both sides of our group for security purposes. We were the very last of the group, which was now led across the tarmac to the main building of the Gander Airport terminal. There were hangers to the right of the terminal and, at the far extreme, the small figure of a uniformed man standing in front of a door. I decided that we should run to that door and to that officer at the last hangar. We proceeded, walking behind the group of passengers, with me carrying one child in my arms and another walking beside me, holding tight to my skirt. I began to slow our pace. When the CSA guard behind us had moved ahead of us, I acted according to my deal with Edik for the running game. Holding Ernestico tightly to my chest, I told Edik the code word GAME.

Initially, he was uncertain because he did not see my indication of which direction to run. After a few seconds, he understood my expressive looks. He noticed that the thumb of my right hand, beneath Ernestico, was pointing towards the hanger with the figure of a uniformed Canadian. Edik did not waste any further time; he let go of my skirt and sprinted as hard as he could in the direction I indicated. After all, speed running was his thing; he loved it and felt confident about winning this game. I did not even dare to look at the CSA guard near me. He must have been stunned by this alarming event. I was certain he would never expect that anything like this might happen. I told Ernestico to hold very tight. He locked his little legs around my waist. With adrenaline kicking quickly through my body, I forgot about the weight of the child in my arms. I took off, running with all my strength, to chase my five-year-old, whose love of the game was evidenced by the speed of his sprinting across the tarmac. I hoped that the guard would be caught by surprise and lose a few seconds in reaction time, but I was too scared to look back at him to see if he was chasing after us. A few times while running, I shouted to Edik, "Stop, Stop, Stop", but he knew, according to the rules of this game, he should not stop until I shouted, "Here." My 'Stop' orders were intended only to confuse the guards. The distance between Edik and me was increasing because by now, my strength with a child in my arms was ebbing fast. Ernestico, being the youngest, was accustomed to travel in this fashion (in my arms), but never before had he experienced such hard running. He was surprised by my violent movements. Still, he continued to hold tightly to me.

The Sea is Only Knee Deep

While running, I dared not look back to confirm if anyone was pursuing us. I was afraid of losing directional motion if I turned my head to look. I was also afraid to find out how close my pursuers were approaching us. However, after I realized that I was slowing down from exhaustion, the instinct for survival made me face reality. After all, we were not escaping Sodom and Gomorrah, so there was no threat that I would be converted into a pillar of salt. I permitted myself to look back and saw one of the CSA guards running after us. My only hope in this desperate chase relied on the assumption that other airline security guards would be afraid to leave the passengers walking across the tarmac towards the airport building. The guard running after us would not understand my real intentions. Instead, he would interpret my actions as a natural, innocent family incident involving an unruly child. I hoped that his misunderstanding of my intentions would become my opportunity; he would run less hard and spare the bullets. I was told by Dr. Nader, my Czech friend in Havana, that CSA guards were instructed by the KGB to shoot and kill to prevent defections.

Seeing the CSA guard running towards us caused a new wave of adrenaline to kick into my bloodstream. I stopped feeling pain and got a second wind, guided by a singular determination to reach the far side of the hangars where the uniformed Canadian stood guard. Ernestico was not a big fat toddler. He had a healthy, slim body. Still, his weight was just too much for sprinting. Our stakes, though, were too high, and this altered my emotional condition: I felt as if my body did not exist, and I was flying in the air above the pain and above the fear, perhaps in a dream. I could not say how much time elapsed to reach the hangar; minutes seemed like an eternity. Edik was the first to approach the uniformed Canadian official standing stone still in front of the hangar. He seemed frozen as he looked at us in astonishment. I shouted to Edik, "Here, Here, Here!"

He stopped right in front of the Canadian official. In a few moments, I was able to catch up with him and lower Ernestico onto the tarmac. After securing the hand of my blessed little runner, we stood together in front of the Canadian official. We needed immediate protection from the CSA security guard who was chasing us. He had now stopped running and was walking fast towards us. Perhaps he was pacified by seeing me in control of my headstrong runner. The middle-aged, blue-uniformed Canadian officer was tall, slim, and angular - like a hockey stick. He was staring at me in disbelief without saying a word. I reached into my brassiere and took out our Soviet passport and the flight tickets.

"We are Soviet citizens. This is our passport. We defected from the Czechoslovakian plane. I am asking for political asylum in Canada,"[58] I said in a low voice while offering our documents. This was the phrase I memorized in English for our special occasion.

"That man," I said, indicating the guard is coming towards us, "will take us away. Please protect us from him."

The Canadian was still not moving, just feeling with his hand for his large mobile radio. I was petrified. Why was the Canadian official not moving? He had an unresponsive facial expression. When I looked back, I saw, as if in some horror film or a bad dream, the approaching CSA guard who was already near. I did not appreciate the fact that the Canadian officer simply felt unsure about what he should do. He was bewildered by the occurrence and needed time to think. For me, everything was clear.

"Please, please, move fast, or they will get us! He is close," I begged.

"Okay, please follow me, ma'am," he answered finally when the CSA guard was almost upon us. He opened the heavy metal door of the hangar behind him. We were let in, to my great relief, and he shut the door securely behind us. Then, while he talked on his mobile radio, we began walking along the endless narrow corridors that linked the airport hangars together, towards the main terminal building. I walked behind him, holding the hands of both children. Finally, I felt relatively safe, thinking that the worst was now behind us, until he suddenly opened the door from the corridors into the terminal hall and let me in with the children. What I saw in front of me was our group of passengers surrounded by the CSA guards and attendants.

It felt as if my eyes jumped out of my head. My legs turned into cotton candy. I lost control of my muscles while my hands were still grasping the children tightly. The terrifying thought that the uniformed Canadian had brought us back to our guards and passengers made my presence there feel unreal. This could only mean that we were dead in the water. My head was spinning, probably from some electrical short circuit in my nervous system. I felt unbearably hot, as if I was boiling in my own juices, unable to regain control of my body. Practically paralyzed by the scene of the guards and passengers staring at us with a surprised expression, my body was no longer responding to my brain's commands. It was running on automatic. I will get at least 15 years in the Gulag.

The only person who was, at that moment, acting cool and exhibiting no emotion was the Canadian officer. He continued to move methodically towards the group as if it was routine and nothing out of the ordinary was happening. He acted as if it was perfectly normal for small children and their mother to sprint across the tarmac. What could I do in such a circumstance? I could not turn around and run back into the hangar because the doors leading to the hangar corridors were probably automatically locked behind us. I was still holding the hands of my two small children. Even if I could find the strength to lift my toddler to carry him again, my already overburdened back, still in pain, would collapse, and I would need to explain to Edik that we must run again and now, for some strange reason, in the opposite direction. He might start arguing because, from his point of view, he won the game already and should be given the promised toy; he will insist. Worst of all were my legs, which seemed to have lost all their muscle strength. I could only continue walking mechanically in my dazed state. I knew there was nothing else I could do but obey the uniformed Canadian's request and walk robotically behind him towards our group of about 130 passengers and guards.

I followed him, dreamlike, my body walking independently of my mind toward our guards. I felt as if my soul was observing everything from above, from outside of my body. I could hear the shouting of my soul: "Run!" but my body was not obeying this order. When our uniformed Canadian officer came close to the CSA guards and passengers, he announced in a stern voice: "Excuse me, please." Then, like Moses leading the Jewish slaves out of Egypt, there was a parting of the Red Sea. The entire mass of waiting people confronting us has divided themselves into two groups to allow the Canadian officer to pass. The children and I walked like puppets directly behind him.

And now, he did something quite unexpected and even violent. Suddenly, without letting anybody recover from their surprise and without wasting a second, he grabbed me by my shoulders and pushed me forward, propelling the three of us through a small opening between two airline counters. An invisible hand opened an inconspicuous metal door from the other side, and the boys and I were thrust into a new room. The Canadian official immediately bolted the door from inside and said to me: "You are safe now ma'am. This is the immigration room of the airport, and no one from your flight can enter here."

Still in shock, I found myself bent towards the children, hugging them with an instinctively protective gesture. The room was very small and austere, with one small window behind the officer's large, plain desk. There were a few hard office chairs. The place looked like an interrogation room. Two men dressed in similar uniforms were behind the desk; one was standing and talking on the phone, and the other was seated and looking at us. The subject at hand was our security situation. Their faces were worried.

All of a sudden, there were violent bangs on our door and shouts in English: "Open the door and return our passengers immediately! You have no right to hold them!"

These would be the CSA flight security officers, who had recovered from their shock and begun to protest. The loud bangs and shouts continued while I looked at the uniformed Canadians locked with us in this room. I wondered why they did not hide us from the attackers.

"Please sit down," said the Canadian officer politely from behind the desk, indicating one of the chairs.

"We can't pacify these intruders," he continued. "You requested political asylum, and you are here under our protection. You are in the immigration room, and no one will be allowed to enter this room until we investigate your request and respond to your government. You cannot leave this room until the plane departs. Would you or your children like a drink? Is water okay? We don't want to open any of the doors of this room in order not to tempt your security agents to force their way in here and try to remove you."

"Thank you; water will be fine," I answered.

"Meanwhile, could we please have your documents, and would you please answer some questions?" said the officer.

I sat down with Ernestico on my lap and invited Edik to sit beside me in front of the Canadian officer's desk. I was still unnerved over the continued hard banging and loud, rude shouts from behind the door.

"Poli, why are they knocking on the doors? Why are they shouting? I won the game; when will I get my toy? Why are we here? I want to go. You promised me a toy if I win, and I won!" Edik brought me down to the ground with his pestering.

"Not right now, my sweet, " I answered. "You will have to wait a bit longer."

A Canadian officer gave us water in plastic cups, and I began answering his questions.

"Your names, country of origin, and where you're traveling and why."

The loud noise behind the door continued. I could not understand why anyone was permitted to make such a scandal in a foreign airport. The Canadian officer behind the desk was talking on the phone all the time. I was very uncomfortable because it was not clear to me if the Canadians had the authority to remove our CSA security agents who were making such a ruckus on the other side of the door.

There were ongoing negotiations between the Canadians and the CSA officials during which the banging would stop for a while. Then it would start again. The flurry of phone calls inside our room continued. The Canadians told me that the CSA flight refused to depart until we were returned to the airplane. This circus continued for hour after hour. Together with our Canadian hosts, we remained locked in this small room. I was worried and tired. Both children, hungry and exhausted, fell asleep in my arms. After an agonizing eternity, the terrifying banging ceased.

It was already in the middle of the night when the phone rang with the news that the CSA plane was departing. There was a new commotion, and somebody unlocked the door of the immigration room and announced that the CSA flight had departed, but the Soviet embassy from Ottawa was furiously demanding my return. Then a phone call came informing our immigration officers that my children and I could now be safely removed from the airport. We were invited to follow our Canadian officials, who drove us, already in the morning light, to a local hotel in Gander. We were brought up into a room with the largest bed (king size) that I had ever seen in my life. The children and I simply dropped dead, in utter exhaustion, on that bed and fell into a deep, peaceful sleep. We did not even bother to undress.

33. You are to be Deported to your Country of Origin

Mentally, emotionally, and physically drained, I was unaware of how long we had slept. It was a deep sleep without nightmares of persecution. We were awakened by the ringing of the phone. At the other end was the voice of a man speaking Russian with a strange accent.

"Hello. My name is Bill Toytman. I am a local businessman."

"Hello, how can I help you?" I muttered unpleasantly, surprised and scared. His language was a mix of Russian and Ukrainian, the way Polish people speak in Russian.

"Gander immigration authorities asked me to talk to you because we don't have any Russian translators in Gander, and they don't understand your English sufficiently."

"Yes, I understand some of your Russian, but not everything because of your accent. If we run into problems of comprehension, we could also switch to Spanish, Ukrainian, German, and only a little bit of English," I suggested.

"We haven't yet had Russian defectors in Gander. We had a few Cubans, many East Germans, and a few Czechoslovakians. This is probably why we do not have any translators for the Russian language in Gander. My wife and I are from Poland, and we both can also speak Yiddish and some Russian. Nobody else in Gander does."

"I would be very grateful and happy to speak with you and your wife," I answered.

"How are you and the children today? We called you yesterday, but you didn't answer, and we decided that you were asleep," he said.

"I can't believe you; were we asleep the whole day? What day is it? How long did we sleep?" I felt disoriented.

"Today is Saturday. Two Canadian officers are waiting to talk to you in the lobby of your hotel. Could we come upstairs to ask you a few questions?" he asked.

"Yes, please. Give us 10 or 15 minutes, and we will be ready."

I was embarrassed; it appeared that we just slept for nearly 24 hours, or I simply misunderstood his Russian. It surprised me that the children were so exhausted that they could sleep as long as I did. I got myself and the boys dressed. There was a knock on the door. I opened it, and three men greeted me. I invited them to my hotel room.

I recognized one of them from the immigration at the airport. He and another officer were wearing the uniform. Bill was the one who just spoke to me on the telephone in Russian. He was a short, lean-framed, and very energetic, middle-aged Jewish fellow. He insisted on speaking Russian; unfortunately, his Russian was not so easy to understand. When I suggested English with Yiddish, he said that he preferred to practice his Russian because there was nobody else in Gander to help with Russian at the airport, and this would provide him with additional income.

I now repeated in Russian the same story I had told in bad and broken English to Canadian immigration at the airport, explaining who we were, from where we came, and where we were going. Bill was translated into English for the Canadian immigration officers. I was asked about my parents and my husband, and where they were working. I answered all of their questions. They did not ask me about my work at all, probably assuming that I was a busy young mother and a housewife.

They spent about an hour politely posing questions. Afterward, Bill asked their permission to bring the boys and me to visit his house and his family in town. I understood that they granted his request because he invited the children and me to accompany him to his store in Gander and later to meet with his family.

"My wife Rose and I are also refugees from Poland," he said, "and we own a store in Gander. All is very good. However, we have no opportunities to practice our Polish or Russian here. If you accept my invitation to come with me to our store, my wife and I would like to invite you and your children to meet with our family for lunch at our home. Would you accept our invitation?" he asked.

"Yes, thank you, I would be delighted," I answered.

After the airport officers had left, we went down to the street level to his car and drove along the streets of Gander, which looked like an old northern town. The buildings were mostly two to four stories tall; the two-storied houses were built of wood, and only a few four-storied new buildings were made of brick. It was already too warm, and the children felt hot in their Moscow outfits. However, we could not change our wear at the hotel since our luggage had departed with Aeroflot to Cuba. All our current possessions remained hidden in my brassiere. These were our most important documents: our passports, birth certificates, medical certificates, and the original of my engineering diploma with the list of all the subjects studied. I also hid in my bra our most precious personal possessions: family photographs cut to fit inside a small envelope. Our clothes were also spotted with some blood marks due to Ernestico's cut fingertip accident two days earlier.

Bill drove us inside the courtyard of a four-story brick building and led us to the entrance of his store. His wife, Rose, opened the door. We were introduced. She looked like a typical young American, a blond girl from a postcard. I found her hospitable, kind, and generous. The store was like a warehouse for all kinds of goods; a general store. She picked up some light clothes for the boys, made of a material unknown to me, and light, pretty slacks and a blouse for me. She suggested we change. I thanked her but refused to accept the clothes because I had no Canadian money to pay for them. She said they were gifts; that the clothes we were wearing, nobody wears any longer in Canada. She insisted that what we were wearing was too warm, too outdated, and marked with blood. I was taken aback because I was particularly fond of my clothes, which Eduardo brought us from England. Finally, we agreed that I would accept her gift for both boys but not for myself. The boys were instructed to change into good-looking, comfortable, and lightweight Canadian clothes: dark blue shorts and light blue pullovers, socks, and sneakers. Additionally, each child was allowed to choose a toy.

"You see," I told Edik, "I promised you a toy if you win the game at the airport, and now you got it because you were such a good boy. The true miracle is not that you are getting this toy without your mommy having the money to pay for it, but that you are such a well-behaved boy and followed my instructions!"

One child picked up a toy car and the other a toy truck to pull by a string behind them. From that moment on, nobody could separate them from their new toys.

After Rose and Bill locked their store, we were invited to their apartment in a new and different four-story brick building. In their home, they introduced us to Paula, their 11-year-old adopted daughter. They confessed that they could not have children of their own, and this little girl was the light of their life. Bill took a couple of Polaroid photographs of us together with Paula in front of their building and gave one to me. Ernestico can be seen in this photo with his little finger still bandaged.

This was our first photo in Canada. How much I would give to be able to send it to Eduardo, who in turn would inform my parents that we made it safely.

Paulina and boys with Paula Toytman in Gander, May 1971

Bill and Rose Toytman came from Poland after the war and kept old religious Jewish food traditions known as '*kosher*'. I had to apologize for knowing nothing about this tradition. Accustomed to eating many traditional Jewish dishes, I had never even heard the word '*kosher*' (the dietary and ceremonial laws governing the purity of food in Jewish religious tradition). They were appalled by my ignorance about religious traditions but were respectful of my version of Judaism. The food was delicious. After the meal, they brought us back to our hotel in their car, and we fell into another healthy and very happy sleep, anticipating a real rest the next day, which was Sunday.

The following morning, we were surprised by insistent knocks at the door, this time without previous warning by phone. I was alarmed. Who could it be on a Sunday morning?

I did not order any room service. While dressing anxiously, I was reminded of an Odessan anecdote about the "knock on the door". It reflected our Soviet mentality. One couple was awakened in the middle of the night by persistent knocks on the door of their apartment. The couple was at first anxious and frightened, only to be happily relieved after opening the door and discovering that it was just their neighbor who came to warn them that their building was on fire.

I was relieved to see the same Canadian officers who had come yesterday, dressed this time in civilian clothes. They told me that the Soviet Government had issued a formal protest and demanded our immediate return to Moscow. They were very worried because, according to them, my defection was threatening bilateral relations. They said that our safety was in peril because the Soviet military attaché, with some employees from the Soviet embassy, arrived yesterday in Gander and were determined to get me back. The Soviet military attaché was very agitated and threatened serious diplomatic retaliation by the Soviet Union.

The Canadian officers were afraid that the Soviets might attempt to kidnap us; therefore, it was for our safety that they decided to transfer us urgently by military helicopter to another city. We were taken through the hotel's rear service entrance to a waiting car. We were driven to the military airport, where a military helicopter was already waiting for us. The Canadian officers kept asking me why the Soviet military attaché was so insistent. He and his team refused to leave Gander Airport until I was returned. The Canadians were puzzled by the severity of the Soviet reaction to the defection of what appeared to them to be a simple housewife and two kids.

After a short flight, the helicopter landed at the military airport in the City of St. John's, Newfoundland. From the airport, we were taken directly to a big square concrete building. We entered and walked along its narrow, brightly lit corridors. Several guards led us into a large concrete hall with some natural light coming through a small window near the ceiling. There were cages with metal bars along both sides of the hall. The cages were all closed and empty. The guards took us near one of these cages and brought in three folding cots for us to sleep on and one chair. They ushered us in and then locked our door. The small window located over the only desk in that hall was far away from our cage. A female guard came to sit at that desk under the window.

I was in shock. We had just been led quietly and without explanation into a prison. I had never even seen a prison or jail before. I could imagine that the Soviets would be capable of doing something like this, but we were in Canada, and these officers were Canadians. What was going on? Didn't I ask for political asylum? Weren't we free in Gander? Then, why are they locking us up in prison?

Now, I was feeling really depressed, unable to understand what was going on. The children were bored sitting in this cage. They brought their new toy vehicles with them and wanted to play by towing them behind. There was no space in our cage to tow their little truck and car. The woman guard came to ask if we needed anything, such as water or a toilet. I asked her how she could help the children to play with their toys. She left to consult with her supervisor, and when she returned, she unlocked our small cell. The boys took their toys outside the cage and started hauling them between the cells of this huge prison hall. It was shocking and amusing to see my little boys towing their miniature vehicles between these awful wire cages. I wished I could take a photograph of how ridiculous these young prisoners looked; surely, such a photograph would win a competition for originality. However, I did not have a camera, and if I did, I am sure the Canadian guards, despite acting with goodwill, would not allow me to take a photo. Later, they brought us hamburgers and French fries for our meal, as well as bedsheets, pillows, and blankets for the night.

The next day, a slender man of average height was

brought by the guards to our cage. He was wearing a currently fashionable dark blue blazer. He was a good-looking, pleasant, polite man in his mid-30s with thinning dark hair and a British accent. He said his name was John, and he requested permission to ask me a few questions. I accepted, and a chair was brought in for him. He sat beside me and took out his notebook to write down my answers. Then, he asked me which language I would prefer to speak with him. He spoke English, Spanish, and Russian. I answered that I was fluent in Russian and Spanish. In this case, he chose Spanish because it was better than his Russian. He began with traditional questions: name, origin, parents, husband, and so on. Then he asked to see my documents. I showed him our certificates and my engineering diploma. He was especially surprised to see my engineering degree and asked:

"You have a professional degree in engineering? How unusual for a woman, especially so young and with small children," he said.

Now it was my turn to be surprised, and I asked, "Why? Don't women work in Canada? I noticed them working at the airport, and even some guards in this prison are women as well." I looked at our guard seated at the desk.

"Were you also working? Where and with whom?" John asked.

"With a Soviet engineering team based with the Ministry of Transport in Havana," I replied.

"What kind of work? And where?" He asked.

"We designed and supervised the construction of a deep-water commercial port and navy base in Cienfuegos," I specified.

"What! You were working in the Cienfuegos commercial port and naval base! During what period?" He was very surprised.

The Sea is Only Knee Deep

"Starting early in 1968 and up until two weeks ago," I replied.

He reacted in shock: "Oh my God! This is very important. Please excuse me. I have to leave immediately, but I will be back shortly."

He stood up and walked away. He left a strong impression on me that I had startled him with my answers. Still, he was polite and kind, and I was hoping that the image of my small children towing their little trucks between the prison cages would alarm him as much as it spooked me. Maybe he could help to find more appropriate conditions for such young children.

The guard brought the food that was unknown to us: breaded fried chicken, which the children devoured. I had no appetite. The prison disheartened me. It was a real mockery to lock the boys and me in prison and force us to live in a cage with lights on during the whole night and female guards watching us while we slept. What kind of danger to Canadians were we? How inappropriate it was to lock us up in prison. I felt so distressed.

John came back early the next day. He said:

"Good morning! I will accompany you today to attend court hearings. There was an embarrassing information leak, and the media are all over the place inquiring about you. Unfortunately, the International Herald Tribune yesterday published a sensational article about your defection and even your photograph. Fortunately, the damage is not critical because the correspondent was not given any details, and some of his data was not entirely correct. Still, any media must be avoided at all costs. You are not allowed to communicate with anyone. Please, we do not need publicity. The Soviet military attaché came to Gander with his large team. He is still there in the airport, demanding your return to the Soviet Union. We don't understand why he needed to bring with him such a big team; maybe they are planning to kidnap you."

"Sorry, but I haven't met anyone from the media," I answered, surprised by this newspaper story. "They must have gotten this information from someone else." I protested. "This photograph of us on the first page of the International Herald Tribune was taken by Bill Toytman during our visit to his family's apartment in Gander. How did the correspondent got your photo to print on the first page of this newspaper? I do not know. Who gave them this information? What court hearings are you talking about?"

"Yours. The immigration judge will decide today on your case," he answered.

"How is it possible?" I asked, surprised. "Nobody told me about it before. Is this why we are in prison? Sure, it is not exactly a nasty and dirty Soviet or Cuban prison. It is not crowded with other prisoners, and the food is very good, but this is not what I expected would happen to me after I managed to defect to freedom. Look at my children and me. Do we look dangerous to anybody in Canada? What happened to my request for political asylum?"

"Yes and no," he answered. "There is a court procedure to establish your legal status. Please get ready to leave shortly. We will be departing for the courthouse."

"Please listen to me with full attention," he instructed me. "You will only answer the judge when he asks you a question. You should never get upset or frightened. I will be accompanying you as your translator. Whatever the judge asks you, I will be translating for you; even if you have understood the question yourself, I will tell you what you need to answer. Think of this as a game because the decision of the judge has nothing to do with your real situation, only with the current law. His decision is only a legal formality. It is not personal, and it is not what is going to happen necessarily. Please trust me. Only repeat exactly what I tell you to say, and you will be fine."

We were driven to the courthouse in the city. The children,

John, and I entered one of the rooms and stood in front of an elderly male judge seated on a high podium. There was no one else in the courtroom except the court clerk, who read to the judge the reason for our detention: "illegal entry into Canada." His words upset me, and my brain went into a confused dream state. Nobody ever told me about court proceedings. My Czechoslovakian friend, Dr. Nader, never mentioned it.

My vision became blurred from emotional distress, which prevented me from seeing the face of the judge clearly. Now, I was seriously alarmed, uncertain of my comprehension of English and distrustful of John, who presented me with the court mandate as a *fait accompli*. The clerk read my name, described the means of our arrival in Canada, and stated that the Soviet embassy issued a formal protest, threatening bilateral relations. John interpreted the English for me, adding that the charge against us was the illegal entry into Canada.

I was disoriented, for I never expected such a twist of events. What about my request for political asylum? If the Canadian court returns us to the Soviet Union, I will receive a long sentence in the Gulag, where I would not survive. Don't Canadians know that? At this point, I wanted to remind the judge that we were not immigrants but refugees. John was still translating what the court clerk was saying.

"Don't say anything, don't argue," John added in Russian and Spanish to assure that I understood him. "Only answer 'yes' when the judge asks you any questions."

What was the use of my protest at this moment if I did not know about my legal rights in Canada? As a Soviet citizen or Cuban resident, I had no access to such information. I felt helpless. I did not have any more strength left after surviving a difficult defection, and now the surprise of this court process. I was frozen in torment, too confused for revolt.

"Paulina Zelitsky, you and your dependent children are accused of entering Canada illegally. Do you admit that you entered this country illegally?" asked the judge.

"Say Yes," was the instruction from John.

"Yes," I repeated.

"The Soviet embassy has demanded your return, so this court has decided that you are to be deported to your country of origin immediately. Do you understand the decision of the court?" asked the judge.

I could not believe what I was hearing. I looked at John. He translated for me and whispered again:

"Trust me. Do not argue. You must say 'yes'."

"What about my request for political asylum?" I almost cried.

"Don't argue, not now. Just say 'yes'. You have to trust me," insisted John. He was becoming alarmed by my resistance.

"Yes," I answered the judge in a low voice, wondering whether I was being framed.

"Canadian authorities will be in charge of the plaintiff and her dependent children," concluded the judge.

Despite assurances from John that the court proceedings did not matter, my Soviet mind began suspecting that something had gone terribly wrong. Was I being cheated? It was quite a horrific feeling. My claim for refugee status was not even acknowledged in the courtroom. Still, there was something about John that made me trust him, and this is why I did not protest in the courtroom. I instinctively trusted him, and so far, I had only positive experiences with Canadian authorities. Anyway, what else could I do? What was the alternative? I did not even know how to register my request for political asylum formally. I was resigned and bewildered. My only solution now was to accept the directives of those in charge of my situation, especially John, who declared our court hearings finished and that the children and I should follow him outside. There was a car waiting for us, and it took us back to the military airport.

"You see, we are not sending you back to Moscow. You are going with us to quite a different place," said John.

34. Tensions in a Safe House

Our car drove directly across the tarmac towards a twin-jet military aircraft. We left the car and boarded the airplane. Inside the cabin, in addition to the uniformed crew, we were greeted by a small group of men dressed in civilian clothes. They introduced themselves as Canadian officers overseeing my case. Jim was a very tall, slim, middle-aged, and stern-looking RCMP officer, with an inscrutable expression on his face. He was dressed like John in a blue blazer. He said he was in charge. Later, I learned that all of them were from the Canadian security service.[59]

They refused to inform me of the destination of our flight or to comment about what happened in the courtroom in St. John's. They did, however, repeat to me that the Soviet embassy in Canada and the Soviet Government in Moscow were demanding my return to the Soviet Union and were threatening serious consequences in their bilateral relationship. Because of Soviet threats, Canadian security was forced to take precautions against possible kidnapping or even assassination of defectors by the KGB on Canadian territory. Various Soviet embassy employees flew from Ottawa to Gander the previous weekend, and, as far as Canadian security was informed, they were still in Gander. Canadians did not understand two circumstances: why was it the Soviet military attaché who personally presented himself in Gander and not a civilian employee of the embassy, and why did the Soviets continue to stay in Gander when their embassy already protested my defection in Ottawa. To assure our safety, Canadian security felt it was necessary to move me around secretly and under military protection. I was happy to leave St.

John's. The jail and court proceedings put me in an uneasy mood about the city. I had not seen anything of St. John's. The prison experience was enough to cancel my curiosity for urban sightseeing.

Our flight took about three hours, and when we landed, it was nighttime. We were driven through the darkness to a safe house located in a three-bedroom apartment where I was never left alone. There was always one or more guards on duty in the apartment. Each day, except for weekends, we were visited by Veronica, the babysitter, a team of investigators, and John, my St. John's translator.

Only later did I learn in which city we were located; it was Ottawa, the Canadian capital. The Canadian security service headquarters was there, and this was the reason we were brought to Ottawa. Veronica, the babysitter for the children, was a middle-aged, soft, and homely woman, originally from Spain. She started quite nicely with the children and me. Her job was to oversee the boys while the team of investigators from Canadian security debriefed me on a nearly daily basis, excluding weekends. Being the only female on the team, Veronica soon became my sole confidant for some personal matters, which normally are discussed only among women, at least in the culture where I came from.

The chief investigator of my case was Jim, a dry, authoritarian, English-speaking Canadian. He laid down rules for life and work inside the safe house where, for the next 72 days, Canadian, American, and UK experts got an opportunity to question me and run their tests to confirm my identity. Strangely, even the children were examined by child psychiatrists. The main purpose of all this debriefing was to discover if I was a false defector, that is, a mole of the KGB.

After my experience at the St. John's courtroom, I no longer felt completely safe. It never occurred to me that Canadian authorities might have legitimate concerns. My truth was so obvious to me; I had brought in my brassiere, all of our documents, and family photographs against which they could check my identity. I observed with some resentment the manipulative tactics to which the experts subjected me. As far as I was concerned, any investigation into the possibility of my belonging to a Soviet spy ring was a waste of time and money. Don't all these investigators know that? It is the truth; my inexperienced mind concluded that they must know that.

I also became annoyed with Jim sometimes, especially when I discovered that my only confidante, the children's babysitter and the only woman I was allowed to see during my nearly three-month safe house incarceration, was reporting to her boss on my every move and utterance. Later, I found out that she was a professional security agent. Her job was to report on all my words and actions, but she also had a secret agenda; she was settling her accounts with John. She conspired against John because she was competing with him for the translator's job. She always argued with him about what I had said or misunderstood, based on my comments to her. The Spanish interpreters were now in their little war between themselves, which engulfed me needlessly in their battles.

Our future freedom depended entirely on how fast and successfully the Canadian security service would conclude their investigations as to whether I was or was not a Soviet spy. If the conclusion of these investigations failed to clear me completely from all suspicions, the Canadian Government would simply act on the existing court judgment to deport us to the Soviet Union. My mental posture was resistant at the start of this exercise because it appeared to be a ridiculous waste of valuable time and resources. Slowly, however, I learned to cooperate with my interrogators because I understood that in this process, the value was not in me but bureaucratic efficiency.

The interrogations included lie detector tests. The

222

investigators fussed a lot, constantly telling me not to be nervous. I was not nervous at all, but curious. I had never seen a lie detector machine, but I was surprised at all this fuss about it.

"Why should I be nervous? Will this machine pinch? Will it bite? Will the electric current punish me if it does not like what I say?" I asked impudently.

"No. None of these punishments."

"Then why are all of you worried? I asked. "Let's play with it. I am suffocating, locked in this apartment, and feeling quite bored; at least the lie detector machine could be fun. I haven't seen such a machine before and feel very curious about how it works technically."

"You must be much more cautious with this machine," John said. "If your answer doesn't match exactly with the programmed evaluation criteria, the machine could draw the wrong conclusion in characterizing your careless statement. You could fail your test, and the evaluation of the machine cannot be revoked," he warned me. This comment unnerved me. Are we back to the "careless behavior" of the denunciation of Boris?

My lie detector tests were conducted in a special laboratory, but they were not as much fun as I had hoped. The main reason was that my answers to the endlessly repeated questions were limited to 'yes' or 'no'. Any deviation was regarded as a failure to answer, which seemed silly when the questions were outright idiotic. There were mostly routine questions like: who are you, and who were you working for, and obvious questions about my family and my contacts in the Soviet Union and Cuba. The questions were designed to determine if I was a Soviet spy. After they finished running all these tests, they would repeat the test for some reason unknown to me and ask the same or similar questions on another day. It became boring and began to irritate me. However, the most distasteful part of the interrogations had to do with very private questions, including a sexual nature, which I particularly disliked and felt were not necessary for a formal government debriefing. Such questions were offensive to me and uncomfortable to answer and record in front of these strange men, even when my answers were negative. I was upset. However, they persuaded me, explaining that it was necessary for their analysis and psychological profiling.

I was not expecting any of the stupid sex questions, as I called them. For me, they were humiliating because I was raised in a country where sex discussions were effectively taboo. In general, the lie detector tests left me unimpressed; polygraphs seemed not to display very sophisticated technologies. I was, after all, an engineer curious to understand the working principle of this mysterious device, which everybody expected to be smarter than those who lied. It appeared to be merely a primitive sensing of the pulse recorded when you are answering questions, except, of course, the analytical software, which had life and logic of its own. I was disappointed because I hoped to see something technically more advanced than merely recording my emotional reactions to the simple but sometimes absurd or offensive personal questions from expert male strangers.

Generally, I experienced a serious perception gap with my interrogators, best described by another Soviet defector and philosopher, Alexander Zinoviev: "For me, the unfolding of history has profound tragic implications; for them, history is of no more consequence than a musical comedy."[60]

While John was translating the questions and my answers, Veronica, my children's babysitter, appeared to conspire against him. Thanks to her, John was constantly upset. He never told me his reasons for being upset until after he was removed from his job altogether. Later, he confided to me that she had denounced him to the boss.

She accused him of sympathizing with me and forming a personal attachment. This was only natural because we were locked in a safe house apartment for so long. She and John were our only permanent human visitors, apart from the debriefings usually conducted in a strictly formal fashion, devoid of human feelings.

That bureaucratic emotional vacuum was very difficult for me. I was a single 25-year-old mother who lost contact with everybody I loved or cared for: my family, friends, and my husband, the only other person in the world who shared the responsibility for our children. I did not know if these people so dear to me had been arrested as a consequence of my defection. The RCMP team and my interrogators were instructed to avoid any emotional involvement. I was dependent, in all aspects of my existence, on the Canadian security service.

Officially, the St. John's court had ordered my return to the Soviet Union. We had no possessions, except one change of dress, courtesy of the RCMP; even all of our documents were removed from me, and we were penniless. What I longed for was a friend's soft shoulder to soak up the bottled feelings that were consuming me. The debriefing procedures required strict and cold emotional non-involvement. Everyone treated me impersonally, except for an embarrassing incident with John, the only person who attempted to give me some hope and demonstrated a human interest.

On various occasions, during breaks, while we were left alone in the room, John attempted to talk with me about my future life and how important it would be for me to stabilize my position in Canada. After two months of interrogation, he congratulated me on passing the lie detector tests. In his opinion, this meant that my release would be imminent after we finished with the technical debriefings. He said about himself that he was transferred to Canada from England only recently to work for the Canadian

Government. He was still not married, which often caused him to feel lonely in a new country. This helped him to understand how I felt. He was hoping that we might meet again after my release so he could offer some support to me if, of course, I would be receptive to his friendly help. He also asked me not to tell anybody that he shared this information with me.

This reminded me of the way my father spoke to me when he often repeated: "Don't tell anyone, please." Are we returning to Soviet secrecy? I did not like that twist. I had made this crazy, dramatic leap into the void, risking our lives and the lives of our families to become free of fear, which paralyzed the existence of all Soviet citizens wherever they were located. Now that we had succeeded in removing our Soviet chains, all I wanted was to be able to say the truth to everybody without fear of repercussions. Wasn't that clear? In my naiveté, I made a further stupid mistake to share my thoughts and emotions with Veronica, the babysitter. I did not know that I was giving her a weapon to get rid of John. She was now on alert, listening covertly to what he was saying.

One day, she took the children into the living room to watch TV, but John and I were still finishing filling out one of the documents in another room for the Canadian security service. This was when John said that it appeared I would be released soon because the Canadian Government decided my case positively. He repeated his hope that he could meet with me in the near future after I was free. To that, I answered with irritation that our future lost any realistic outlook after being locked up for all this time. John misinterpreted my frustration with this lengthy clearance procedure and my outburst as being upset about him; he looked at me, embarrassed, and left the room.

Actually, he was quite shy, never used inappropriate gestures or wording, and was careful in his behavior. Still, the brief but personal nature of his conversation with me was, evidently, strictly prohibited. I did not know that and felt guilty for my response. His indiscreet but kind offer of friendship prompted my indignation and misdirected my rebellious instincts. I struck out against the only humane and honest gesture in that safe house. It was easier than attacking the security bureaucracy on which my very existence depended.

Veronica was eavesdropping on our conversation and promptly reported the incident to Jim. This resulted in a commotion. Jim made a big fuss about a completely innocent but apparently forbidden personal conversation. The whole operation was temporarily shut down, and I was warned by Jim that, unless I testified as to what John said, their evaluation of this incident would result negatively for me. To be returned to the Soviet Union after all that I had been through, only because of an innocent incident, at least from my vantage point, was too much to lose. Despite John's request not to tell anyone, I repeated our conversation for Jim and, with this admission, killed John's new career, who, subsequently, was replaced as a translator by Veronica. I felt guilty but had no choice.

I learned about all the repercussions from John himself when he came to say goodbye. I was embarrassed to see him so upset. When we were alone, John asked me to accompany him to the staircase landing outside of our apartment, where he explained to me that Veronica had reported him because she wanted his job as a translator, which paid much better than the job of a babysitter. The Canadian security service went along with her manipulation and forced me to testify to John's superiors about his indiscretions. I became annoyed with Veronica and found it difficult to share our private living space while she was snitching on me to her superiors.

In Cuba, I risked everything by refusing to do that very same thing to my colleagues, and here she was doing it in a free country, only to compete for a better job. This was revolting to me, and I did not want to see her again, but nobody was asking my opinion. She became my translator, which was a fresh problem because she did not have the necessary technical vocabulary required at this new technical stage of my debriefings.

The dark apparition of the St. John's courtroom still lingered. Will they act on the decision of the court to return us to the Soviet Union? Or, will the Canadian Government grant us political asylum? I did not know anything for sure, and Jim was not forthcoming. Now that I had passed, according to John, the Canadian security tests and was no longer considered a Soviet spy, why couldn't we start our new independent life, free of fears and spies? I was becoming impatient. Later, I learned that most of the previous Soviet defectors shared a similar experience, and the majority felt ignored and vulnerable.[61]

Finally, after almost three months of these pointless games (from my perspective), Jim declared that the Canadian Government made its decision. He officially congratulated me on passing the tests. I made him understand that I was not surprised: "Passed what? Test on what?" He explained that the tests proved that I was not lying when I denied being a Soviet spy.

"I am glad that the machine concluded that I was not a false defector sent as a mole by the Soviet Government," I added ironically. I was pretty tired of spending an entire Canadian summer locked up with the children in a safe house by then.

Jim asked: "Which country would you like to choose for your residence - Canada, the United States, or some other? You are given the right to choose."

"Thank you. This choice is a total surprise for me, but I already made up my mind for Canada."

"Are you sure? The US Government is offering you

asylum and even assistance. Some sectors of the US Navy expressed an interest in debriefing you, of course, with your agreement. They might even offer you a job."

I thought that enough was enough; enough debriefings, enough suspicions, enough dependencies, enough fear. I wanted to be finally free and independent. I wanted to control my life and move forward. I did not want another government to tell me what to do. I did not need any new military privileges (those in Havana were a sufficient lesson for me). Canadian security officers told me that I would appear on the 'KGB Wanted List'. I knew instinctively that such a list might be valid until one of us dies: me or the current Soviet system.

My father always taught me that survival depended on counting only upon myself and not upon trusting others as my protectors. The high price we just paid for our freedom strengthened my conviction that civilian insecurity, and maybe even poverty until I found a job in Canada, were better than a sanctuary in the USA, where I would have to rely on and strictly obey orders from military or security bureaucrats whose record of effectiveness, from my Cuban perspective, was questionable. I asserted:

"No, I am sure. My original choice was Canada, and it is Canada. I am very impatient to start our new independent and free life in this country. We have so much to learn, and I would like to begin as soon as possible."

This was the first time I was told that I would be offered a choice. Honestly, I did not know anything about any of these countries. The available information in the Soviet Union about Western countries was simply pure and slanderous propaganda. I was concerned about KGB vengeance. They could kidnap us, just as they have done with other Soviet defectors. None of the Western intelligence services gave me much confidence. In the USSR and in Cuba, where I lived and worked, the information about those services was derogatory.

Everything I knew about the CIA was unfavorable, mocking, and cynical. Their agents were considered incompetent, a laughing stock in both Moscow and Havana. The news about Cuban double agents working for the CIA, who had informed on hundreds of their poor Cuban collaborators that the Cuban Government subsequently executed, was loudly rumored throughout the Soviet community in Cuba. To my mind, such stories seemed unbelievable and scandalous. Initially, I even thought this was merely anti-American propaganda. However, the rumors turned out to be true. In 1987, Cuban television aired an eleven-part documentary, *The CIA War Against Cuba*, which confirmed all those early rumors. A total of 38 double agents and 179 CIA agents, and thousands of Cuban informers were identified on Cuban national television.

The British Secret Intelligence Service (SIS), known as MI6 (Military Intelligence, Section 6), was the main vehicle of pride and achievement for the Soviet KGB. Legendary KGB double agents - including Kim Philby, Donald Maclean, Guy Burgess, and Anthony Blunt – known as the Cambridge Five spy ring, successfully undermined and redirected all Western intelligence information to the Soviet Union for over 35 years. All the Western foreign services greatly underestimated the level of penetration of the West by the security services of the Soviet alliance.

Additionally, I heard some nasty stories, which were possibly Soviet propaganda, about Americans even torturing Soviet defectors because they were afraid that these defectors might have been implanted to stay dormant in the US until the Soviets reactivate them (sleeper cells). Why should I subject myself to such risks?

However, more objective doubts had to do with my confidence level. How could any defector trust that Americans could protect them if they failed to protect even their own President Kennedy? Concerning defectors,

American security services "alternated between indifference and benign neglect; they pretended friendliness, but expressed actual annoyance and contempt."[62] Nor could I forget my own shocking experience with the St. John's courtroom. Earlier, I successfully suppressed my feelings to gather the strength to fly over the abyss. Now, my worries resurfaced about the consequences of my defection for my family back home and the uncertainty of our future in Canada. I was in emotional turmoil from renewed fear, guilt, and loneliness.

35. The Sun Shines Brighter after a Shower[67]

The U.S. State Department (Office of The Historian) describes the period of détente from 1969 to 1979:

"Between the late 1960s and the late 1970s, there was a thawing of the ongoing Cold War between the United States and the Soviet Union. This détente took several forms, including increased discussion on arms control. Although the decade began with vast improvements in bilateral relations, by the end of the decade, events had brought the two superpowers back to the brink of confrontation."[63]

My defection was a personal initiative and was not arranged or assisted by either side of the parties to détente. I was merely an inconvenient incident for the negotiating bureaucracies. The publicity surrounding my defection, triggered by *the International Herald Tribune* (*IHT*) article, was unwelcome news for the security services of Canada and the United States.[64]

The American administration was working hard to conclude these agreements, confirming that the Soviet Union had reached parity with the United States in strategic nuclear weapons. Enormous efforts invested in these negotiations were not about to be diverted by reports of defectors, even when those reports merited serious attention and related to the treaties themselves. It was very important for the American administration to reach results; given that, and under Soviet pressure to turn defectors back, the new guidelines of Western governments called for minimizing their importance and avoiding publicity.

At the same time, the RCMP security service in Canada was collaborating with the FBI in Operation GRIDIRON, which, since 1969, was implemented to identify the Soviet mole in the RCMP security service that had caused a lot of damage in both the USA and Canada.[65] The RCMP and FBI were driven to a state of paranoia but were unable to identify the mole (Sergeant Gilles Brunet, the son of an RCMP deputy commissioner) until 1980. Given the present uncertainty, they preferred to return Soviet defectors rather than risk harboring another Soviet sleeper.

Politically, it was easier to do without publicity, and this is why my minders became so angry about the publication in *The International Herald Tribune* of June 4, 1971, reporting on my defection. They would prefer a news blackout on any defection from the USSR, being able to pretend that it never happened. No one other than Bill Toytman, who snapped the Polaroid, and his wife Rose could have shared with the correspondent of the *International Herald Tribune (IHT)* the photograph of the children and me. This photograph appeared on the first page with a brief description of our successful jump to freedom in Gander. The news about my successful defection spread like wildfire abroad throughout Warsaw Pact communities and produced a subsequent torrent of defections in Gander from Warsaw Pact airlines. A happy young mother and her kids on the front page of the *IHT* unwittingly provided global publicity for Gander. Thanks to the conscious humanitarian approach of the Canadian Government and the compassionate help of Gander Airport officials, this small city in Newfoundland became a practical gateway for defectors from totalitarian regimes from the early 1970s through to the 1990s.

During the period of détente negotiations, the attitude of the American Government toward defectors was that they were a nuisance to be avoided: "Ideally, U.S. diplomats in these days of bridge-building would like to have no defectors from the Communist bloc."[66] While I was in the Soviet Union, I had heard rumors that the American and Soviet administrations, in their effort to bring about détente, had made a secret deal to return defectors and minimize all publicity. Now, these rumors appeared to be confirmed when my investigators displayed their irritation and exasperation over the *IHT* defection story.

However, I was not sure that bringing my defection into the limelight was bad. Vladimir Krasnov, in his book *Soviet Defectors, The KGB Wanted List,* concludes: "Even in a country whose government and citizens show hospitality, defectors can never feel completely safe in the hands of bureaucrats unless their plight is widely publicized."[67]

From this perspective, my Polish hosts, Bill and Rose Toytman in Gander, unknowingly did me a favor. I learned only much later that the Canadian Government did not yet have an official policy of protecting Soviet defectors in those early days. The RCMP security service had also been embarrassed by numerous scandals involving Soviet sleeper agents. Many KGB agents were stationed in the Canadian cities of Ottawa and Montreal because of their proximity to the United States and the comparatively lax immigration practices of the Canadian Government. To protect themselves from KGB and GRU penetration in the guise of false defectors, the RCMP security service returned the occasional defector to the USSR.

From what I experienced, almost all investigative procedures that took place in my debriefings were dedicated to a standard bureaucratic evaluation of my identity. Despite their initial enthusiasm when the security service pulled me out of the St. John's jail, I had the impression that the investigators in Ottawa, including the foreign agents or specialists who came to interrogate me, were unfamiliar with technical naval fields. They showed little interest in understanding or investigating the Soviet submarine base in Cienfuegos. Their questions failed to address the important issues related to our work in Cienfuegos. Whenever I attempted to interject with some information that I considered of strategic value, I was always told to wait until these specific questions were asked. I quickly understood that any initiative on my part would be regarded as counterproductive. I was honestly puzzled by their apparent lack of appreciation for technical and military matters during my debriefing.

Of course, any verbal information had to be evidenced by documents (drawings, plans, or photographs). Without material evidence, according to my investigators, verbal statements were of little use, even when this information had very serious implications for the whole issue of détente, or, maybe, because of it. Cold War negotiators were searching for good news and seemed reluctant to hear anything that might complicate their bureaucratic mission. I remembered how urgently the Swiss spy in Havana begged me to take photographs of our Cienfuegos documentation and drawings. Nevertheless, I was not certain whether he was not a Soviet provocateur. Even in my eyes, such photographs would be evidence of outright treason. Not just me, but my family and Eduardo would be tortured into oblivion if the Soviets caught me taking photographs of these top-secret documents. This is why the Swiss spy was willing to pay a lot of money. Without photographs, it is only my word. Perhaps this is why they are investigating my psychology to such extremes. Certainly, I could describe and even draw from memory for my investigators the facilities in Cienfuegos, but only photographs or documented evidence are considered reliable proof. Probably, the main objective of my investigators was only to verify that I was not a Soviet spy. They hardly aimed at anything more substantive. In my estimation, this safe house interrogation was a waste of time and resources for both of us.

I was becoming very frustrated, spending my nights building resistance to their procedures. In the end, however, I decided to err on the side of caution and tolerate their bureaucratic tactics. I realized that we were dealing with the apparent mindlessness of American Government diplomacy, which was fearful of anything that might interrupt their ongoing negotiations with the Soviets. They were overly self-confident and reluctant to recognize that Soviet nuclear weapons were threatening their backyard again. Such news was politically inconvenient. They do not want public exposure or leaks of evidence.

For myself, there were three realistic possibilities:

Either Canadian authorities would deport me following the St. John's court decision. In this case, I could be subjected to torture by the KGB, as happened to some other Soviet defectors.

Or, the Canadian security service would let us stay in Canada but might leak information about my whereabouts, thanks to Soviet or Cuban moles inside the Canadian security services, exposing me to a KGB kidnapping.

Or, the RCMP security service would recommend that the Canadian Government grant us asylum and permit us to become regular Canadian immigrants.

I was afraid that my worst-case scenario, in the current bureaucratic context of large government intelligence agencies, was that the RCMP, FBI, and KGB would negotiate a diplomatic solution in an attempt to achieve a quiet deal by exchanging a defector for a spy. As the defector, I could be returned to the Soviet Union in exchange for a spy. It would be so simple for them - just acting upon the existing court decision in St John's. How could I trust this process if I was not offered legal assistance or even allowed to claim refugee status? In light of the decision by the St. John's court, why should I trust bureaucrats? Are they not all self-serving careerists? I became quite skeptical about their ability to formulate priorities, as one might expect from any serious foreign intelligence agency. What kind of trust could a defector have in these agencies when even the members of the Canadian security team did not trust one another? I had in mind the firing of John.

What I did not know at the time was that the RCMP Security Service was in serious trouble with the FBI (in charge of counterintelligence for North America), which accused the RCMP of allowing the penetration of a KGB mole. In response, the RCMP security service had to compartmentalize all their security information related to the US military. This meant that my case was kept secret and isolated, even from the Royal Canadian Mounted Police bureaucracy.

I should have been very grateful for such discreet and careful handling of my case, given what I learned about the mole only nine years later in 1980. It was a highly embarrassing scandal for the RCMP, which, indeed, had been infiltrated by a Soviet mole on a very senior level. He informed the KGB in Canada and Washington of the whereabouts of Soviet defectors around the world. As a result, these defectors were effectively located, kidnapped, and returned to Moscow; unless, of course, they were killed outright by the 'wet department" of KGB assassins whose mandate was to eliminate every defector on the KGB's wanted list.[68]

Still, despite all these concerns and machinations, I was worried about my parents and Eduardo. I spent countless nights fretting and losing sleep. I desperately desired to learn what happened to them. However, I was strictly forbidden to communicate with anyone from the safe house location. I could not even call the aunts of Eduardo in Spain.

I appreciated, only later, how fortunate we were to be isolated. At the time, however, the thoughts about my parents and Eduardo were like a sharp knife, turning in my heart every sleepless night, and I could not proceed into the future without resolving my fears about their safety. The Canadian security team did not understand how important it was for me, much more important than food or daily comforts. Every night, I analyzed their situation in my mind. There was no way to confirm whether my secret visit to Odessa had been detected by the KGB. It was not likely, but possible that they obtained this information after my defection.

To allow me to travel unsupervised was a serious mistake on the part of the KGB's agents. How will they cover it up? This train of thought brought me to the idea that I had become a real embarrassment for the KGB because they committed irregularities and blunders in my case. They proved to be sloppy. Somebody would be paying dearly for these errors unless they tried to cover them up somehow. Nevertheless, according to Canadian security officers on my case, the Soviet embassy in Canada was still, aggressively and persistently, demanding my return.

I was hoping that if the KGB were not informed of my visit to Odessa, they would not blame my father and Shura for my defection. The new Soviet law did not provide for the arrest of family members. However, they might be fired from their jobs at the Black Sea Institute. Papa had told me that this outcome would not affect them too seriously since they were already receiving small pensions. After all, even the draconian *Article 58.1c* of the Soviet Criminal Code stipulated three years of shared residence as a condition for the prosecution of family members. My father could easily demonstrate that we had not lived together over the last three years.

As for Eduardo, he was probably safe since Cubans were considerably more lenient about defections than the Soviets. They had to be because almost every Cuban family, including Fidel Castro's, counted relatives in the USA who escaped or left officially. Eduardo and I were now formally divorced, and Eduardo would claim that he had no previous knowledge of my plans to escape. He would argue that if he had such knowledge, he would not allow his two sons to leave Cuba. Defections in Cuba were commonplace, as opposed to the Soviet Union.

Still, despite the comfort of my highest hopes, I was anxious to obtain news from my family. I wanted to call Maria, Eduardo's mother, in Havana and ask her how Eduardo was doing and if they had heard from my parents. I became obsessed with this need to communicate. I begged our boss from Canadian security to help me to contact Maria, but he plainly and categorically refused, forbidding any form of outside communication. His order was straightforward: no contact at all with the outside world at any cost! To this, he added that the team working on my case was ordered to be extremely secretive, even within the RCMP.

The decision of the St. John's immigration court continued to hang over my head like the sword of Damocles. The court decision had not been revoked, and the Canadian security team refused to discuss this matter with me. John was the only person who sympathized with me and gave me hope that everything would end positively; now, he has been fired. I felt tormented by the prospect that the Soviet Government, worried that I would disclose information about the Cienfuegos submarine base, was negotiating with Canada an attractive deal for my return, which would be hard for Canadians to turn down.

I longed desperately for news about my parents and normal life. The children were tired as well, having been locked inside the safe house apartment the whole summer. They begged for permission to play outside and could not understand the reason why not. It had been dragging on for too long. The short Canadian summer was almost over when, suddenly, Jim came to announce that the Canadian Government awarded my children and me permanent resident status. This meant that we were granted the asylum I had asked for. Afterward, Jim accompanied us on our first release from the safe house apartment to visit a Canadian immigration office in Ottawa, issuing us a temporary residence permit.

The next day, Jim brought us to a small one-bedroom apartment in Ottawa's older but central neighborhood. The apartment was on the second floor of a small, tired-looking two-story building. The apartment was scarcely furnished with a kitchenette, but no appliances, and no TV. We had no possessions and only a small stipend from the Canadian Government that paid for the apartment and utilities, plus an allowance of 170 Canadian dollars for food. This was meant to cover our expenses before starting a subsidized, intensive 60-day English course for new immigrants, which came with a cash stipend. Upon my graduation from this English course, I was expected to function entirely on my own, find a job, and provide for the children who attended a free daycare center for new immigrants during the language course.

My fears of being hunted down in Ottawa by the KGB haunted me constantly. I thought about leaving our apartment as soon as possible to confuse our tracks for the KGB, whose agents may already know that I was in the Ottawa area. Anyway, I did not like this tiny, bleak, old apartment, especially its narrow, dark wooden staircase leading to the main floor. Still, I was delighted that the apartment had a telephone. The first thing to do when they dropped the children and me at the apartment was to call Maria, the mother of Eduardo, to ask her about Eduardo and to say that we were fine, in good health, and in a safe place. The presence of a working telephone was just too much temptation for my longing to find out what happened to Eduardo. I did not even think to call the Soviet Union, but Cuba, I hoped, could be a different affair because there was not the same widespread telephone tapping by security. As soon as the Canadian security agents departed, I grabbed the telephone and asked the operator to dial the phone number I had for Maria in Havana. As soon as she picked up the phone, I cried:

"*Mami, Mami*, it is Paulina. The children and I are fine. Would you please tell Eduardo that we made it out well? Tell him that we are safe in Canada. Auntie will know how to contact us. How are you and Eduardo?"

"*Hija* (daughter in Spanish), we are all fine," said Maria after a pause. "Please, never, ever call here again," she hung up the phone.

I thought that maybe we got disconnected. I called again,

but the operator was unable to reconnect. I understood that Maria was refusing to talk to me because she was afraid. She must have a good reason to prohibit me from contacting them in Cuba. So, I called Maria's sister, Eduardo's aunt, in Spain, and she confirmed that she heard that Eduardo was interrogated but was not arrested and was doing fine. I told her that the children and I were in Ottawa, Canada, and left my phone number with her for emergencies. I warned her not to disclose my number to anyone except Eduardo or my father if either should call her. What I did was extremely dangerous, but I felt certain about Eduardo's aunt's loyalty in Spain.

A short while after my phone call, Jim, the head of my Canadian security team, stormed into our apartment to rebuff me for these phone calls. He was very angry and prohibited me from doing anything like that ever again until the Canadian security services would inform me of their official permission, which they never did.

However, Jim told me a few days later that he received a positive report from someone in the Soviet Union (probably from their embassy or other contacts) about my parents, who continued to reside at their previous address in Odessa. He refused to explain where this information came from. He reported that my parents were no longer working, which meant that they were fired from their jobs, but they were not arrested and were still living in our original communal apartment.

The resulting relative peace of mind allowed me, for the first time, to enjoy our new life in this wonderful country, Canada. I began learning proper English and slowly assimilated with other students in my English class. The boys and I spent most of our free time in the local neighborhood park to compensate for three months of virtual house arrest. It was easy to adjust to the cordial and outgoing Canadian ambiance. Thanks to the general humanitarian spirit, high level of civilization, and multicultural tolerance, Canada proved to be our true homeland, not by birth but by choice.

Montreal.

Paulina and the boys are playing in their first snow in Canada.

Coincidentally, the first engineering work that I found in the city of Montreal was connected with Latin America, where my fluent Spanish, once again, became an important asset, allowing me to continue an adventurous and challenging technical professional life. Our integration into Canadian society did not take long. We were young, and Canada is a progressive and generous country radiating fresh energies.

Following a successful professional engineering career in Canada, over the next 15 years, the greatest surprise of my life was a personal invitation to contribute to the reforming of Soviet society. This new opportunity came about in anticipation of the implementation of Perestroika and Glasnost under the new Soviet First Secretary, Mikhail Gorbachev. The architect of Soviet economic and social reform was Alexander Yakovlev, the Soviet Ambassador to Canada and Gorbachev's mentor. The Canadian connection was instrumental in Yakovlev's political and economic education and, ultimately, in the implementation of Soviet reforms.[69] My return to the USSR in a new and constructive capacity is another big adventure, which deserves its own story.

Our new life in Montreal

For my parents, there was also a happy conclusion. The KGB was not aware of my visit to Odessa: my relatives admitted nothing when questioned, and my parents were not accused of anything. Shortly after my defection, my father was detained briefly and interrogated by the KGB in Odessa. He understood that the KGB was not informed of my visit to Odessa, and he adamantly insisted that he was completely unaware of my visit to Moscow. He was lucky that the KGB was no doubt embarrassed by their sloppiness and tried to camouflage their mistakes. He was released unharmed after he testified that we had not lived together for more than three years and that he had no previous knowledge of my plans.

Still, both were fired from their jobs. Taking into account that they were already receiving a retirement pension, the damage to them was minimal.

Then, four years later, in 1975, I was able to arrange for my parents an invitation from the so-called "relatives in Israel", and they were permitted to emigrate. To leave the Soviet Union, they were required to pay the Soviet state the costs of their education (20 years each of their salaries). It was a lot of money, and they were forced to sell everything, including Shura's dacha in Arcadia. Their pension payments were terminated, and our apartment in Odessa was confiscated by the state.[70]

Strip-searched at Moscow's airport on exit; they flew to Vienna, where HIAS (Hebrew Immigrant Aid Society), acting on their claim that they wanted to reunite with their daughter in Canada, sponsored their flight to Rome for re-processing to Canada. Through private fundraising from members of Jewish communities worldwide, HIAS has assisted in relocating nearly five million Jewish and other refugees whose lives and freedom were believed to be at risk around the world. Without HIAS and JAFI (Jewish Agency for Israel) assistance, the Soviet exodus would not have been possible. My parents stayed for three months in Rome while the Canadian Embassy there processed their entrance visas to Canada based on my sponsorship. They spent those three months visiting all the museums and many other public historical and cultural sites. Their sacrifice of losing everything they owned and everything familiar, as well as their pensions and health insurance, and being banned forever from returning to the Soviet Union, could not spoil their happiness at reuniting with their grandchildren and me in Canada.

I sponsored their coming to Canada, and for the rest of their lives, we lived together in this wonderful country that we proudly call our home. At their advanced age, they diligently took courses in English to be able to communicate with their grandchildren and Canadian friends. They formed new friendships with neighbors and other seniors, particularly in the Jewish community, where they later met other ex-Soviet Jewish immigrants. The Jewish community in Canada generously offered new immigrants from the USSR social and cultural support, particularly essential for older immigrants. My parents were able to enjoy numerous cultural and social activities and travel opportunities organized for seniors, all of which helped to temper their nostalgia for Odessa.

Paulina's parents and children were finally together in Canada in 1975

Despite the challenges of all the new learning, technical and otherwise, including 11 examinations to upgrade my engineering qualifications and earn postgraduate degrees in Canada; despite the relocations to different cities where my engineering projects were based; despite all the moving around with various Canadian engineering companies and Canadian government departments; despite all these demanding circumstances, I managed to keep, thanks to my parents who joined us in Canada, a loving home, and a stimulating environment, allowing all of us to develop as balanced and independent individuals.

There were, of course, some tough moments as well, which landed me with a fair measure of guilt. The most difficult was all the home moving and travel, which was hard for my children and my parents. As a female immigrant, I needed to compete for jobs with local men who were much better connected than I was and fit more tightly into the male-dominated, Anglo-Saxon engineering culture. (The local professional engineering associations addressed me in correspondence as "Mr." and when I complained, they answered that they had no category for "Mrs."). Usually, I picked up those jobs that were unwanted by locals because of their low pay or undesirable location, such as projects in the Canadian Arctic that required travel to the field. It was always very painful to leave my young children at home for a week with my older, defenseless parents while I traveled long distances to inspect my projects. Truly, I hated having to travel on business and to leave all of them at home without my protection, but I had no choice; I was responsible for earning our living and supporting everyone in the family. Still, in my absence, they managed quite well to care for themselves and our home. In retrospect, these business trips had a positive outcome because they forced the children to learn responsibilities more quickly and to become more mature and independent. My absences also helped my parents to develop a strong bond with their grandchildren and to learn the ropes of survival in Canada faster than under my continuous protection. Necessity rules invention.

Both boys have done very well, academically and in the marketplace. They graduated from Canadian universities with technical and scientific degrees and felt free to work for themselves from the very start in the high-tech entrepreneurial sector. I was proud of their quest for independence and their desire for lifelong learning. I kept reminding our boys that they should take full advantage of their freedom and full responsibility for their destiny. I encouraged them to use our dearly purchased freedom to develop their talents to be able to do what they like and to express what they feel; if not for themselves, then out of respect for the millions of victims who perished at the hands of those dystopian totalitarian regimes from which we were so fortunate to escape. I admire their aspirations and achievements: they are confident, responsible, and independent individuals.

When I defected, Eduardo was called for interrogations with the Soviet and Cuban security services. He was, however, released right away when he demonstrated that he was divorced and did not share a residence with me after our divorce. He claimed that he knew absolutely nothing of my intentions. He continued to be entrusted by the Cuban Government for foreign assignments, but with less frequency due to the failing economy.

Unfortunately, Eduardo's mother never told him about my phone call and did not give him my message. She was afraid that if she did, Eduardo would attempt to get in touch with me, and this would blow his alibi. I also called an aunt of Eduardo in Spain and asked her to let him know our whereabouts. She was very sweet to me, but she also failed to give Eduardo my message. It looked as though their family decided that Eduardo should stay and support his mother in Cuba. Desperate to learn about our destiny, Eduardo traveled to Moscow and Odessa, where my parents and my relatives met with him but could tell him little about our lives in Canada. None of us corresponded because we anticipated that our mail would be read by the KGB.

All they told him was that the KGB reported that we had defected to Canada. Eduardo traveled by Aeroflot via Montreal several times but never attempted to defect for a variety of reasons, chief among them his responsibility for the support of his mother.

I did not judge Eduardo. Despite our disagreements, I understood and respected his decision to stay in Cuba with his mother. He had a right to have his own mind. A year after my defection, he met his current wife, Charo, and a year later, they were married and had a baby boy. When I learned about it from his aunt in Spain, with whom I was in touch, I felt betrayed and angry. I had maintained the hope that he would join us in Canada. Eventually, I recovered from the news and decided to move ahead with my life. Rather than dwell on the past, I concentrated on achieving professional status in Canada, learning new skills, getting new degrees, and better remuneration.

New adventures and remarkable experiences continued throughout my professional career, but these belong to other stories. Our boys and I met with Eduardo and Charo only 26 years later. None of them, including his mother Maria and his sister, are not living in Cuba any longer. Like many other Cubans, more than two million of them, who decided to abandon the island, Eduardo and his family made a successful transition and became productive citizens of a world free from exploitation and coercion. It was not easy for them to separate themselves from their former identity and their familiar culture and to arrive penniless in completely different worlds, but so it was for countless other refugees who are fortunate and grateful to obtain asylum from the oppressive regimes of their native countries.

These refugees, apart from abandoning their loved ones and all of their possessions, have also assumed serious risks to themselves and their families. No reasonable person would undertake such extreme measures simply because of economic incentives in the affluent West. I was born into a relatively privileged middle-class family in Odessa, which I considered to be the best and most beautiful city in the Soviet Union. Growing up, I had no personal knowledge of anyone else in the Soviet Union living in better conditions than mine; therefore, my incentives to defect were not economic but social and political. I refused to live in constant fear under a cruel and mendacious system that bred corruption and cynicism, and where *Oprichnicki*[71] of old times or the security agents of new times could dictate the destinies of the rest of us at their will. The free choice to control my destiny, and not economic motives, was what obliged me to take the leap in Gander. Those who have experienced the fear of slavery can best appreciate my sentiments.

Since childhood, I have experienced how utopian ideologies lead humanity to disaster, and I refused, categorically, to participate, even at the risk of my life. The word *utopia* derives from the Greek root meaning 'no place'. I have always declined to go there; in this aspect, I feel like a true Odessan. For me, **the ocean is only knee-deep on my way to freedom.**

Warm again in Canada with my papa

Epilogue: Reset for the Cold War Waltz

During 1971, while I was being debriefed in Ottawa, the game of *koshki-mishki* (cat and mouse) between the Soviet Union and the United States was in full swing. The game, begun in 1968, lasted until 1991 when the Soviet Union was dissolved. Those players who were knowledgeable about the actual state of affairs were intensely curious regarding the true reasons behind the apparent naiveté of successive American administrations, who kept quiet about Soviet breaches of all four international agreements between the Cold War adversaries:

- The informal deal between the superpower leaders (Khrushchev and Kennedy), following the Cuban Missile Crisis of 1962, whereby the Soviets would take their missiles permanently out of Cuba, and the US would remove its missiles from Turkey and refrain from attacking Cuba.[72]

- The Treaty of Tlatelolco of 1967 (Treaty on the Prohibition of Nuclear Weapons in Latin America and Caribbean States).[73]

- The Treaty on the Prohibition of the Emplacement of Nuclear Weapons on the Seabed was signed in Moscow in February 1971 by the Soviet Union and the United States.[74]

- SALT (Strategic Arms Limitation Talks) was based on two rounds of bilateral talks and corresponding international treaties regarding arms control involving the United States and the Soviet Union.[75]

Despite these agreements, the Soviet nuclear submarine station in Cienfuegos used the geostrategic position of Cuba as a base to maintain the presence of Soviet nuclear weapons in the American backyard: in the Caribbean and Atlantic regions. Furthermore, since the 1970s, the Soviets were tracking the movement of US warships from the Soviet SIGINT in Cuba (signals intelligence collection facility at Lourdes, Cuba). In fact, over 75% of the global military's strategically important information for the Soviet Union came from this SIGINT center at Lourdes.

Soviet SIGINT at Lourdes

Soviet experts continued to marvel at why it was that the American Government, over more than 20 years, never publicly protested the operation of the Soviet naval base in Cienfuegos. This base was used to service Soviet vessels consisting of submarine cruisers (attack submarines), equipped with strategic nuclear ballistic and guided torpedo and cruise missiles with the capacity to cover all of North America.

The persistent reluctance by the American Government to respond to provocative Soviet breaches of existing agreements appeared to be intentional, hidden under the table for the purpose of servicing internal political objectives. In a similar vein, the US Government chose to ignore those relentless rumors about Cuban intelligence having orchestrated one of the most daring and damaging crimes in American history - the assassination of President John Kennedy. The former CIA agent Brian Latell described in his book *Castro's Secrets: The CIA and Cuba's Intelligence Machine,* how Fidel Castro used the Mexican cover granted to Cuban intelligence in Mexico to set up Lee Harvey Oswald as the future assassin. Latell conducted a detailed investigation of declassified CIA documents in the US National Archives. A retired American historian who served as a CIA Cuba analyst for over 30 years and lately as a Director of the Center for the Study of Intelligence can demonstrate that even in such a critical case as the assassination of an American president, internal political conveniences may result in a cover-up.

A few years before the 2012 publication of Latell's book, the celebrated German filmmaker Wilfried Huismann, with scriptwriter Gus Russo in their documentary *Rendezvous with Death: JFK and the Cuban Connection,* undertook a detailed investigation of the connections among Cuban and Mexican intelligence services, Robert Kennedy and Cuban-American double agents, the Soviet ties to Oswald, and the assassination of JFK. The justification for the American cover-up is shockingly revealed in front of the camera by former Secretary of State General Alexander Haig. The former high official relates that when he sat in on a top-level White House meeting and told his colleagues that he had information about the Cuban/Mexican connection to the assassination, he was admonished bluntly to shut up and never again to speak of the matter. Haig explained that the violent reaction to his admission of conspiratorial information was a result of the political awareness on the part of President Lyndon Johnson, who believed Cuba was to blame and decided not to tell the American people. Haig says in the film that Johnson believed that if the American public ever became aware of Castro's complicity in the death of JFK, there would be a swing to the right that would keep the Democratic Party out of power for a very long time.

The remains of the Soviet submarine base can be observed today

After the demise of the USSR, Soviet sources reported that, between 1971 (the year of my defection) and 1991 (the year the Soviet Union collapsed), Cienfuegos provided 29 service and support maintenance operations for Soviet nuclear submarines ranging between 40 and 120 days. The stealth technology of later models of Soviet submarines was rapidly improving, thereby minimizing their acoustic, magnetic, radar, and visual signatures. Hidden beneath the surface of the sea, these underwater nuclear-powered giants were each carrying dozens of missiles armed with multiple nuclear warheads.[76] Despite such blatant treaty breaches, no official public American protest ever took place.

During my debriefing in Ottawa in 1971, I assumed that my information about the military naval base in Cienfuegos was not a unique eye-opener for the American Government. Still, at the SALT Summit between Americans and Soviets in Moscow in May 1972, there was no mention of the presence in Cuba of Soviet submarines with nuclear ballistic missiles or of the presence of a Soviet tender to service nuclear submarines. Besides the interview with Henry Kissinger in the *New York Times* in 1970, and his own article published in *Time Magazine* in 1977, there was no official mention of this issue at all. Actually, the American administration was consistent in denying the further presence, after 1970, of Soviet missiles in Cuba.

Nor did the Americans protest the presence of Soviet combat brigades, the many thousands of whom were guarding and handling tactical nuclear weapons in the Punta Movida Complex linked to Cienfuegos by rail; nor did they object to the Cuban/Soviet monitoring of American military transmissions in the Lourdes SIGINT center. Studies by American researchers demonstrated that all five American administrations (from Nixon to the elder Bush) intentionally chose to ignore these breaches of international treaties.[82]

A consistent US policy of strict secrecy and cover-up of Soviet military operations in Cuba permitted subsequent American administrations to avoid politically embarrassing and risky confrontations with the Soviets; at least, this was the calculated gamble perpetuated by Henry Kissinger.

President Carter was informed about Soviet batteries of modified SA/2 anti-aircraft missiles on the Cuban northeast coastline facing the United States. These missiles could be deployed quickly in surface-to-surface mode. They had an operational range exceeding 150 miles and could reach ground targets in Florida with precision. However, Carter was so anxious to sign the SALT II Agreement that he accepted the status quo. The Soviet navy squadrons were also supported by the air force TU-95D "Bears" and TU-142 "Backfire" bombers carrying nuclear bombs and missiles, and based in St. Antonio de Los Baños. They were effectively coordinated for military action thanks to four Soviet SIGINT centers operating in Cuba. In 1978, in addition to six Soviet airfields in Cuba for Backfire strategic bombers, an additional two squadrons with 75 fighter bombers (MIG 23/27) were stationed in Cuba.

Soviet base in San Antonio de Los Baños

Additionally, the third phase of the underwater terminal for Soviet submarines, which entered into service in 1978, was servicing undetected until 1991, Soviet nuclear-powered stealth submarines equipped with ballistic nuclear warhead missiles with underwater launch capability. In light of such a vast continuous buildup of Soviet military might on the Island of Cuba during and after superpower arms limitation treaties, why did the US Government remain silently submissive after 1971? Perhaps the US, following its successful defusing of the 1962 Cuban Missile Crisis, did not believe that the Soviets had any intention of launching a nuclear first strike. Also, the Americans would have been well informed about the fragile nature of Soviet society during the Khrushchev and Brezhnev years. Behind technologically, economically weak, mismanaged, corrupt, and overextended globally, the leaders of the Soviet Union were not anxious to start a nuclear war. However, if such a war did break out, they wanted to ensure themselves that they could win. This is why the Soviet leadership was determined to negotiate détente from a position of power. The Cienfuegos base offered this security and helped to justify it to the Soviet Politburo, claiming strategic advantage, which, if needed, would assure the Soviets the first strike in a nuclear war.

We have to wonder at the concealed diplomacy of the American administration in those years, when the US allowed

Henry Kissinger to negotiate discreetly to mitigate another nuclear war crisis. Of course, this was also a time of grave political protest in America over the Vietnam War, which was going badly for the US military. The American political leaders did not need to deal publicly with another international military crisis in their backyard. The behind-the-scenes diplomatic theater allowed the United States to conduct negotiations over a period of 20 years while ignoring Soviet military bullying. The decisions of Soviet leaders, after the death of Stalin, could not be made exclusively by a single obsessed maniac, but only by a group of competing, experienced members of the Politburo, each of whom had to watch over his own shoulders.

Obviously, this was not the case with Fidel Castro. Both Soviets and Americans came to appreciate that the rule of an absolute single dictator in Cuba - *Jefe Maximo* - could be perilously irrational. Ultimate decisions regarding global survival were vulnerable to the capricious moods of a single man. This man could not be trusted. In the end, however, it was Cuba that appeared to benefit the most from this situation. Never again did the island have to worry about an American invasion despite Fidel's politically convenient exhortations to the contrary. At least this time, Fidel Castro was not able to launch a wild missile, since control of these missiles was now better secured inside submarines.

New acoustically sophisticated, nuclear-powered Soviet submarines permitted uninterrupted surveillance of the American coast. Still, the American Navy was technologically superior in the Gulf of Mexico, if not in numbers, then in capability. This underwater Cold War waltz lasted until the morally degraded and economically decrepit Soviet Union disintegrated from its own weight. Its collapse was the accumulated consequence of low productivity, inept management, massive corruption, and the deep demoralization of the artificially constructed new Soviet man (*Homo Sovieticus*). The Soviet ruling class, the nomenklatura,[84] was now deeply despised and resented by the majority of decent and intelligent people in the Soviet

Union, who had adopted a passive attitude of pretending to work and to participate in the social and economic life of their country. In reality, they undermined the national economy and spirit. The sum of this lethal mix slowly eroded and finally destroyed the economic and political power of the brutal Soviet regime.

While Russia has evolved considerably since the Stalinist era of the Soviet empire, many threads of the *Homo Sovieticus* mentality remain. Despite a brief flirtation with free speech and open markets during Perestroika, the country has bounced back, like the *Vanka-vstanka* (roly-poly) doll, into authoritarianism with its legacy of corruption, human rights violations, and criminal violence.[77] Currently, the Russian media and school history manuals, both approved and controlled by the Russian Government, teach that Stalin was its great leader and the misfortunes of the world were and are instigated by the United States and its allies. These are the old tricks, traditionally used in Russia, designed to distract attention from the nation's internal mismanagement and towards external enemies.

Instead of re-examining their history and assuming responsibility for it in order to ensure that the darkest days will never be repeated, the country, run by and for the FSB (Federal Security Services) – a modern successor of the KGB, is seeking to reassert the traditional power of its empire. Putin accepted publicly that some excesses in governing took place during Stalin's rule, but they were necessary, he said, because Stalin wanted to accelerate the industrialization of the Soviet Union. Adolf Hitler also claimed that the atrocities committed by fascists were designed to benefit the German nation. It is convenient to blame just one dead man for national savagery on the scale of genocide.

However, it is necessary to recognize that such genocide could not happen without the complicity of a large group of powerful people (the bureaucrats) who benefited from the oppression of others and, therefore, supported and implemented these criminal actions against humanity. A similar group of technocrats at the time of Russian Tsar Ivan the Terrible, were called *oprichniki*; during the Russian Revolution, Lenin's operatives were called *commissars*; and after Stalin came to power, on a lower bureaucratic level, they were called *apparatchiks,* and on a very senior level, *nomenklatura.* A new class of *nomenklatura* in modern Russia is called *siloviki.* They are alive and well and in control of Russia, ensconced in privilege, surrounded by wealth, and protected by their government. They are experienced in the art of disinformation, always ready to mislead the docile masses with lies, theatrics, and promises. They are the real ruling class of Russia that has inherited the resources and assets from the Revolution. According to Mikhail Volensky, in his analysis of this subject in his book *Nomenklatura*[78] Russia's new ruling elite returned the country to a method of traditional authoritarian Asian state capitalism with control over an obedient population and expansionist pretensions.

Since the demise of the USSR, few Russians have shown an appetite for the establishment of a "Truth and Reconciliation Commission" that would recognize and examine the crimes of Soviet history with a view to healing the Russian nation through truth-telling, mutual understanding, and forgiveness. Perhaps this lack of commitment to such a process derives not just from the reluctance of new political leaders to open up Soviet archives (and Soviet wounds), but also from the powerful sense of collective guilt felt, at least subconsciously, by generations of Soviet people. As well, it takes an independent mind, a strong stomach, and a brave heart to digest the full horrors of Soviet terror.

Another challenge for Russians is their hurt national pride. Traditionally, Soviet and Russian children were programmed, from daycare through the school years, with xenophobic hate propaganda against the West. The reforms, which Gorbachev intended, were designed to create a democratic socialist state. Instead, Russia morphed into a cynical autocratic state capitalism whose power elite make up their own rules and convenient ethics. It is useful to recall the famous quotation from Vladimir Ilyich Lenin himself: "If we offer a good price, the capitalists will sell us the rope on which we will hang them." The wording used today by ex-KGB politicians and ex-Soviet *nomenklatura* has changed, but their objectives remain the same.

A long history of tyranny, mistrust, and conspiracy has created a culture of cynicism and hostility incomprehensible to Western well-wishing liberals. This mentality will continue to imbue Russian society until a critical mass of a new generation of Russians comes of age and refuses to live in a society of fear and dependency from which I was able to liberate myself only by abandoning it.

Meanwhile, Soviet deep-water submarine technology continues to progress, having reached parity with the US in the late 1970s and 1980s. In deep-water technology, Russia became even more advanced than America and more numerous. Soviet nuclear deep-water supply stations, development of which started in the early 1970s to serve as an underwater service station for nuclear-powered submarines, evolved with a unique technological advantage due to the Russian titanium poly-spherical hull. One of the variations of this technology is modified for scientific applications. It is known as AC-12 Losharik, Projects 10831-10833, Class Norsub-5.

Currently, it is used for geological probing of the ocean bottom beneath the Arctic Ocean ice. There are two of these, built recently, out of six ordered by the Russian navy. They are designed to operate with geological drilling probes at extreme water depths down to 6000 meters. Russia is planning to claim an additional 1,200 square miles of Arctic Ocean bottom beyond their 200-mile economic zone because they believe that the underwater seabed structure - Lomonosov and Mendeleyev Ridges - are a continuation of the Siberian continental platform.

The total of Russian Arctic claims represents 25% of the

world's oil and natural gas global reserves. In September 2012, the expedition of "Sevmorgeo" and "AARI", with the help of the Russian navy, drilled 3 shallow bore holes on the Arctic Ocean bottom at water depths between 2,000 and 2,500 meters over 20 days.[79] They collected various geological samples from the bedrock with the use of two Russian research icebreakers and the nuclear deep-water supply station Losharik, a Class Norsub-5 navy submarine. The resulting data will be provided to the United Nations Commission on the Continental Shelf, including the results of seismo-acoustic profiling. It is a promising and lucrative opportunity, but not an immediate opportunity for Russia because, as we say in Canada, it is as expensive to drill in the Arctic as it would be on the moon.

China, which has deep pockets, may choose to financially bankroll Arctic development. Rosneft (the Russian state oil company with the license rights for all Arctic reserves) has offered this investment opportunity to China. Clearly, it is a worrisome collaboration because Russian and Chinese industrial ambitions have always taken precedence over environmental concerns.

The Arctic is a fragile ecosystem for oil and gas reserves exploitation. Moscow has unveiled the Arctic 2035 strategy by planning to develop huge new energy projects in its remote Arctic areas, creating tens of thousands of jobs and using the Northern Sea Route to export oil and gas to overseas markets as the region becomes increasingly free of ice. Current Russian Arctic large producing fields, Prirazlomnoe and Shtochmanskoe, are preparing to implement these technologies. Still, we can take some solace from the fact that this remarkable Russian deep-water submarine technology is being deployed for peaceful purposes.

Still, sadly, the ghost of imperial struggle for global power has not faded away. Once again, threatening clouds appeared on the horizon. The Cold War confrontation waltz is back in fashion in Russia, riding on a wave of chauvinist hype.

The disinformation wars are conducted in Russia and by Russia worldwide in a variety of fields: political, economic, cultural, and in the media, incessantly brainwashing innocent, rebellious, though well-intended, minds.

An obvious candidate for a Pulitzer Prize in bias and propagandistic distortion is Russian Television (RT), whose foreign broadcasting services in English, Spanish, and Arabic, based in Washington, DC, and in other major cities around the world, transmit a steady stream of unbalanced and slanted reporting against Western democracies. From RT's point of view, only in Russia is democratic government flawless and majestic. RT recently re-opened its Spanish-language broadcast in Cuba, brainwashing the Cuban public in Russian might and right free of charge.

And again, Cuba is at the forefront of veiled Russian expansionism. Under the pretext of selfless, benevolent efforts to help Cuba, Russia announced plans to rebuild, at the Russian state's expense, its old military, a naval base in Cienfuegos, and its military airport base in San Antonio de Los Baños, including modern SIGINT facilities (intelligence collection center targeting the United States).[80]

According to Russian press sources, the Russian Foreign Intelligence Service (SVR) has officially restarted in Cuba the Russian Intelligence Digital Intelligence Gathering Center SIGINT for its agent network in North and South America[81] and the new Russian Global Navigation Communications System GLONASS. All of this is a good fit for Cuba's true rulers *Los pinchos*, (translated as "brochette", meaning the meat of Cuban citizens on the skewer of the Cuban military), in Cuba's long-running cold war with the United States.

AGI Victor Leonov (the main AGI Spy Ship Vischego Klassa of the Russian Navy) periodically visits Havana for the coordination and collection of digital data. Recently, once again, it arrived on March 3, 2020, in a secret and unsafe manner, by turning off the transmitter signals over AIS (Automatic Identification System) and its lights, not answering inquiries from other ships to avoid a collision in high-traffic areas.   **https://www.cubanet.org/noticias/cuba-barco-espia-ruso-reaparece-en-puerto-de-la-habana/.**

During her previous Cuban visit in December 16,17 and 18 of 2019, AGI Victor Leonov provoked numerous protests from passing vessels and the US Coast Guard with some experts suggesting that it is gathering US military information from US naval bases, digital signatures of US subs, radars and sensors, information from undersea cables and even the surveillance of US coastline for "Kanyon targeting". **https://www.washingtonexaminer.com/opinion/what-russias-unsafe-spy-ship-might-be-up-to**

Putin, Medvedev, and Borisov officially announced the commencement of their operations last December in Cuba personally; not a single Western media outlet noticed this fact. **https://twnews.com.ua/ru-news/borisov-soobshchil-o-zapuske-pervoi-na-kube-stantsii-glonass**

On February 22, 2020, the head of the Russian Navy, Admiral Nikolay Evmenov, returned to Moscow from 6 days working visit to Cuban ports and Cuban Navy enterprises on the invitation of Raul Castro and Miguel Diaz-Canel in response to their own working visit to Moscow in 2019. The Russian and Cuban media reported the visit of Russian Navy Admiral Nikolay Evmenov to Cuba in Russian and Spanish languages, with Russian media announcing the return of the Russian Navy submarine base in Cienfuegos.

The deal is described as being made on the behest of the Cuban state. Russia promised to invest over 1 billion Euros into rebuilding and modernizing Cuban harbor facilities (in Jagua Bay?) to service Russian navy submarines and the Cuban navy military industry. To that effect, the Russian media asserted that the Cuban civil residents of the Bay of Jagua and Cienfuegos will be relocated from the coastal areas. One billion Euros would be the largest ever investment in militarizing Cuba.

Being aware of the current dismal state of the economy, when the Russian state cannot pay for the medical services of Russian veterans and pensioners, I decided to check this claim and found the confirmation in Cuban media of last year, made upon the return of Raúl and Miguel Diaz-Canel from Moscow. The Cuban government announced to the residents in the area of Bay of Jagua and Cienfuegos relocation to the interior of Cuba for climatic reasons. **https://www.cubanet.org/noticias/unas-11-420-familias-seran-reubicadas-en-cienfuegos/**

In conclusion, the Russian Navy announced its return to providing a base in Cuba for Russian submarines with nuclear-tipped cruise missiles, as well as for the Russian Navy surface fleet. According to Putin, the Cuban base is similar to Tartus, a Russian navy base in Syria.

That is in addition to the even more dangerous Russian technology: SKIF - Russian nuclear-tipped cruise missiles located on the ocean floor in the offshore of Cuban territorial waters of its Northern coast. These missiles are controlled remotely from the already mentioned brand new Russian SIGINT/GLONASS center, which Russian V-President Dmitry Medvedev personally officially opened and announced as functional in Cuba on October 4, 2019.

Adm. Mark Ferguson, the United States Navy's top commander in Europe, said that the intensity of Russian submarine patrols had risen by almost 50 percent over the past year, citing public remarks by the Russian Navy chief, Adm. Viktor Chirkov. Analysts say that tempo has not changed since then. The patrols are the most visible sign of a renewed interest in submarine warfare by President Vladimir V. Putin, whose government has spent billions of dollars on new classes of diesel and nuclear-powered attack submarines that are quieter, better armed, and operated by more proficient crews than in the past.

The tensions are part of an expanding rivalry and military buildup, with echoes of the Cold War, between the United

States and Russia. Moscow is projecting force not only in the North Atlantic but also in Syria and Ukraine and building up its nuclear arsenal and cyber warfare capacities in what American military officials say is an attempt to prove its relevance after years of economic decline and retrenchment. *"Russia Bolsters Its Submarine Fleet, and Tensions With U.S. Rise,"* affirmed Eric Schmitt, in his article in The New York Times.

Independent American military analysts see the increased Russian submarine patrols as a legitimate challenge to the United States and NATO. Even short of tensions, there is the possibility of accidents and miscalculations. Many are skeptical regarding data from Putin's "disinformation" services, hoping that the reference to Russian strategic nuclear missiles is only intended to intimidate the Americans to negotiate larger Russian benefits in the missile shield negotiations.

Will the US military strategy count on betting that the Russian military will collapse from economic bankruptcy before it causes irreversible damage? Only time will tell if the new submerged Russian missiles, once again, will aim at the US coastal facilities from Cienfuegos or, rather, from the new Cuban ocean bottom-based location, such as Boca de Jaruco, for example. After all, the Russian Government surprised its own oil experts by promising to invest 35 billion US dollars in the development of Boca de Jaruco offshore oil field despite the recognition that it is exhausted and dry after continuous sour oil production for the last 30 years. Hardly viable during the époque of low oil prices, this sounds like another Kremlin disinformation campaign in a contemporary Caribbean asymmetric war.

For the impoverished Cuban people, however, it will be business as usual, as they scratch their heads and wonder why the Russian Government needs to rebuild an airport in San Antonio de Los Baños, located only 10 kilometers from Havana's international airport, particularly when Havana's new and large international airport (a gift from Canada) handles very little traffic. Russian media claim that these big, new logistical hubs will stimulate Russian tourism or improve the Cuban economy.

Perhaps the submarines and the bombers with nuclear missiles will become the objects of tourism for the Russian armed forces, and why not? During the previous Soviet missions to Cuba in 1962 and during 1970-1990, all Soviet personnel related to those missions had their visas stamped as agricultural or technical assessors. It is now possible that the Soviet military personnel will have their visas stamped as tourists. It is not difficult to imagine Soviet military deals being made with the Cuban military, which is in total control of Cuba, despite the camouflage exercise of a projected transition to a future civilian government. The economic gains from these military projects for the Cuban people will be minimal, while Russia consolidates, for the third time, its strategic hemispheric power base in the Gulf of Mexico. The Cold War waltz is again on the upswing. The brilliant future of international co-operation will continue to wait on stand-by.

Paulina Zelitsky, Paul Weinzweig

Appendix 2: Excerpt from the article of Boris Ioffe "Special Secret Mission"

The New World, The World of Science #5, 1995, Moscow.

The Academician Boris Ioffe was a Russian theoretical physicist and a Corresponding Member of the USSR Academy of Sciences. He was one of the pillars of Soviet nuclear physics and one of the inventors and developers of Soviet high-energy physics. Boris Ioffe was instrumental in the development of the theory of nuclear reactors and the hydrogen bomb. He patented numerous inventions and authored over 300 scientific papers on elementary particle physics.

Translation to English by Paulina Zelitsky

"I am sure that the main purpose of Stalin was world domination, or at least as a first step towards this goal - the seizure of several territories in Europe and in Asia (Turkey, Korea, access to the southern seas; think of the communist army engaged in Greece, Indochina, Malaysia, the Philippines, etc.). The attack on South Korea was the first serious test of strength. From the outset of hostilities, I realized from the statements of Soviet propaganda that Stalin was directing and organizing the aggression of North Korea; that the war was provoked by South Korea is a pure lie. I also understand that Stalin was using this war for an early reconnaissance of Western, and especially US, military response. I am convinced that in the early 50s, Stalin planned to launch and win a third world war. Time was critical. Stalin had not much time left - in 1949, he was seventy years old - and needed to act quickly.

Recently, there was an important confirmation of this view. The article by Lieutenant-General N. Ostroumov, who was then Deputy Chief of Operations of the Air Force, states that in the spring of 1952, Stalin ordered the creation of 100 new divisions with tactical bombers. According to Ostroumov, Stalin was preparing for another war. In the Czech Republic, a memoir was published by General Chepichka. Chepichka was the defense minister in the communist government of Czechoslovakia under Klement Gottwald in the late 1940s and early 1950s. In particular, Chepichka's memoir relates that in 1952, Stalin had called a meeting of defense ministers of the socialist countries of Eastern Europe. At this meeting, Stalin said that he expected World War III to start in the next year or two and demanded that the Soviet allied armies must be ready for it.

In order to implement these goals, it was necessary to solve two difficult problems: the military - to create nuclear weapons; and the political - to prepare the people for war. The decision regarding the latter problem was particularly difficult, and Stalin understood this: it would seem impossible to motivate the people to wage a new war only 8-10 years after the end of the hardest and bloodiest war in the history of Russia, and moreover, against America, Russia's former ally, and using conventional means of propaganda. Even the traditional gears of terror used against Soviet citizens by its government might be insufficient. It was necessary to wake people and make them emotionally very angry. However, it should not be just an abstract anger against someone overseas, about whom the average person hears only on the radio. It was essential that each person saw the objects of his hatred close to him, threatening Soviet citizens and their families, and these enemies were sent and led from across the ocean.

To find a suitable object for the hatred of the people was not hard - it was the Jews. The Jews are ideally suited for this purpose: everyone has seen a Jew, everyone could have a number of Jews for an object of their hatred, and the old

Russian tradition of anti-Semitism has not been forgotten. The peace pact with Hitler, before the war, and the refresher course in anti-Semitism during the war by the German occupiers, helped Stalin and his obedient party and state apparatus to deliberately foment anti-Semitism in the second half of the 1940s (by calling it anti-cosmopolitanism, publicizing arrests and shootings of Jewish cultural workers and members of the scientific community as 'killing pests', etc.). The anti-Semitic campaign, which dangerously intensified up to the moment of Stalin's death, was not just another episode in the Stalinist policy of repression of people to whom he would take a dislike - it was an instrument he needed for his next ambitious goal.

A new and very important step towards this goal was the 'Doctors' Plot'. At the end of 1952, a group of 37 professors, leading medical experts, was arrested. All of them, except for one or two, were Jews. They were accused of acting on orders from the American Jewish donors to JAC (Jewish Anti-Fascist Committee). Under the guise of treatment, they were trying to kill the leaders of the Communist Party and the Soviet State. Since the advent of the first message about the 'Doctors' Plot', it has become clear to me that this was a fake, fabricated by Stalin, with the purpose of starting a new persecution campaign.

The accusations of the 'Doctors' Plot' were falsely fabricated from start to finish, not immediately recognized as false by everyone, even among intellectuals, because some of those arrested have, under extreme torture, signed the false confessions prepared by their interrogators. The 'Doctors' Plot' was conceived from the premise that it would demonstrate that the Jews are the killers, even when they are from the noblest profession, such as doctors. And, it was not intended just to arrest and jail three dozen prominent physicians in the Soviet Union: the propaganda and rumors were spread across the country that all the Jewish doctors were criminals and the enemies of the people.

I myself have heard on the street, in shops, etc., statements like: 'We have a doctor in the clinic - a Jew. I do not go to him, he would poison me'; or 'So and so died in the hospital - he was killed by a Jewish doctor'. And this hatred (of Jews) was extended not only to the physicians, but to the rest of Soviet society.

The sequence of the play had multiple stages:

Act One: sentencing after full confessions are extorted under torture;

Act Two: a public execution by hanging in Red Square;

Act Three: pogroms (called forth as 'spontaneous' actions of the people against the Jews throughout the country);

Act Four: Jewish personalities, famous in the world of culture, would write letters to Stalin and to the Soviet Government, in which they would recognize the collective responsibility of Jews as a nation. However, the authors of the letter would ask for the protection of the Jewish people from pogroms, to which end they will be permitted to leave the big cities and go back to the land.

Act Five: mass deportation of Jews to the areas of the Far East. Relevant camps or barracks were already prepared or were under construction.

It was easy to predict the sharp reaction of America, which, of course, would have stood up to defend the Jews. America and Western Europe would support them. And then, according to Stalin's plan, there will be a switch of people's fury from the internal enemy to the external.

The requirement for the solution of the second problem - the military: in the late 40s, the Soviet Union had an absolute superiority in ground forces in Europe. But that was not enough: Stalin's plan required, if not parity in nuclear weapons with the United States, then at least the American public outcry, fearing Soviet nuclear attack on the United States, warning against the use of the atomic bomb in the event of another war in Europe.

Since 1949, the USSR had nuclear weapons. But they were not enough, and in this respect, we are greatly inferior to America. In 1945, it was announced that the US was working on creating a much more powerful weapon - the hydrogen bomb, which was far from complete. I want to emphasize that, I believe, Stalin's aim was to create a Soviet hydrogen bomb in order to win a nuclear war against America.

I think that Stalin realized that the overtaking of Americans would be impossible. His aim was different: creating a hydrogen bomb almost simultaneously with the Americans, to test it and demonstrate that we also have nuclear weapons. The Americans will not know how many hydrogen bombs we have - two, three, or five. And when the war begins in Europe with conventional weapons (in which case, of course, the Soviet Army is superior), it would be likely that the US would refrain from the use of nuclear weapons, fearing the impact of hydrogen bomb retaliation on its territory. Thus, the Soviet hydrogen bomb would serve as a means of nuclear blackmail at the beginning of this war in Europe.

Further developments fully confirm this scenario. By the end of 1952, it became clear that the hydrogen bomb will be ready in a short time (from six months to a year): all the fundamental issues had been resolved, only its realization remained. The plan foresees to start design, construction, and commissioning of reactors to produce tritium - the main component required for the hydrogen bomb in the early 1950s. Simultaneously, there were organized political events: the public execution can be expected sometime in the spring-summer of 1953.

The test of a hydrogen bomb in the Soviet Union took place in August 1953; perhaps, it was somewhat delayed due to the death of Stalin and later by other disturbances (the execution of Beria, changes in the leadership of the nuclear industry, etc.). So I am deeply convinced that if it were not for the intervention of fate - the death of Stalin in March 1953 - World War III could have broken out somewhere in 1953 or 1954 and the world would have been on the brink of (or beyond) disaster. Therefore, the creation of a hydrogen bomb in the USSR in the early 50s, from my point of view, represented a grave danger to humanity."

About the Authors

Paulina Zelitsky is a Canadian Professional Engineer in the security, transportation, and energy sectors. She obtained her initial M. Eng. degree in Coastal Marine Engineering from National Marine University in Odessa, Ukraine, and in Permafrost Engineering at the University of Alberta, Canada.

Paulina started her career as a port designer for Soviet, Cuban, and later in the 70s for private Canadian engineering companies across Canada. After Paulina's naturalization and certification as a Canadian Professional Engineer, she jump-started her new career in Arctic Engineering in the energy sector, initially with the Northern Canada Power Commission in Edmonton and later with Petro-Canada as a Systems Engineer and with Ports Canada as a Program Manager. From 1984, Paulina served as a Safety and Risk Analysis Engineer at EMR COGLA in Ottawa and the National Energy Board (NEB), where she participated in the development of Canadian Onshore Pipeline Regulations and Canadian Diving Regulations.

Paul Weinzweig grew up in Toronto, Canada, where he earned a Ph.D. in Sociology from the University of Toronto and went on to do volunteer research work in West Africa at a community mental health project. He has taught in the social sciences at several Canadian universities and helped to pioneer and present televised distance education. Paul served as Associate Director of the Ontario

Confederation of University Faculty Associations, where he managed negotiations between university teachers and the new provincial distance education authority (TV Ontario) that laid the ground rules for the participation of university teachers in the new electronic educational media. Paul has researched many areas, including private school education, the role of international non-governmental organizations in peace and disarmament, the plight of Canada's indigenous peoples migrating from rural to urban areas, and cultural programming for Toronto's Harborfront development.

In 1987, during the advent of Perestroika, Paul was invited to the Soviet Union, where his book on creativity and self-realization was published in Russian. The book became a best-seller, and he was encouraged to make a television series for Soviet Central Television based on the book's themes. The 14-part TV series ("To the Promised Land..."), blending Russian performing arts with talks on social and psychological change, became part of a fund-raising effort by Paul and his wife, Paulina, to support the renowned but struggling Natalya Sats Musical Theater.

Paulina Zelitsky, Paul Weinzweig

Other Published Books by the Authors:

- *The Sea is Only Knee Deep- Volume 1,*
- *Dog Days in Cuba,*
- *Moscow Book of Promises,*
- *The Dreamer Whose Dream Came True,*
- *A Practical Antidote for The Ills of Capitalism,*
- *Technology and Humanism,*
- *Odessaphile,*
- *Adios Angelina,*
- *Chaos & Redemption: Reflections on Economy, Technocracy, and Humanism,*
- *A Fare to Remember: Taxi Stories, School Confessions, and Family Reflections*

ENDNOTES

1   Lyrics from *Sugarcane*, a popular Caribbean folk song.

2   Chicken Little is a folk tale with a moral about the deadly consequences of illusory fear and the failure of courage. The story is about a chicken who believes, hysterically, that the world is ending. The chicken's mistaken belief in impending disaster is expressed in its repeated cries that "The sky is falling!"

      Gallego is a colloquial Cuban reference to someone obsessed with his Spanish ancestry.

4   Lyrics and music by Annie Lennox and Dave Stewart.

5   *Hispanidad* refers to the presumed cultural and economic alliance among all Spanish-speaking countries.

6   *Niños* is the name given to over 3000 Spanish children who were evacuated to the Soviet Union during the Spanish Civil War. As young men, they became cadets at Soviet military schools. One of the special schools was situated in the town of Ivanovo and was known as the E. D. Stasova International School. Some graduates of this school later turned up as Fidel Castro's personal bodyguards, and some became leading figures in the Cuban intelligence service - the most aggressive in the world, often exceeding its teachers in the Soviet security services in both cruelty and cunning. The GRU and KGB used some of the school's graduates as spies. However, the majority of the first generation of Spanish children remained in the Soviet Union with no possibility of leaving. The Soviet Government, for operations abroad, used the second generation of Spaniards. One of their tactics was to send some young Soviet Spaniards to Cuba, give them time to get used to

the country and culture, and then send them to Africa and Central America as Cubans to fight against "American Imperialism".

7   Michail Voslenski, *Nomenklatura*, MP October, Soviet Rossia, 1991, 167-178.

8   Cubana's flights CU-T668, Havana-Prague-Moscow, were using four Bristol Britannia turboprops purchased in Britain. These aircraft had to be leased in 1962 to CSA Czechoslovakian Airlines to allow this route to be operated by CSA instead of Cubana. The main reason for this change of operators was the problem with Cuban pilots who were defecting during the refueling stops in Gander. These Eastern European transatlantic routes were very important for the Cuban Government since the majority of foreign recruits from Latin and North American countries enrolled in Cuban international terrorist training came to Cuba via Prague. Bristol Britannia turboprops did not have the fuel capacity to cover the Havana-Prague distance and had to be refueled in Gander, Newfoundland, Canada. On their way back from Prague to Havana, these flights made an additional refueling stop in Shannon, Ireland, about which I found out only later.

9   Michail Voslenski, *Nomenklatura*, London, Overseas Publications Interchange Ltd., 1990, p.88.

10   *Kaddish* is a traditional Jewish prayer for the dead.

11   The NKVD Order № 00486 gave instructions about the repression of wives and children of enemies of the people. "Socially dangerous" children were to be placed in labor camps, corrective labor colonies, or special-regimen orphanages.

12   *Haskalah* was a rational reform Jewish movement, inspired by the European Enlightenment and designed to integrate Jews into the larger society. It was created by

the German Jewish philosopher Moses Mendelssohn in the mid-18th Century.

13 Robert Weinberg. "The Pogrom of 1905 in Odessa: A Case Study" in *Pogroms: Anti-Jewish Violence in Modern Russian History*, John D. Klier and Shlomo Lambroza, editors. Cambridge University Press, 1992, 248-89.

14 Hasidism began as a Jewish revivalist mystic movement in which charismatic spiritual leadership replaced legalistic doctrine. Hasidism was founded in the 18th Century Eastern Europe by a cabbalist named Israel Baal Shem Tov (1700-1760). Early on, it attracted a following among both uneducated and scholarly Jews in Eastern Europe and the Ukraine. The emphases of the movement on encouragement, optimism, fervent prayer, kindness, and good deeds filled spiritual needs among the common people and provided a creative outlet for their spiritual beliefs. Hasidism is extremely orthodox, requiring followers to adhere rigidly to every basic doctrine and principle in traditional Jewish belief and practice. Still, it retains a strong mystical element, which emphasizes personal communion with God. Thus, mysticism is not an esoteric gift for a minority of ascetic Jews, but rather an integral part of the community of believers.

15 http://en.wikipedia.org/wiki/Odessa_pogroms

16 Semyon Petliura was a publicist, writer, journalist, Ukrainian politician, statesman, and national leader who led Ukraine's struggle for independence following the Russian Revolution of 1917. During the period of Ukrainian independence, 1918-1920, he was head of the Ukrainian State.

17 Nestor Makhno was a Ukrainian anarcho-communist revolutionary and a leader of a peasant independent anarchist army in Ukraine during the Russian Civil War.

18 Anton Denikin, a Russian general who led the anti-Bolshevik ("White") forces on the southern front during the Russian Civil War (1918–20).

19 The Pale of Settlement was decreed by Tsarina Ekaterina II in 1791 as a territory in the Russian steppes (plains) where Russian Jews were permitted to reside. Even within the Pale, Jews were prohibited from leasing or owning land or operating taverns. They were denied access to middle or higher education, but they had to pay double tax and serve in the Russian army from the age of 12. Those who were drafted into the army never returned to their families. Only after the overthrow of the Czarist regime in 1917 was the Pale of Settlement abolished.

20 Ataman Struck from Chernobyl was a captain of the tsarist army who occasionally led the battalions of the Petliura army, and other times, the White Army of Denikin. He was infamous for extreme cruelty and recognized as a bandit by all participating sides.

21 The 1st Cavalry Army was the famous Red Army cavalry formation. It was also known as Budyonny's Cavalry Army. When the Russian Civil War broke out in 1918, a soldier named Semyon Buyonny organized a small cavalry force out of local Cossacks in the Don region. The force grew rapidly in numbers, sided with the Bolsheviks, and eventually became the 1st Cavalry Army. It was transformed from a guerrilla force into a proper military unit under the command of Semyon Budyonny and the political guidance of Kliment Voroshilov.

22 SMERSH (Russian acronym for "Death to Spies") was the Counter-Intelligence Agency in the Soviet Army. SMERSH, in fact, was less concerned about counter-intelligence (well served by NKGB "Special Services") than about the loyalty of the Red Army's own servicemen and commanders.

Afficionados of the early Ian Fleming novels and James Bond films will recognize the Russian acronym SMERSH, the archenemy of 007 and the British Secret Service. In later films, SMERSH was replaced by SPECTRE, a global terrorist organization.

23   The Soviet Union was utterly unprepared for the defense of the country against the German invasion. Stalin refused to pay any attention to the multiple (over 30) warnings coming from the operatives of the Comintern (NKVD: International Affairs Security, spies of the Communist International) and from INU (Foreign Intelligence Directorate of Soviet State Security, NKGB) in Germany and Europe, and even from Roosevelt and Churchill. All those who warned the Soviet Union of Hitler's plans to attack ended up arrested and shot by the NKVD or the Gestapo. The Soviet Union, despite an international prohibition against arming Germany, was supplying Germany with raw materials and military hardware (aircraft, ships, tanks, artillery, and ammunition) in order to help Germany escalate the war in Europe. Meanwhile, for a decade before the war, the Soviet Union was secretly training German military pilots and officers in order to enable Germany to damage Europe as much as possible. According to Victor Rezun (pen name Victor Suvorov), a Soviet defector from GRU, in his book *Day-M* (London: Hamish Hamilton, 1990), the reason for the incomprehensible confusion of the Soviet leadership during the first two weeks of the war was that they never considered the defense of the USSR. Since all their efforts were directed towards their own secret European invasion plan, prepared by Stalin and his senior generals, to be launched on July 6, 1941, they were oblivious to German intentions. Stalin and his lieutenants dedicated all efforts and resources of the nation to their own delusional plan to invade Europe. Hitler learned of Stalin's plans from German intelligence, which reported that the entire might of the

Soviet military was massed on the European border of the Soviet Union without any provisions for defense, only for attack. This information forced Hitler to make a pre-emptive attack on the Soviet Union two weeks prior to the planned Soviet invasion of Europe. This was much earlier than the date forecast in Hitler's strategic plans. The German army was already involved in fighting the war on two fronts; a third front was a classic masterpiece in self-destruction, but Hitler was panicked by the news about Soviet aggression planned for July 6[th,] 1941. Ultimately, it came down to a question of who first. Despite standard military knowledge that the simultaneous opening of a third front is a suicidal strategy, Hitler decided to attack the Soviet Union on June 21, 1941. German forces were already thinly spread, but Hitler felt he had no option but to pre-empt Stalin's own invasion plans and to invade the Soviet Union.

It was Stalin's plan, first to win a war against Germany, then to become the liberator of a weakened Europe. After "liberating" Europe, his troops would not leave until he had assured their Soviet satellite status (as was done in Eastern Europe). Stalin's obsession with world domination rendered him delusional. Like Genghis Khan, who set wild fires behind his troops to drive them to victory, Stalin rejected all strategies for the defense of the Soviet Union to conquer the whole of Europe and later to proceed on to Asia and America. When German forces attacked Ukraine from Poland on June 22, 1941, on three different fronts, they benefited from open access to the major transportation infrastructure prepared by Stalin for his own planned aggression against Europe.

24   Anne Applebaum. *Gulag, a History*, New York: Anchor Books (Random House), 2004, 557.

25 http://www.port.odessa.ua/index.php/en/history/development-stages

26   According to Soviet historians Mikhail Heller and
Alexandr Nekrich:

"Soviet foreign policy failures in Korea, Berlin, and
Yugoslavia, and domestic economic difficulties led
Stalin to reapply an already tested method for combating
the growing discontent among the population: whipping
up national hysteria, especially anti-Semitism. Anti-
Semitism had increased in the USSR, mainly in the
southern regions, under the impact of Soviet-Nazi
friendship in 1939-1941 and during the Nazi occupation.
Stalin's anti-Semitism was also intensified by U.S.-
Soviet antagonism and U.S. support for the Jewish
victims of Genocide and the Zionists who were
establishing the state of Israel. (Israel had refused to
become a Soviet satellite as Stalin was hoping)."

Utopia in Power: The History of the Soviet Union from
1917 to the Present, New York: Summit Books, 1986,
501.

27   Anne Applebaum. *Gulag, a History*. Op. cit., 420-444.

28   Minority nationalities deported to the extreme northern
remote areas of the Soviet Union, included: Italians,
Greeks, Turks, Kurds, Germans, English, Romanians,
Poles, Hungarians, Tartars, Kalmyks, Armenians,
Karelians, Iranians, Azerbaijanis, Afghans, Chechens,
Ingush, Koreans, Chinese, Finns, Lithuanians, Latvians,
Estonians, and Khazars.

29   Solomon Mikhoels, Yiddish actor, director of the
Moscow State Yiddish Theater, and chair of the Soviet
"Jewish Anti-Fascist Committee". He was assassinated
on orders of Stalin.

30   The Jewish Anti-fascist Committee (JAC) was formed
on Stalin's orders in April 1942, with the official
support of the Soviet authorities. Its objective was to
influence international public opinion and organize

political and financial support for the Soviet Union, particularly from the West. In 1952, after this Committee accomplished a successful large fundraising, members were arrested on trumped-up spying charges, tortured, and executed by firing squad after a secret mock trial. They were officially rehabilitated (exonerated) in 1988.

31   On December 1, 1952, Stalin made an announcement at the Politburo meeting:

"Every Jew in the Soviet Union is a nationalist and the agent of American Secret Services. Jewish nationalists - and they are all nationalists - think that the Jewish nation is being helped by the USA. This is why they consider that it is their obligation to assist the American imperialists." And then he added: "There are too many Jewish nationalists in medical, scientific and cultural fields."

Quoted in the Russian language weekly newspaper *New Russian Word*, May 7, 1993; also, excerpts from *"Notes of the Meeting of the Politburo"* on December 1, 1952, from the diaries of Stalin's minister V.A. Malishev, were published by The Moscow daily newspaper *Nezavisimaya Gazeta* of September 29, 1999. Essentially, Malishev recorded the same words as Stalin at that meeting.

32   Doctor Victor Kogan-Yasny (Ukraine) was the first in the Soviet Union to treat diabetes with insulin.

33   On the plan to deport Soviet Jews, Alexander Yakovlev wrote:

"Stalin gave a commission in 1952 to A.N. Chesnokov, Chief Editor of the magazine *Philosophical Issues*, to write a theoretical justification for the need to deport the Jews. This theoretical work was published in one million copies under the title 'Why it is necessary to deport the entire Jewish population far from the Soviet industrial centers'. It was decommissioned and burned after Stalin's death. In this work, Chesnokov justified, from the point of view of Marxist-Leninist positions, the historical need and justification for the measures of deportation of Jews to be undertaken by the Communist Party and Stalin personally. Chesnokov 'proved' that the Jews, by their nature, are the enemies of the people and of socialism, according to the personal experience of Stalin and his friends who liquidated the opposition, who happened to be all Jewish, in the early 1920s and 30s. For his outstanding work, Chesnokov was given the special honor of becoming Chief Editor of *Kommunist* magazine and was elected into the Politburo at the 19th Communist Party conference in early October of 1952." *Like the Relics, Like the Holy Oil.* Moscow: Eurasia, 1996, 108.

34   http://www.sakharov-center.ru/asfcd/auth/?t=book&num=2010

35   Nikita Khrushchev, "Khrushchev Remembers". Moscow Weekly magazine *Ogonyok* 1990, #7, 263.

36   Utopia in Power: The History of the Soviet Union from 1917 to the Present, 501-506.

37   Alexander Solzhenitsyn. *Gulag Archipelago.*

38   Quote from Dr. Yakov Eizenshtat's testimony regarding KGB senior operative N. N. Poliakov, the secretary of the special committee reporting directly to Stalin about the preparations ordered by Stalin for the deportation of Soviet Jews:

"There was a plan to instigate pogroms nationwide. This plan began with 37 Moscow Jewish doctors and their families who were arrested, tortured, and indicted along with hundreds of other prominent Jewish intellectuals. All these Jews who were arrested were slated for execution by hanging in major cities across the Soviet Union. These executions were designed to spark violent mob attacks against Jews throughout the country."

See also: Andrei Sakharov, "Memoirs" in weekly magazine *Zname*, № 12, 1990, and P. Sudoplatov, *Special operations: Lubyanka and Kremlin, 1930-1950.* Moscow: Omega Press, 1998.

39   Svetlana Alliluyeva, *Only One Year*. London: Harper Collins, 1969, 135.

40   Nikita Khrushchev, "Memoirs". *Ogonyok* #7, 1990, Moscow.

41   Arkady Vaysberg, *From Hell to Paradise and Back*. Moscow: Olympia Press, 2003, 157-193.

42   Different authors, "File of medical doctors, forty years after", Archives of Andrei Sakharov Center website:

     http://www.sakharov-center.ru/projects/bases/gulag.html

43   Dr. Y.Y. Etinger (son of Dr. Y. Etinger, one of those Moscow doctors arrested and tortured to death) interviewed with Marshal Nikolay Bulganin in the 1970s. Bulganin was the Minister of Armed Forces and later the Prime Minister of the Soviet Union (1955-1958). He was with Stalin at his last drinking party the night he was paralyzed.

http://www.sakharov-center.ru/asfcd/auth/?t=book&num=2010

The interview was initially published in Moscow magazine *Novoe Vremia*, #2, 1993, 47-49, where Marshal Nikolay Bulganin testified that the rumors regarding mass deportations of Jews to the Far North and Far East corresponded to reality:

"All paperwork to that effect was ready;

Bulganin received orders from Stalin to provide all major Soviet cities with a sufficient number of military cattle trains to deport the entire Jewish population;

And at the same time, to organize train crashes and pogroms in various cities. (There was a history of deportee train crashes because the capacity of unheated barracks built in the Far East was sufficient for less than 50% of the deported.

Stalin, Malenkov, and Suslov were the main architects of this plan, but a larger group of other Soviet leaders was involved as well."

Bulganin refused to say who because they were still in power in the 1970s when the interview took place, and Bulganin said that he wanted to die a natural death without their help.

In 2001, the New York publisher "World" published a book *Impossible to Forget* authored by the Soviet historian Y.Y. Etinger (an orphan adopted by the famous physician Yakov Gilyarievich Etinger, who, in 1952, jointly with his wife and son, was imprisoned and tortured under the "Moscow Doctors Plot"). Etinger, the son, describes these events in detail. He was exonerated in 1954.

44   Alexander Yakovlev. *Like The Relics, Like The Holy Oil*, 108.

45   Utopia in Power: The History of the Soviet Union from 1917 to the Present, 504-506.

46   Soviet physicist, Academician Boris Ioffe. "Special Secret Mission" in *The New World, the World of Science,* #5, 1995. This publication is attached in Appendix 2.

47   Stalin's father, Vissarion Dzhugashvili, a South Ossetian descendant of slaves, was a morose and frightening

drinker. A man consumed by anger, he got drunk quickly. His mother, Keke (Catherine), also a descendant of slaves, was pretty with a light complexion and freckles. She was religious, literate, and loved music. Joseph (Stalin), their fourth and only surviving child, had a striking resemblance to his father: dark and lean with a low brow and morose character. Vissarion spent their meager income on alcohol, and when drunk, he mercilessly beat his son and his wife. As a result, little Joseph suffered physical and emotional scars. His confidence was not helped by his physical deficiencies: he was short in stature, quite dark in complexion, his left foot was webbed, and his left arm was shorter than the right arm and stiffened at the elbow as the result of a youthful accident and reconstructive surgery; his face was covered with deep pockmarks from childhood smallpox.

According to the author Edward Radzinsky in his biography of *Stalin* (New York: Random House, 1997), based on new documents from Russia's secret archives, both mother and son used to take refuge with neighbors from Vissarion's rages. After Vissarion abandoned them, Keke, with the help of her local Jewish friend and neighbor Nana Moshiashvili, found jobs as a laundress and maid with local Jewish merchant families in town. These work assignments helped her and her son to survive. Nana described the toll taken on the young Joseph as a result of this impoverished and brutal lifestyle:

"His harsh home life left him embittered. He was an embittered, insolent, rude, and stubborn child with an intolerable character. His mother was head of the family now, and the fist that had subdued his father was now applied to the upbringing of their son. She beat him unmercifully for disobedience."

Another author, Roman Brackman, describes in *The Secret File of Joseph Stalin: a Hidden Life* (London, Frank Cass, 2001) how young Joseph took revenge on his father by testifying against him in court on a charge of abuse. As a result, his father was imprisoned for 10 years. However, this punishment was not sufficient for Joseph, and when he met his father again, after his release from prison, he was filled with hatred, disgust, guilt, and fear, which he could not sustain. He arranged for the assassination of his father by his friend, code-named Kamo (real name, Simon Ter-Petrosian), who murdered him with an axe in March of 1906.

Stalin's revenge against his father set the stage for a lifetime of murderous persecutions where he was the victim, and **everyone else was the criminal. This reversal of roles or** distortion of reality is a standard defense mechanism (psychotic in Stalin's case), an unconscious psychological strategy to protect himself from his own shame and guilt. He began to employ his pathological methods professionally by providing services to *Ochrana* (Russian Tsarist Secret police) for over 14 years as an agent provocateur. He spent the rest of his life shielding his reputation from scandal.

N. Kipshidze, a doctor who treated Keke, Stalin's mother, in her old age, described the exchange between her and her son during his only visit before her death:

"Why did you beat me so hard?" he asked his mother.

"That's why you turned out so well," Keke answered.

"And Joseph - who exactly are you now?" his mother asked him.

"Remember the tsar? Well, I'm like a tsar."

To which she said something so naive that the whole country laughed heartily:

"You'd have done better to have become a priest."

To the end of his days, Joseph went on naively settling accounts with his poverty-stricken childhood. It was then, in his childhood, that his beloved mother's humiliation, their everlasting hunger, their poverty, sowed hatred and resentment in the morbidly touchy boy's mind. Hatred above all for them - those rich Jewish traders. Joseph's feelings were reinforced by jealousy and resentment."

http://www.washingtonpost.com/wp-srv/style/longterm/books/chap1/stalin.htm

48   Anastas Mikoyan, Foreign Affairs Minister and the President of the Supreme Soviet, *Так Было* (*How it was*). Moscow: Vagrius, 1999, page 536.

49   *Oif a meisseh fregt kain kasheh nit* (Don't ask questions about fairy tales) is a Yiddish proverb.

50   SALT 1 is the common abbreviation for the "Strategic Arms Limitation Talks Agreement". The first series of Strategic Arms Limitation Talks extended from November 1969 to May 1972. During that period, the United States and the Soviet Union negotiated the first agreements to place limits and restraints on some of their central and most important nuclear armaments. In a "Treaty on the Limitation of Anti-Ballistic Missile Systems", they moved to end an emerging competition in defensive systems that threatened to spur offensive competition to still greater heights. In an "Interim Agreement on Certain Measures With Respect to the Limitation of Strategic Offensive Arms", the two nations took the first steps to check the rivalry in their most powerful land- and submarine-based offensive nuclear weapons.

51   Honey Pot or Honey Trap are terms the intelligence services employ when sexual entrapment is used as a

tool to obtain confidential information or recruit a foreign official. Seduction is a classic technique; "swallow" was the KGB tradecraft term for women and "raven" the term for men, both trained to seduce intelligence targets.

52   Lyrics from a popular WW2 Odessan song: *You are the Odessan Mishka* about having to abandon Odessa.

53   Protocol #50 of 2/09/1920 of The Organizing Bureau of the Central Committee of the Russian Communist Party, Archives of KGB, USSR, Fond 1, v 4, art. #82.

54   http://www.armymuseum.ru/archiv-russkoy-imperatorskoy-armii-i-revoliutsii-1917-g

55   Mikhail Heller and Alexandr Nekrich. Utopia in Power: The History of the Soviet Union from 1917 to the Present.

56   Roman Brackman. *The Secret File of Josef Stalin: A Hidden Life*. London: Frank Cass, 2001.

57   *Noit brecht eizen* (Necessity breaks iron): a Jewish proverb.

58   Pavlik Morozov was adopted as a patron child saint by the Young Pioneers. His life exemplified the duty of all good Soviet citizens to become informers, even at the expense of family ties. His story was a fabrication of Soviet propaganda aimed at converting children into fanatical instruments of state security.

59   After the Velvet Revolution in 1989, Prague International Airport was named after Franz Kafka. In 2012, it was renamed after Václav Havel. Both are writers who did much to raise the international cultural profile of Czechoslovakia.

60 Charles J. Halperin. "Soviet Historiography on Russia and the Mongols," Russian Review 41, no.3 (1982), 306-322.

61 Permission was granted to Soviet Jews who could legally demonstrate the evidence of having direct family in Israel and could present a legal invitation from their family relatives. However, the majority of Soviet Jewish applications to immigrate to Israel (repatriate on grounds of reunification of family) were turned down, especially for those with a higher education or responsible jobs. They were refused permission to leave by OVIR (the MVD department responsible for the provisioning of exit visas).

A typical excuse offered was that the applicants, who had been given access at some point in their careers to information vital to Soviet national security, could not be allowed to leave the country. My family did not have anybody in Israel, and most importantly, neither they nor I had any chance to get permission to exit on the pretext that we had access to information vital to Soviet national security, as well as the presumably high costs of our higher education. Those who applied to emigrate but were refused by OVIR were harassed and persecuted. They were fired from their jobs and refused any possibility to work again. Those who were not working, not only starved, but also were liable for arrest as *tuneyatsi* - people who don't work. Once arrested, they received hard labor sentences in forced labor camps for *treason*. After completing these hard labor sentences, they could forget about applying for permission to emigrate because now they had a criminal record for being *tuneyatsi*.

These people were called *refusniks* (somebody who was turned down). This situation was eased in 1972 when the government imposed the so-called "diploma tax" for would-be emigrants who received their higher education in the USSR. In some cases, the fee was as high as twenty annual salaries. This measure was apparently designed to combat the brain drain caused by the growing emigration of Soviet Jews and other members of the intelligentsia to the West. Still, my parents and I, even if we had so much money to pay, which we did not, would not be permitted to exit because of the issue of "access to sensitive state information at any point of time".

62   Political asylum came under Article 14 of the United Nations Universal Declaration of Human Rights: "Everyone has the right to seek and to enjoy in other countries asylum from persecution." The United Nations 1951 Convention Relating to the Status of Refugees and the 1967 Protocol relating to the Status of Refugees guide national legislation concerning political asylum. Under these agreements, a refugee is a person who is outside his or her own country's territory (or place of habitual residence if stateless) owing to fear of persecution on protected grounds. Protected grounds include race, nationality, religion, political opinions, and membership and/or participation in any particular social group or social activities. Canada was a signatory to the 1967 Protocol.

63   Canadian Security Intelligence Services were under the RCMP (Royal Canadian Mounted Police) until 1984, when the Government of Canada passed an Act of Parliament for the creation of a separate civilian security intelligence service. This legislation not only gave birth to CSIS (Canadian Security Intelligence Service), but it also clarified the differences between security intelligence activities and law enforcement work, bringing to an end the 120-year interlocking of Canada's security intelligence service with the federal police force (RCMP).

64   Alexander Zinoviev. *Homo Sovieticus*. London: Paladin Grafton Books, 1986, 62.

65   Dr. Vladislav Krasnov. *Soviet Defectors: The KGB Wanted List*. Stanford, California: Hoover Institution Press, Stanford University, 1985.

66   *Soviet Defectors: The KGB Wanted List*. 164.

67   *Di zun sheint lichtiker noch a regen* (The sun shines brighter after a shower): an old Yiddish Proverb.

68   http://history.state.gov/milestones/1969-1976/Detente

Even the understanding of this term "détente" is different in English and in Russian. In the West, it is understood as "a relaxation of tensions", but in *the Soviet Short Political Dictionary,* it states that *razryadka* (détente) "is the steady strengthening of the position of the countries of the socialist camp and a defeat for the imperialist forces.*"* This translates, according to communist ideology, into: "agreement is a method for gathering forces". Actually, Brezhnev declared to the Soviet public that he hoped that détente would help solve the economic bottlenecks in the Soviet economy through trade and American investment. However, the reality was that the Soviet economy was not producing because it was infested with incompetence, corruption, and enormous waste as a result of covering the costs of international colonial interventions that often soured. Conflict with China on the Soviet side and the Vietnam War on the American side contributed to a political desire on both sides to take a respite from the Cold War.

The American administration, in pursuit of détente with the Soviets failed to understand how Soviet motives for détente were conditioned by a series of crises on many levels in the Soviet Union: in economy, ideology, and politics. From 1966 to 1968, when over a million surviving prisoners were released from the Gulag camps, the Soviet Union lost not only its nearly free labor force but also simultaneously bankrupted its ideological grip over the general population. Only when the surviving million *zecks* (prisoners in the Gulag) flooded the country and surreptitiously told their stories, did the rumors about the nation's brutality against its citizens become substantiated. Millions of innocent people were kidnapped and tortured by the state while the lives of their families and relatives were crippled, only to fulfill slave labor quotas for the purpose of "pyramid-building" rather than for the nation's economic welfare. The prisoner release resulted in a moral collapse among the general population, a collapse that was unacknowledged but widely experienced even when it was unseen and unspoken. Though ordinary people were well aware that it would be suicidal to criticize these state crimes publicly, or to attempt to rectify injustices, or to try to change the system, nevertheless, during the 1960s, the majority of the Soviet population turned into cynics, conformists, and pragmatists. They were not enthusiastic producers for the economy. The emergence of small dissident groups or human rights movements resulted in the KGB launching a new nationwide terror campaign against dissent with the same Gulag consequences as before, in addition to a new use of mental institutions as repressive punishment and torture prisons.

69   The American and Soviet administrations were deeply engaged in the politics of détente during the decade following the late 1960s. In 1968, the Non-Proliferation Treaty was signed. In 1971, a treaty prohibiting the installation of any kind of weapons of mass destruction on the ocean floor was signed; followed by a signed agreement, later in 1972, between the United States and the Soviet Union on strategic arms limitations.

70   The final report of the McDonald Commission (Inquiry into certain activities of the Royal Canadian Mounted Police) issued in 1981, indicated that there had been 20

cases of persons charged with espionage offences under the Official Secrets Act and that 42 diplomats had been expelled from the country for espionage-related activities since 1945.

http://www.thecanadianencyclopedia.com/articles/intelligence-and-espionage

71   *Soviet Defectors*, 152.

      Ibid, 154.

73   Since the late 1960s, it was suspected that there was a Soviet infiltrator in the ranks of Canadian intelligence. Suspicion fell initially upon the Canadian ambassador in Moscow, Leslie James Bennett, but in the 1980s, it was discovered that the mole had actually been Sergeant Gilles Brunet, the son of an RCMP deputy commissioner.

74   Alexander Nikolaevich Yakovlev, Soviet politician, historian, and diplomat, was the spiritual and intellectual architect behind Glasnost and Perestroika. He had been a long-time member of the Politburo and the Secretariat of the Communist Party of the USSR. He was Head of the Department of Ideology and Propaganda, from where he was ousted for his published criticism of Russian chauvinism and anti-Semitism. Subsequently, he was appointed for a decade as Soviet Ambassador to Canada. Yakovlev (dubbed by American journalist and author David Remnick as "Gorbachev's good angel") was befriended by Prime Minister Pierre Trudeau and became attracted to the virtues of democracy while in Canada. It was thanks to numerous low-key private meetings with Canadian Ukrainian farmers organized by Canada's Minister of Agriculture, Eugene Whalen, that Alexander Yakovlev became convinced of the need to reform the social-political-economic structure of the Soviet Union. He became Gorbachev's principal mentor on reforming the country. The bond between these two

men was forged in Canada in 1983 when Yakovlev was
Soviet Ambassador to Ottawa and Gorbachev was
visiting Canada as the Soviet Minister of Agriculture.
(See Christopher Shulgan, *The Soviet Ambassador, The
Making of the Radical Behind Perestroika.* Toronto:
McClelland and Stewart, 2009).

75   For a brief history of the exodus of Jews from the Soviet
Union, see the link:
http://en.wikipedia.org/wiki/HIAS#The_Soviet_Jewry_Exodu
s

76   The *Oprichniki* were the members of an organization
responsible for the torture and murder of internal
enemies of the Russian Tsar Ivan IV (Ivan the Terrible).
Notorious for their violent means of enforcement, they
could be compared to modern "death squads" or secret
police. Guided by Tsar Ivan, they devastated civilian
populations.

77   The understanding of 1962 between Nikita Khrushchev
and John Kennedy differed significantly between its
published Western and Soviet versions:

WESTERN VERSION: The Soviets promised to dismantle,
remove, and not to install all Soviet offensive weapons
in Cuba again in exchange for a US public declaration
and agreement never to invade Cuba. The US also
agreed (secretly, to save face) to dismantle all US-built
Jupiter IRBMs (Intermediate-range ballistic missiles),
deployed in Turkey and Italy, which it did. Both sides
declared that they complied.

SOVIET VERSION: Fidel Castro made an ultimatum to the
US Government, demanding the fulfillment of a non-
invasion promise and the removal of the Guantanamo
US base in Cuba, dismantling of all US-built Jupiter
IRBMs deployed in Turkey and Italy, or the US would
face Soviet military might in their own backyard. John
Kennedy got terrified and promised to comply. Yet, he

has not removed the Guantanamo base from the island as he promised, and, therefore, Americans can never be trusted.

78   Treaty on the Prohibition of Nuclear Weapons in Latin America and Caribbean States (the Treaty of Tlatelolco) obligates Latin American parties not to acquire or possess nuclear weapons, nor to permit the storage or deployment of nuclear weapons on their territories by other countries. On February 14, 1967, the Treaty was signed at a regional meeting of Latin American countries at Tlatelolco, a district in Mexico City, by 33 Latin American countries. Cuba asserted support for the principle since 1962 but stipulated conditions: that Puerto Rico and the Panama Canal Zone be included in the Treaty, and that foreign military bases, especially Guantanamo Naval Base, be eliminated. Finally, Cuba ratified the Treaty in 2002.

http://2001-2009.state.gov/t/ac/trt/4796.htm#signatory

79   Treaty on Prohibition of Nuclear Weapons on the Seabed, signed February 11, 1971, between USSR and USA.

80   Strategic ballistic means that it affects the larger war context, such as destroying a city to prevent the production of military equipment for the entire war, and not just a single battle. Strategic weapons are larger missiles, either on submarines or air-launched. A strategic weapon could also be used for a tactical purpose and vice versa. The tactical ballistic missiles are those for short-range use (typically, less than 300 kilometers).

81   Russian Sources:

•   Vadim Truchachev. "Russia will restore its foreign navy bases", published in the newspaper *Pravda* on January 24, 2009.

Paulina Zelitsky, Paul Weinzweig

http://www.pravda.ru/world/asia/middleeast/24-01-2009/299641-navy-0/

- Sergey Telegin. "Cuba that we are losing" published in the newspaper *Soviet Rossya* of 27.12.2001
  http://cubafriend.narod.ru/bibleo/telegin.htm

- *Krasnaya Zvezda* of : 20.07.1969, 14.05.1970, 11.09.1970, 06.02.1971, 23.05.1971, 21.10.71

- *Izvestia* of: 28.05.1970, 15.09.1970, 08.12.1970

- *Morskaya Gazeta*, attachment to *"Fleet"* of 01.07.1999, page 1.

- *Na Strazhe Zapoliaria* of 18.03.2000, page 2.

- Alexander Rozin. "Second Cuban Crisis", page 9 in *Autonomka:*http://avtonomka.org/vospominaniya/istorik-rozin-aleksandr-vladimirovich/412-vtoroy-kubinskiy-krizis.html

- S.S. Berezhnoy. "Nuclear submarines of BMF and Rossia", *Special Review 2001*.

- Sergey Brilev. "How many Caribbean crises were there?" in *Komsomolskaya Pravda*.

- Capitanets. "BMF After the War Period" published in the magazine *Navy Collection #2, 1994*.

- Vladimir Chozikov. "Assembly line for Submarine cruisers", *Shipbuilding #6 of 1997*.

- http://www.cnw.mk.ua/weapons/navy/submarin/667.htm

- Yury Apalkov. Submarines of Soviet Fleet of 1945-1991, Morkniga, 2011.

82   Christopher Whelan. "The Soviet Military Buildup In Cuba", *Heritage Foundation Backgrounder*, Washington, Issue 189, page 10.

83   Extract from Letter Of Nikita Khrushchev to Fidel
           Castro of Oct. 30, 1962.

           http://www.marxists.org/espanol/khrushchev/1962/oct/30.htm

           "If, by yielding to popular sentiments, we had allowed
           ourselves to be drawn into the most inflamed among the
           populace, and if we had refused to reach a reasonable
           agreement with the US Government, war would have
           broken out that would have resulted in millions of
           deaths. The survivors would blame the leaders for not
           taking measures to prevent this war of extermination.
           The prevention of war and an attack on Cuba depended
           not only on the actions taken by our government, but
           also upon the analysis and review of the actions of the
           enemy near their territory".

84   *Nomenklatura,* in Soviet political terminology, meant
           the special list of those who were trusted, not for
           professional qualifications, but for political obedience.
           These individuals were nominated for all the important
           positions within the government, as well as in the
           economy, in science, and in the arts. Soviet
           Nomenklatura (Soviet true ruling class) enjoyed many
           perks and privileges and helped themselves liberally to
           the national resources, which they controlled and
           appropriated.

85   Russian *Vanka-Vstanka* is a traditional Russian
           handcrafted egg-shaped bouncing doll (roly-poly) that
           contains heavy material inside its wooden cavity, which
           allows the doll to always bounce back to its original
           position under gravity, despite all attempts to incline the
           doll by force.

86   See Endnote 10.

87   Sevmorgeo Northern Marine Geology Research and
           AARI (Arctic Antarctic Research Institute). Both R&D

institutions were traditionally engaged in Arctic development.

88   Recent official Russian media reports related to the revival of Russian military bases:

- http://fognews.ru/putin-rossiya-vozvrashhaetsya-na-kubu.html

- Vadim Truchachev. "Russia will restore its foreign navy bases", published in the newspaper *Pravda* on January 24, 2009.

  http://www.pravda.ru/world/asia/middleeast/24-01-2009/299641-navy-0/

- http://topwar.ru/27392-set-zarubezhnyh-baz-vmf-sssr.html

- Vitaly Ankov. "Russian Navy to get over 50 new warships and nuclear submarines in 2016", *Rianonovosti* of 03-01-2013
  http://en.ria.ru/military_news/20130103/178558846/Russian_Navy_to_Get_Over_50_New.html

- http://ria.ru/defense_safety/20130420/933664053-print.html

- http://rutube.ru/video/7a42242232e46408a14c18789743aa2d/

- Tomas Niesen. "More nukes in Kola", *Berentobserver* of January 11, 2013
  http://barentsobserver.com/ru/bezopasnost/2013/01/novoe-yadernoe-vooruzhenie-na-kolskom-poluostrove-10-01

- Oleg Vorobiov. "Russia will build new airport in Cuba", published in the newspaper *Izvestia* on April 15, 2013, http://izvestia.ru/news/548619

- http://www.amic.ru/news/215563/

- "Russian Chief of Staff reviews the Cuban weapons", *Martinoticias*, April 19, 2013
  http://www.martinoticias.com/content/general-gerasimov-cuba-visita-oficial-/21703.html

- "Chief of Staff arrived in Cuba for working visit", *RIA NOVOSTI*, April 19, 2013
  http://ria.ru/defense_safety/20130419/933440157.html

- Luba Lulko. "Russia will restore its military bases", *Pravda*, July 30, 2012

- http://www.pravda.ru/world/30-07-2012/1123320-military_base-0/

- http://www.agentura.ru/dossier/russia/people/soldatov/lourdes/

- http://www.pseudology.org/razbory/Na_dne.html

- http://blogs.fas.org/security/2013/05/russianssbns/

- http://www.warandpeace.ru/ru/exclusive/view/74611/

  - http://fognews.ru/putin-rossiya-vozvrashhaetsya-na-kubu.html

  - http://www.youtube.com/watch?v=1oW4ObwDUwshttp://www.youtube.com/watch?v=hRTqulvVcXl

  - http://www.globalresearch.ca/russias-s-300-surface-to-air-missile-already-deployed-and-functional-in-syria-the-ordnance-bothering-the-allies/5336882

[2] Chicken Little is a folk tale with a moral about the deadly consequences of illusory fear and the failure of courage. The story is about a chicken who believes, hysterically, that the world is ending. The chicken's mistaken belief in an impending disaster is expressed in its repeated cries that the "The sky is falling!"

[3] *Gallego* is a colloquial Cuban reference to someone obsessed with his Spanish ancestry.

4   Lyrics and music by Annie Lennox and Dave Stewart.

5   *Hispanidad* refers to the presumed cultural and economic alliance among all Spanish-speaking countries.

6   *Niños* is the name given to over 3000 Spanish children who were evacuated to the Soviet Union during the Spanish civil war. As young men, they became cadets at Soviet military schools. One of the special schools was situated in the town of Ivanovo and was known as the E. D. Stasova International School. Some graduates of this school later turned up as Fidel Castro's personal bodyguards, and some became leading figures in the Cuban intelligence service - the most aggressive in the world, often exceeding its teachers in the Soviet security services in both cruelty and cunning. The GRU and KGB used some of the school's graduates as spies. However, the majority of the first generation of Spanish children remained in the Soviet Union with no possibility of leaving. The Soviet Government, for operations abroad, used the second generation of Spaniards. One of their tactics was to send some young Soviet Spaniards to Cuba, give them time to get used to the country and culture, and then send them to Africa and Central America as Cubans to fight against "American Imperialism".

7   Michail Voslenski, *Nomenklatura*, MP October, Soviet Russia, 1991, 167-178.

8   Cubana's flights CU-T668, Havana-Prague-Moscow, were using four Bristol Britannia turboprops purchased in Britain. These aircraft had to be leased in 1962 to CSA Czechoslovakian Airlines to allow this route to be operated by CSA instead of Cubana. The main reason for this change of operators was the problem with Cuban

pilots who were defecting during the refueling stops in Gander. These East European transatlantic routes were very important for the Cuban Government since the majority of foreign recruits from Latin, and North American countries enrolled in Cuban international terrorist training, came to Cuba via Prague. Bristol Britannia turboprops did not have the fuel capacity to cover the Havana-Prague distance and had to be refueled in Gander, Newfoundland, Canada. On their way back from Prague to Havana, these flights made an additional refueling stop in Shannon, Ireland, about which I found out only later.

[9] Michail Voslenski, *Nomenklatura*, London, Overseas Publications Interchange Ltd., 1990, p.88.

[10] The NKVD Order № 00486 gave instructions about the repression of wives and children of enemies of the people. "Socially dangerous" children were to be placed in labor camps, corrective labor colonies, or special-regimen orphanages.

[11] *Haskalah* was a rational reform Jewish movement, inspired by the European Enlightenment and designed to integrate Jews into the larger society. It was created by the German Jewish philosopher Moses Mendelssohn in the mid-18th Century.

[12] Robert Weinberg. "The Pogrom of 1905 in Odessa: A Case Study" in *Pogroms: Anti-Jewish Violence in Modern Russian History*, John D. Klier and Shlomo Lambroza, editors. Cambridge University Press, 1992, 248-89.

[13] Hasidism began as a Jewish revivalist mystic movement in which charismatic spiritual leadership replaced legalistic doctrine. Hasidism was founded in 18th

Century Eastern Europe by a kabbalist named Israel Baal Shem Tov (1700-1760). Early on, it attracted a following among both uneducated and scholarly Jews in Eastern Europe and Ukraine. The emphases of the movement of encouragement, optimism, fervent prayer, kindness and good deeds filled spiritual needs among the common people and provided a creative outlet for their spiritual beliefs. Hasidism is extremely orthodox, requiring followers to adhere rigidly to every basic doctrine and principle in traditional Jewish belief and practice. Still, it retains a strong mystical element which emphasizes personal communion with God. Thus, mysticism is not an esoteric gift for a minority of ascetic Jews, but rather an integral part of the community of believers.

[14] Semyon Petliura was a publicist, writer, journalist, Ukrainian politician, statesman, and national leader who led Ukraine's struggle for independence following the Russian Revolution of 1917. During the period of Ukrainian independence, 1918-1920, he was head of the Ukrainian State.

[15] Nestor Makhno was a Ukrainian anarcho-communist revolutionary and a leader of a peasant independent anarchist army in Ukraine during the Russian Civil War.

[16] Anton Denikin, a Russian general who led the anti-Bolshevik ("White") forces on the southern front during the Russian Civil War (1918–20).

[17] The Pale of Settlement was decreed by Tsarina Ekaterina II in 1791 as a territory in the Russian steppes (plains) where Russian Jews were permitted to reside. Even within the Pale, Jews were prohibited from leasing or owning land or operating taverns. They were denied access to middle or higher education, but they had to pay

double tax and serve in the Russian army from the age of 12. Those who were drafted into the army never returned to their families. Only after the overthrow of the Czarist regime in 1917, was the Pale of Settlement abolished.

[18] Ataman Struck from Chernobyl was a captain of the tsarist army who occasionally led the battalions of the Petliura army, and other times, the White Army of Denikin. He was infamous for extreme cruelty and recognized as a bandit by all participating sides.

[19] The 1st Cavalry Army was the famous Red Army cavalry formation. It was also known as Budyonny's Cavalry Army. When the Russian Civil War broke out in 1918, a soldier named Semyon Buyonny organized a small cavalry force out of local Cossacks in the Don region. The force grew rapidly in numbers, sided with the Bolsheviks, and eventually became the 1st Cavalry Army. It was transformed from a guerrilla force into a proper military unit under the command of Semyon Budyonny and the political guidance of Kliment Voroshilov.

[20] Kaddish is a traditional Jewish prayer for the dead.

[21] SMERSH (Russian acronym for "Death to Spies") was the Counter-Intelligence Agency in the Soviet Army. SMERSH, in fact, was less concerned about counter-intelligence (well served by NKGB "Special Services"), than about the loyalty of the Red Army's own servicemen and commanders.

Aficionados of the early Ian Fleming novels and James Bond films will recognize the Russian acronym SMERSH, the archenemy of 007 and the British Secret

Service. In later films, SMERSH was replaced by
SPECTRE, a global terrorist organization.

22 The Soviet Union was utterly unprepared for the defense
of the country against the German invasion. Stalin
refused to pay any attention to the multiple (over 30)
warnings coming from the operatives of the Comintern
(NKVD: International Affairs Security, spies of the
Communist International) and INU (Foreign Intelligence
Directorate of Soviet State Security, NKGB) in
Germany and Europe and even from Roosevelt and
Churchill. All those who warned the Soviet Union of
Hitler's plans to attack ended up arrested and shot by the
NKVD or the Gestapo. The Soviet Union, despite an
international prohibition against arming Germany, was
supplying Germany with raw materials and military
hardware (aircraft, ships, tanks, artillery, and
ammunition) to help Germany escalate the war in
Europe. Meanwhile, for a decade before the war, the
Soviet Union was secretly training German military
pilots and officers to enable Germany to damage Europe
as much as possible. According to Victor Rezun (pen
name Victor Suvorov), a Soviet defector from GRU, in
his book *Day-M* (London: Hamish Hamilton, 1990), the
reason for the incomprehensible confusion of the Soviet
leadership during the first two weeks of the war, was
that they never considered the defense of the USSR.
Since all their efforts were directed towards their own
secret European invasion plan, prepared by Stalin and
his senior generals, to be launched on July 6 of 1941,
they were oblivious to German intentions. Stalin and his
lieutenants dedicated all efforts and resources of the
nation to their own delusional plan to invade Europe.
Hitler learned of Stalin's plans from German
intelligence, which reported that the entire might of the
Soviet military was massed on the European border of

the Soviet Union without any provisions for defense, only for attack. This information forced Hitler to make a pre-emptive attack on the Soviet Union two weeks before the planned Soviet invasion of Europe. This was much earlier than the date forecast in Hitler's strategic plans. The German army was already involved in fighting the war on two fronts; a third front was a classic masterpiece in self-destruction, but Hitler was panicked by the news about Soviet aggression planned for July 6[th,] 1941. Ultimately, it came down to a question of who first. Despite the standard military knowledge that the simultaneous opening of a third front is a suicidal strategy, Hitler decided to attack the Soviet Union on June 21, 1941. German forces were already thinly spread, but Hitler felt he had no option but to pre-empt Stalin's own invasion plans and to invade the Soviet Union.

It was Stalin's plan, first to win a war against Germany, then to become the liberator of a weakened Europe. After "liberating" Europe, his troops would not leave until he had assured their Soviet satellite status (as was done in Eastern Europe). Stalin's obsession with world domination rendered him delusional. Like Genghis Khan, who set wild fires behind his troops to drive them to victory, Stalin rejected all strategies for the defense of the Soviet Union to conquer initially the whole of Europe and later to proceed on to Asia and America. When German forces attacked Ukraine from Poland on June 22, 1941, on three different fronts, they benefited from open access to the major transportation infrastructure prepared by Stalin for his own planned aggression against Europe.

[23] Anne Applebaum. *Gulag, a History*, New York: Anchor Books (Random House), 2004, 557.

24   http://www.port.odessa.ua/index.php/en/history/development-stages

25   Solomon Mikhoels, Yiddish actor, director of the Moscow State Yiddish Theater, and chair of the Soviet "Jewish Anti-Fascist Committee". He was assassinated on orders of Stalin.

26   The Jewish Anti-fascist Committee (JAC) was formed on Stalin's orders in April 1942, with the official support of the Soviet authorities. Its objective was to influence international public opinion and organize political and financial support for the Soviet Union, particularly from the West. In 1952, after this Committee accomplished successful large fundraising, members were arrested on trumped-up spying charges, tortured, and executed by firing squad after a secret mock trial. They were officially rehabilitated (exonerated) in 1988.

27   On December 1, 1952, Stalin announced at the Politburo meeting:

      "Every Jew in the Soviet Union is a nationalist and the agent of American Secret Services. Jewish nationalists - and they are all nationalists - think that the Jewish nation is being helped by the USA. This is why they consider that it is their obligation to assist the American imperialists." And then he added: "There are too many Jew-nationalists in medical, scientific and cultural fields."

      Quoted in the Russian language weekly newspaper *New Russian Word*, May 7, 1993; also, excerpts from "Notes of the Meeting of the Politburo" on December 1, 1952, from the diaries of Stalin's minister V.A. Malishev, were published by The Moscow daily newspaper

Nezavisimaya Gazeta of September 29, 1999.
Essentially, Malishev recorded the same words as Stalin at that meeting.

28   Dr. Y.Y. Etinger (son of Dr. Y. Etinger, one of those Moscow doctors arrested and tortured to death) interview with Marshal Nikolay Bulganin in the 1970s. Bulganin was the Minister of Armed Forces and later the Prime Minister of the Soviet Union (1955-1958). He was with Stalin at his last drinking party the night he was paralyzed.

http://www.sakharov-center.ru/asfcd/auth/?t=book&num=2010 The interview was initially published in Moscow magazine *Novoe Vremia*, #2, 1993, 47-49) where Marshal Nikolay Bulganin testified that the rumors regarding mass deportations of Jews to the Far North and the Far East corresponded to reality:

"All paperwork to that effect was ready;

Bulganin received orders from Stalin to provide all major Soviet cities with a sufficient number of military cattle trains to deport the entire Jewish population;

And at the same time to organize train crashes and pogroms in various cities. (There was a history of deportee train crashes because the capacity of unheated barracks built in the Far East was sufficient for less than 50% of the deported).

Stalin, Malenkov, and Suslov were the main architects of this plan, but a larger group of other Soviet leaders was involved as well."

Bulganin refused to say who because they were still in power in the 1970s when the interview took place, and

Bulganin said that he wanted to die a natural death without their help.

In 2001, the New York publisher "World" published a book *Impossible to Forget* authored by the Soviet historian Y.Y. Etinger (an orphan adopted by the famous physician Yakov Gilyarievich Etinger who in 1952, jointly with his wife and son, were imprisoned and tortured under the "Moscow Doctors Plot"). Etinger, the son, describes these events in detail. He was exonerated in 1954.

[29]   Alexander Yakovlev. *Like The Relics, Like The Holy Oil*, 108.

[30]   Nikita Khrushchev, "Khrushchev Remembers". Moscow Weekly magazine *Ogonyok* 1990, #7, 263.

[31]   Utopia in Power: The History of the Soviet Union from 1917 to the Present, 501-506.

[32]   Doctor Victor Kogan-Yasny (Ukraine) was the first in the Soviet Union to treat diabetes with insulin.

[33]   On the plan to deport Soviet Jews, Alexander Yakovlev wrote:

"Stalin gave a commission in 1952 to A.N. Chesnokov, Chief Editor of the magazine *Philosophical Issues*, to write a theoretical justification for the need to deport the Jews. This theoretical work was published in one million copies under the title 'Why it is necessary to deport the entire Jewish population far from the Soviet industrial centers'. It was decommissioned and burned after Stalin's death. In this work, Chesnokov justified, from the point of view of Marxist-Leninist positions, the historical need and justification for the measures of deportation of Jews to be undertaken by the Communist

Party and Stalin personally. Chesnokov 'proved' that the Jews, by their nature, are the enemies of the people and of socialism, according to the personal experience of Stalin and his friends who liquidated the opposition - who happened to be all Jewish - in the early 1920s and 30s. For his outstanding work, Chesnokov was given the special honor of becoming Chief Editor of *Kommunist* magazine and was elected into the Politburo at the 19th Communist Party conference in early October of 1952." *Like the Relics, Like the Holy Oil.* Moscow: Eurasia, 1996, 108.

[34]   According to Soviet historians Mikhail Heller and Alexandr Nekrich:

"Soviet foreign policy failures in Korea, Berlin, and Yugoslavia and domestic economic difficulties led Stalin to reapply an already tested method for combating the growing discontent among the population: whipping up national hysteria, especially anti-Semitism. Anti-Semitism had increased in the USSR, mainly in the southern regions, under the impact of Soviet-Nazi friendship in 1939-1941 and during the Nazi occupation. Stalin's anti-Semitism was also intensified by U.S.-Soviet antagonism and U.S. support to the Jewish victims of Genocide and the Zionists who were establishing the state of Israel. (Israel had refused to become a Soviet satellite as Stalin was hoping)." Utopia in Power: The History of the Soviet Union from 1917 to the Present, New York: Summit Books, 1986, 501.

[35]   Anne Applebaum. *Gulag, a History*. Op. cit., 420-444.

[36]   Minority nationalities deported to the extreme northern remote areas of the Soviet Union, included: Italians, Greeks, Turks, Kurds, Germans, English, Romanians, Poles, Hungarians, Tartars, Kalmyks, Armenians,

Karelians, Iranians, Azerbaijanis, Afghans, Chechens, Ingush, Koreans, Chinese, Finns, Lithuanians, Latvians, Estonians and Khazars.

[37] Svetlana Alliluyeva, *Only One Year*. London: Harper Collins, 1969, 135.

[38] Nikita Khrushchev, "Memoirs". *Ogonyok #7*, 1990, Moscow.

[39] Arkady Vaysberg, *From Hell to Paradise and Back*. Moscow: Olympia Press, 2003, 157-193.

[40] Different authors, "File of medical doctors, forty years after", Archives of Andrei Sakharov Center website: http://www.sakharov-center.ru/projects/bases/gulag.html

[41] http://www.sakharov-center.ru/asfcd/auth/?t=book&num=2010

[42] Alexander Solzhenitsyn. *Gulag Archipelago*.

[43] Quote from Dr. Yakov Eizenshtat's testimony regarding KGB senior operative N. N. Poliakov, the secretary of the special committee reporting directly to Stalin about the preparations ordered by Stalin for deportation of Soviet Jews: "There was a plan to instigate pogroms nationwide. This plan began with 37 Moscow Jewish doctors and their families who were arrested, tortured, and indicted along with hundreds of other prominent Jewish intellectuals. All these Jews who were arrested were slated for execution by hanging in major cities across the Soviet Union. These executions were designed to spark violent mob attacks against Jews throughout the country." See also: Andrei Sakharov, "Memoirs" in weekly magazine *Zname*, № 12, 1990 and

P. Sudoplatov, *Special operations: Lubyanka and Kremlin, 1930-1950*. Moscow: Omega Press, 1998.

[44] Utopia in Power: The History of the Soviet Union from 1917 to the Present, 504-506.

[45] Soviet physicist Academician Boris Ioffe. "Special Secret Mission" in *The New World, the World of Science,* #5, 1995. This publication is attached in Appendix 2.

[46] Stalin's father Vissarion Dzhugashvili, a South Ossetian descendant of slaves, was a morose and frightening drinker. A man consumed by anger, he got drunk quickly. His mother Keke (Catherine), also a descendant of slaves, was pretty with a light complexion and freckles. She was religious, literate, and loved music. Joseph (Stalin), their fourth and only surviving child, had a striking resemblance to his father: dark and lean with a low brow and morose character. Vissarion spent their meager income on alcohol and when drunk, mercilessly beat his son and his wife. As a result, little Joseph suffered physical and emotional scars. His confidence was not helped by his physical deficiencies: he was short in stature, quite dark in complexion, his left foot was webbed, and his left arm was shorter than the right arm and stiffened at the elbow as the result of a youthful accident and reconstructive surgery; his face was covered with deep pockmarks from childhood smallpox.

According to the author Edward Radzinsky in his biography of *Stalin* (New York: Random House, 1997), based on new documents from Russia's secret archives, both mother and son used to take refuge with neighbors from Vissarion's rages. After Vissarion abandoned them, Keke with the help of her local Jewish friend and neighbor Nana Moshiashvili, found jobs as a laundress and maid with local Jewish merchant families in town. These work assignments helped her and her son to survive. Nana described the toll taken on the young Joseph as a result of this impoverished and brutal lifestyle:

"His harsh home life left him embittered. He was an embittered, insolent, rude, stubborn child with an intolerable character. His mother was head of the family now, and the fist which had subdued his father was now applied to the upbringing of their son. She beat him unmercifully for disobedience."

Another author, Roman Brackman, describes in *The Secret File of Joseph Stalin: a Hidden Life* (London, Frank Cass, 2001), how young Joseph took revenge on his father by testifying against him in court on a charge of abuse. As a result, his father was imprisoned for ten years. However, this punishment was not sufficient for Joseph, and when he met his father again, after his release from prison, he was filled with hatred, disgust, guilt, and fear which he could not sustain. He arranged for the assassination of his father by his friend, code-named Kamo (real name, Simon Ter-Petrosian), who murdered him with an ax in March of 1906.

Stalin's revenge against his father set the stage for a lifetime of murderous persecutions where he was the victim, and everyone else was the criminal. This reversal of roles or distortion of reality is a standard defense mechanism, (psychotic in Stalin's case), an unconscious psychological strategy to protect himself from his own shame and guilt. He began to employ his pathological methods professionally by providing services to *Ochrana* (Russian Tsarist Secret police) over 14 years as an agent provocateur. He spent the rest of his life shielding his reputation from scandal.

N. Kipshidze, a doctor who treated Keke, Stalin's mother, in her old age, described the exchange between her and her son during his only visit before her death:

"Why did you beat me so hard?" he asked his mother.

"That's why you turned out so well," Keke answered.

"And Joseph - who exactly are you now?" his mother asked him.

"Remember the tsar? Well, I'm like a Tsar."

To which she said something so naive that the whole country laughed heartily:

"You'd have done better to have become a priest."

To the end of his days, Joseph went on naively settling accounts with his poverty-stricken childhood. It was then, in his childhood, that his beloved mother's humiliation, their everlasting hunger, their poverty, sowed hatred and resentment in the morbidly touchy boy's mind. Hatred above all for them - those rich Jewish traders. Joseph's feelings were reinforced by jealousy and resentment."

http://www.washingtonpost.com/wp-srv/style/longterm/books/chap1/stalin.htm

[47] Anastas Mikoyan, Foreign Affairs Minister and The President of the Supreme Soviet, *Так Было* (*How it was*). Moscow: Vagrius, 1999, page 536.

[48] SALT 1 is the common abbreviation for the "Strategic Arms Limitation Talks Agreement". The first series of

Strategic Arms Limitation Talks extended from November 1969 to May 1972. During that period, the United States and the Soviet Union negotiated the first agreements to place limits and restraints on some of their central and most important nuclear armaments. In a "Treaty on the Limitation of Anti-Ballistic Missile Systems", they moved to end an emerging competition in defensive systems that threatened to spur offensive competition to still greater heights. In an "Interim Agreement on Certain Measures With Respect to the Limitation of Strategic Offensive Arms", the two nations took the first steps to check the rivalry in their most powerful land- and submarine-based offensive nuclear weapons.

[49] Honey Pot or Honey Trap are terms the intelligence services employ when sexual entrapment is used as a tool to obtain confidential information or recruit a foreign official. Seduction is a classic technique; "swallow" was the KGB tradecraft term for women and "raven" the term for men, both trained to seduce intelligence targets.

[50] Protocol #50 of 2/09/1920 of The Organizing Bureau of the Central Committee of the Russian Communist Party, Archives of KGB, USSR, Fond 1, v 4, art. #82.

[51] http://www.armymuseum.ru/archiv-russkoy-imperatorskoy-armii-i-revoliutsii-1917-g

[52] Mikhail Heller and Alexandr Nekrich. *Utopia in Power: The History of the Soviet Union from 1917 to the Present.*

[53] Roman Brackman. *The Secret File of Josef Stalin: A Hidden Life.* London: Frank Cass, 2001.

54   Pavlik Morozov was adopted as a patron child saint by the Young Pioneers. His life exemplified the duty of all good Soviet citizens to become informers, even at the expense of family ties. His story was a fabrication of Soviet propaganda aimed to convert children into fanatical instruments of state security.

55   After The Velvet Revolution in 1989, Prague International Airport was named after Franz Kafka. In 2012, it was renamed after Václav Havel. Both are writers who did much to raise the international cultural profile of Czechoslovakia.

56   Charles J. Halperin. "Soviet Historiography on Russia and the Mongols," **Russian Review** 41, no.3 (1982), 306-322.

57   Permission was granted to Soviet Jews who could legally demonstrate the evidence of having direct family in Israel and could present a legal invitation from their family relatives. However, the majority of Soviet Jewish applications to immigrate to Israel (repatriate on grounds of reunification of family) were turned down, especially for those with a higher education or responsible jobs. They were refused permission to leave by OVIR (the MVD department responsible for the provisioning of exit visas). A typical excuse offered was that the applicants, who had been given access at some point in their careers to information vital to Soviet national security, could not be allowed to leave the country. My family did not have anybody in Israel, and most importantly, neither they nor I had any chance to get permission to exit on the pretext that we had access to information vital to Soviet national security as well as the presumably large costs of our higher education. Those who applied to emigrate, but were refused by OVIR, were harassed and persecuted. They were fired

from their jobs and refused any possibility to work again. Those who were not working, not only starved, but also were liable for arrest as *tuneyatsi* - people who don't work. Once arrested, they received hard labor sentences in forced labor camps for *tuneyatsvo*. After completing these hard labor sentences, they could forget about applying for permission to emigrate because now they had a criminal record for being *tuneyatsi*. These people were called *refusniks* (somebody who was turned down). This situation was eased in 1972 when the government imposed the so-called "diploma tax" for would-be emigrants who received their higher education in the USSR. In some cases, the fee was as high as twenty annual salaries. This measure was apparently designed to combat the brain drain caused by the growing emigration of Soviet Jews and other members of the intelligentsia to the West. Still, my parents and I, even if we had so much money to pay, which we did not, would not be permitted to exit because of the issue of "the access to sensitive state information at any point of time".

[58] Political asylum came under Article 14 of the United Nations Universal Declaration of Human Rights: "Everyone has the right to seek and to enjoy in other countries asylum from persecution." The United Nations 1951 Convention Relating to the Status of refugees and the 1967 Protocol relating to the Status of Refugees guides national legislation concerning political asylum. Under these agreements, a refugee is a person who is outside his or her own country's territory (or place of habitual residence if stateless) owing to fear of persecution on protected grounds. Protected grounds include race, nationality, religion, political opinions and membership and/or participation in any particular social

group or social activities. Canada was a signatory to the 1967 Protocol.

59   Canadian Security Intelligence Services were under the RCMP (Royal Canadian Mounted Police) until 1984 when the Government of Canada passed an Act of Parliament for the creation of a separate civilian security intelligence service. This legislation not only gave birth to CSIS (Canadian Security Intelligence Service), it also clarified the differences between security intelligence activities and law enforcement work, bringing to an end the 120-year interlocking of Canada's security intelligence service with the federal police force (RCMP).

60   Alexander Zinoviev. *Homo Sovieticus*. London: Paladin Grafton Books, 1986, 62.

61   Dr. Vladislav Krasnov. *Soviet Defectors: The KGB Wanted List*. Stanford, California: Hoover Institution Press, Stanford University, 1986.

62   Dr. Vladislav Krasnov. *Soviet Defectors: The KGB Wanted List*. 164.

63   http://history.state.gov/milestones/1969-1976/Detente

Even the understanding of this term "détente" is different in English and in Russian. In the West, it is understood as "a relaxation of tensions", but in *the Soviet Short Political Dictionary,* it states that *razryadka* (détente) "is the steady strengthening of the position of the countries of the socialist camp and a defeat for the imperialist forces. "* This translates, according to communist ideology, into: "agreement is a method for gathering forces". Actually, Brezhnev declared to the Soviet public that he hoped that détente will help solve the economic bottlenecks in the Soviet economy through trade and American investment. However, the reality was that the Soviet economy was not producing because it was infested with incompetence, corruption, and enormous waste as a result of covering the costs of international colonial interventions which often soured. Conflict with China on the Soviet side and the Vietnam War on the American side contributed to a political desire on both sides to take a respite from the Cold War.

The American administration in pursuit of détente with the Soviets failed to understand how Soviet motives for détente were conditioned by a series of crises on many levels in the Soviet Union: in the economy, ideology, and politics. From 1966 to 1968, when over a million surviving prisoners were released from the Gulag camps, the Soviet Union lost not only its nearly free labor force but simultaneously bankrupted its ideological grip over the general population. Only when the surviving million *zeks* (prisoners in the Gulag) flooded the country and surreptitiously told their stories, did the rumors about the nation's brutality against its citizens become substantiated. Millions of innocent people were kidnapped and tortured by the state while the lives of their families and relatives were crippled, only to fulfill slave labor quotas for the purpose of "pyramid-building" rather than for the nation's economic welfare. The prisoner release resulted in a moral collapse among the general population, a collapse that was unacknowledged but widely experienced even when it was unseen and unspoken. Though ordinary people were well aware that it would be suicidal to criticize publicly these state crimes or to attempt to rectify injustices, or to try to change the system, nevertheless, during the 1960s, the majority of the Soviet population turned into cynics, conformists, and pragmatists. They were not enthusiastic producers for the economy. The emergence of small dissident groups or human rights movements resulted in the KGB launching a new nationwide terror campaign against dissent with the same Gulag consequences as before, in addition to a new use of mental institutions as repressive punishment and torture prisons.

64   The American and Soviet administrations were deeply engaged in the politics of détente during the decade following the late 1960s. In 1968, the Non-proliferation Treaty was signed. In 1971, a treaty prohibiting the installation of any kind of weapons of mass destruction on the ocean floor was signed; followed by a signed agreement, later in 1972, between the United States and the Soviet Union on strategic arms limitations.

65   The final report of the McDonald Commission (Inquiry into certain activities of the Royal Canadian Mounted Police) issued in 1981, indicated that there had been 20 cases of persons charged with espionage offenses under the Official Secrets Act and that 42 diplomats had been expelled from the country for espionage-related activities since 1945.

http://www.thecanadianencyclopedia.com/articles/intelligence -and-espionage

66   Dr.Vladislav Krasnov. *Soviet Defectors*, 152., Hoover Institution, Stanford University, 1986

67   Ibid, 154.

68   Since the late 1960s, it was suspected that there was a Soviet infiltrator in the ranks of Canadian intelligence. Suspicion fell initially upon the Canadian ambassador in Moscow, Leslie James Bennett; but in the 1980s, it was discovered that the mole had actually been Sergeant

Gilles Brunet, the son of an RCMP deputy
commissioner.

[69] Alexander Nikolaevich Yakovlev, Soviet politician,
historian, and diplomat, was the spiritual and intellectual
architect behind Glasnost and Perestroika. He had been a
long time member of the Politburo and the Secretariat of
the Communist Party of the USSR. He was Head of the
Department of Ideology and Propaganda from where he
was ousted for his published criticism of Russian
chauvinism and anti-Semitism. Subsequently, he was
appointed for a decade as Soviet Ambassador to Canada.
Yakovlev, (dubbed by American journalist and author
David Remnick as "Gorbachev's good angel"), was
befriended by Prime Minister Pierre Trudeau and
became attracted to the virtues of democracy while in
Canada. It was thanks to numerous low-key private
meetings with Canadian Ukrainian farmers organized by
Canada's Minister of Agriculture, Eugene Whalen,
which Alexander Yakovlev became convinced of the
need to reform the social-political-economic structure of
the Soviet Union. He became Gorbachev's principal
mentor on reforming the country. The bond between
these two men was forged in Canada in 1983 when
Yakovlev was Soviet Ambassador to Ottawa and
Gorbachev was visiting Canada as the Soviet Minister of
Agriculture. (See Christopher Shulgan, *The Soviet
Ambassador, The Making of the Radical Behind
Perestroika.* Toronto: McClelland and Stewart, 2009).

[70] For a brief history of the exodus of Jews from the Soviet
Union, see the link:
http://en.wikipedia.org/wiki/HIAS#The_Soviet_Jewry_Exodus

[71] The *Oprichniki* were the members of an organization
responsible for the torture and murder of internal
enemies of the Russian Tsar Ivan IV (Ivan the Terrible).

Notorious for their violent means of enforcement, they could be compared to modern "death squads" or secret police. Guided by Tsar Ivan, they devastated civilian populations.

[72] The understanding of 1962 between Nikita Khrushchev and John Kennedy differed significantly between its published Western and Soviet versions:

WESTERN VERSION: Soviets promised to dismantle, remove and not to install again all Soviet offensive weapons in Cuba in exchange for a US public declaration and agreement never to invade Cuba. The US also agreed (secretly, to save face) to dismantle all US-built Jupiter IRBMs (Intermediate-range ballistic missiles), deployed in Turkey and Italy, which it did. Both sides declared that they complied.

SOVIET VERSION: Fidel Castro made an ultimatum to the US Government, demanding the fulfillment of a non-invasion promise and the removal of the Guantanamo US base in Cuba, dismantling of all US-built Jupiter IRBMs deployed in Turkey and Italy or the US will be facing Soviet military might in their own backyard. John Kennedy got terrified and promised to comply. Yet, he has not removed the Guantanamo base from the island as he promised and, therefore, Americans can never be trusted.

[73] Treaty on the Prohibition of Nuclear Weapons in Latin America and Caribbean States (the Treaty of Tlatelolco) obligates Latin American parties not to acquire or possess nuclear weapons, nor to permit the storage or deployment of nuclear weapons on their territories by other countries. On February 14, 1967, the Treaty was

signed at a regional meeting of Latin American countries at Tlatelolco, a district in Mexico City, by 33 Latin American countries. Cuba asserted support for the principle since 1962 but stipulated conditions: that Puerto Rico and the Panama Canal Zone be included in the Treaty, and that foreign military bases, especially Guantanamo Naval Base, be eliminated. Finally, Cuba ratified the Treaty in 2002. http://2001-2009.state.gov/t/ac/trt/4796.htm#signatory

[74]   Treaty on Prohibition of Nuclear Weapons on the Seabed, signed February 11, 1971, between USSR and USA.

Strategic ballistic means that it affects the larger war context, such as destroying a city to prevent the production of military equipment for the entire war, and not just a single battle. Strategic weapons are larger missiles, either on submarines or air-launched. A strategic weapon could also be used for a tactical purpose and vice versa. The tactical ballistic missiles are those for short-range use (typically, less than 300 kilometers).

[75]

[76]   Russian Sources:

•   Vadim Truchachev. "Russia will restore its foreign navy bases", published in the newspaper *Pravda* on January 24, 2009. http://www.pravda.ru/world/asia/middleeast/24-01-2009/299641-navy-0/

- Sergey Telegin. "Cuba, which we are losing" published in newspaper *Soviet Rossya* of 27.12.2001 http://cubafriend.narod.ru/bibleo/telegin.htm

- *Krasnaya Zvezda* of : 20.07.1969, 14.05.1970, 11.09.1970, 06.02.1971, 23.05.1971, 21.10.71

- *Izvestia* of: 28.05.1970, 15.09.1970, 08.12.1970

- *Morskaya Gazeta*, attachment to *"Fleet"* of 01.07.1999, page 1.

- *Na Strazhe Zapoliaria* of 18.03.2000, page 2.

- Alexander Rozin. "Second Cuban Crisis", page 9 in *Autonomka* http://avtonomka.org/vospominaniya/istorik-Rozin-Aleksandr-vladimirovich/412-vtoroy-kubinskiy-krizis.html

- S.S. Berezhnoy. "Nuclear submarines of BMF and Rossia", *Special Review 2001*.

- Sergey Brilev. "How many Caribbean crises were there?" in *Komsomolskaya Pravda*.

- Capitanets. "BMF After the War Period" published in magazine *Navy Collection #2, 1994*.

- Vladimir Chozikov. "Assembly line for Submarine cruisers", *Shipbuilding #6 of 1997*.

- http://www.cnw.mk.ua/weapons/navy/submarin/667.htm

- Yury Apalkov. *Submarines of Soviet Fleet of 1945-1991*, Morkniga, 2011.

[77] Russian *Vanka-Vstanka* is a traditional Russian handcrafted egg-shaped bouncing doll (roly-poly) that contains heavy material inside its wooden cavity which

allows the doll always to bounce back to its original position under gravity, despite all attempts to incline the doll by force.

[78] *Nomenklatura,* in Soviet political terminology, meant the special list of those who were trusted, not for professional qualifications, but for political obedience. These individuals were nominated for all the important positions within the government, as well as in the economy, in science and the arts. Soviet *Nomenklatura* (Soviet true ruling class) enjoyed many perks and privileges and helped themselves liberally to the national resources, which they controlled and appropriated.

[79] Sevmorgeo Northern Marine Geology Research and AARI (Arctic Antarctic Research Institute). Both R&D institutions were traditionally engaged in Arctic development.

[80] Recent official Russian media reports related to the revival of Russian military bases:

- http://fognews.ru/putin-Rossiya-vozvrashhaetsya-na-kubu.html

- Vadim Truchachev. "Russia will restore its foreign navy bases", published in the newspaper *Pravda* on January 24, 2009. http://www.pravda.ru/world/asia/middleeast/24-01-2009/299641-navy-0/

- http://topwar.ru/27392-set-zarubezhnyh-baz-of-sssr.html

- Vitaly Ankov. "Russian Navy to get over 50 new warships and nuclear submarines in 2016", *Rianonovosti* of 03-01-2013 http://en.ria.ru/military_news/20130103/178558846/Russian_Navy_to_Get_Over_50_New.html

- http://ria.ru/defense_safety/20130420/933664053-print.html

- http://rutube.ru/video/7a42242232e46408a14c18789743aa2d/

- Tomas Niesen. "More nukes in Kola", *Berentobserver* of January 11, 2013, http://barentsobserver.com/ru/bezopasnost/2013/01/novoe-yadernoe-vooruzhenie-na-kolskom-poluostrove-10-01

- Oleg Vorobiov. "Russia will build new airport in Cuba", published in the newspaper *Izvestia* on April 15, 2013, http://izvestia.ru/news/548619

- http://www.amic.ru/news/215563/

- "Russian Chief of Staff reviews the Cuban weapons", *Martinoticias*, April 19, 2013, http://www.martinoticias.com/content/general-Gerasimov-Cuba-visita-official-/21703.html

- "Chief of Staff arrived in Cuba for working visit", *RIA NOVOSTI*, April 19, 2013, http://ria.ru/defense_safety/20130419/933440157.html

- Luba Lulko. "Russia will restore its military bases", *Pravda*, July 30, 2012

- http://www.pravda.ru/world/30-07-2012/1123320-military_base-0/

- http://www.agentura.ru/dossier/russia/people/soldatov/lourdes/

- http://www.pseudology.org/razbory/Na_dne.html

- http://blogs.fas.org/security/2013/05/russianssbns/

- http://www.warandpeace.ru/ru/exclusive/view/74611/

[81] http://fognews.ru/putin-Rossiya-vozvrashhaetsya-na-kubu.html

Paulina Zelitsky, Paul Weinzweig

www.ingramcontent.com/pod-product-compliance
Lightning Source LLC
Chambersburg PA
CBHW070759280326
41934CB00012B/2975